WITHDRAWN

DS
119.7
C643
1973

Colloquium on the
New World Balance
and the Search for
Peace in the Middle
East, New York,
1973.

The new world
balance and peace

DATE			

The New World Balance and Peace in the Middle East: Reality or Mirage?

The New World Balance and Peace in the Middle East: Reality or Mirage?

A Colloquium

HELD UNDER THE AUSPICES OF THE
INSTITUTE FOR MEDITERRANEAN AFFAIRS

on

Friday and Saturday, May 4 and 5, 1973

at

Carnegie Endowment for International Peace
New York City

Edited by Seymour Maxwell Finger

Rutherford • Madison • Teaneck
Fairleigh Dickinson University Press
London : Associated University Presses

© 1975 by Associated University Presses, Inc.

Associated University Presses, Inc.
Cranbury, New Jersey 08512

Associated University Presses
108 New Bond Street
London W1Y OQX, England

Library of Congress Cataloging in Publication Data

Colloquium on the New World Balance and the Search for Peace in the
Middle East, New York, 1973. The new world balance and peace in the
Middle East.
    Proceedings of the colloquium.
1. Jewish-Arab relations—Congresses.   2. Near East—Foreign relations—
Congresses.   I. Finger, Seymour Maxwell, 1915– . II. Institute for
    Mediterranean Affairs, New York.   III.   Title.
        DS119.7.C643 1973   320.9'56'046   75–1807
            ISBN 0–8386–1675–5

TO

HELEN, My Wife

The good, the true, the beautiful

Contents

List of Participants

His Excellency Ambassador I. A. Akhund
  Permanent Representative of Pakistan to the United Nations
Mr. M. Arad
  Deputy Consul General of Israel, New York, New York
Mr. Manoutchehr Ardalan
  Counselor, Imperial Embassy of Iran, Washington, D.C.
Hon. Alfred LeRoy Atherton, Jr.
  Assistant Secretary of State for Near Eastern and South Asian Affairs, Washington, D.C.
General E. L. M. Burns, *former Chief-of-Staff of the United Nations Emergency Force; Carleton University, Ottawa, Canada*
Rt. Hon. Lord Caradon, *former Minister of State and Permanent Representative of the United Kingdom of Great Britain and Northern Ireland to the United Nations*
His Excellency Ambassador Sir Colin Crowe
  Permanent Representative of the United Kingdom of Great Britain and Northern Ireland to the United Nations

  * Not all participants took an active part in the discussion.

9

Mr. Francois de La Gorce
Minister of Embassy of France to the United States, Washington, D.C.

His Excellency Ambassador Jacob Doron
Deputy Permanent Representative of Israel to the United Nations

His Excellentcy Slaheddine El Gouli
Tunisian Ambassador to the United States, Washington, D.C.

His Excellency Ambassador Robert Fack
Permanent Representative of the Netherlands to the United Nations

His Excellency Ambassador Seymour Maxwell Finger
Former Senior Advisor to the Permanent Representative of the United States to the United Nations; Professor of Political Science, Staten Island Community College and the Graduate School, City University of New York.

His Excellency Ambassador Sergio Armando Frazao
Permanent Representative of Brazil to the United Nations

Mr. S. P. Garasenko
First Secretary of Embassy of the U.S.S.R.
Department of Middle Eastern Affairs, Washington, D.C.

His Excellency Ambassador Fereydoun Hoveyda
Permanent Representative of Iran to the United Nations

His Excellency Ambassador Peter Jankowitsch
Permanent Representative of Austria to the United Nations

Senator Jacob Javits

Mr. Robert Wilson Kitchen, Jr.
Minister-Counsellor, Economic & Social Council
Permanent Mission of the United States to the United Nations

Mr. Miljan Komatina
Minister-Counsellor, Deputy Permanent Representative of the Socialist Federal Republic of Yugoslavia to the United Nations

Mr. German Matveevich Kosenkov
Second Secretary, Permanent Mission of the Union of Soviet Socialist Republics to the United Nations

Mr. Yitzhak Leor
Consul of Israel, New York, N.Y.

Mr. Abrahim Lif, Counsellor,
Israeli Embassy, Washington, D.C.

Mr. J. C. Moberly, Counsellor,
British Embassy, Washington, D.C.

Mr. Richard H. Nolte, *former U.S. Ambassador to Egpyt; Director, Institute of Current World Affairs*

His Excellency Ambassador Osman Olcay
Permanent Representative of Turkey to the United Nations

Mr. Mahmoud M. Osman
Second Secretary of the Permanent Mission of Egypt to the United Nations

His Excellency Dr. Richard Sergeyevich Ovinnikov
Senior Counsellor, Political Affairs
Permanent Mission of the Union of Soviet Socialist Republics to the United Nations

Major General Indar Jit Rikhye
Former Chief-of-Staff of the United Nations Emergency Force; International Peace Academy, N.Y.

His Excellency Ambassador William E. Schaufele, Jr.
Senior Adviser to the Permanent Representative of the United States Mission to the United Nations

Dr. William Schneider
Legislative Assistant to Senator James L. Buckley of New York, Washington, D.C.

Mr. William D. Smith, New York Times *Correspondent*

Mr. Peter Stavrionos
Assistant to Senator James Abourezk of South Dakota, Washington, D.C.

Professor T. R. Adam, *Political Scientist*

Mr. George Agree, *Director of the Committee for the Democratic Process*

Mrs. George Agree

Dr. Gil Carl Alroy, *Department of Political Science, Hunter College*

Dr. David Arons, *Executive Vice-President, Dropsie College*

Prof. Lawrence L. Barrell, *Chairman, Administrative Committee Board of Governors, American College of Jerusalem; Member of Board, I.M.A.*

Mr. Rustum Bastuni, *former member of the Knesset*

Mr. Y. Ben Ami, *Executive, International Trade*

Mrs. Y. Ben Ami

Mr. Peter H. Bergson, *Investment Banker; Member of Board, I.M.A.*

Mrs. Lionel Berman, *Director, Arab-Israeli Research and Relations Project*

Mrs. Walter Bishop, *Institute for Mediterranean Affairs*

Mr. Sam Pope Brewer, *Foreign Correspondent,* The New York Times

Miss Helen Caruso, *Council on Foreign Relations*

Mr. Leo Cherne, *Executive Director, Research Institute of America*

Professor Lawrence B. Cohen, *Department of Industrial & Management Engineering Columbia University*

Mr. Ronald Colven, The Washington Post, *Washington, D.C.*

Professor Joseph Dunnor, *Chairman, Department of Political Science, Yeshiva University*

Mr. Peter W. Eccles, *Vice-President, Goldman Sachs International Corp.*

Mrs. Peter W. Eccles

Mr. Clark Eichelberger, *Commission to Study the Organization of Peace*

Professor Luther H. Evans, *Director of International & Legal Collections, Columbia University*

Mrs. Luther H. Evans

Mr. Alfred W. Feiler, *Industrialist; Board Member & Secretary of I.M.A.*

Mrs. Alfred W. Feiler, *Literary Translator*

Dr. Henry L. Feingold, *City University of New York*

Professor Marnin Feinstein, *Classical Languages & Hebrew, City College of New York*

Mrs. Marnin Feinstein

Miss Bena Finberg, *Stockbroker*

Dr. Bruno Foa, *Economic Consultant*

Mr. Jack Friedgut, *Vice-President of First National City Bank*

Professor Louis L. Gerson, *Department of Political Science, University of Connecticut; Board Member, I.M.A.*

Dr. Harry D. Gideonse, *Chancellor, The Graduate Faculty, The New School for Social Research*

Mr. Max Gilman, *Author*

Mrs. Max Gilman

Professor Gidon Gottlieb, *School of Law, New York University*

Mrs. Gidon Gottlieb

Mr. Alvin Grauer, *Public Relations Consultant*

Mrs. Alvin Grauer

Dr. George Gruen, *American Jewish Committee*

Heskel M. Haddad, M.D., *Clinical Professor of Ophthalmogy, New York Medical College*

Professor John H. Herz, *Political Science Department, City College of New York*

Mr. Milton Handler, *Lawyer (Kaye, Fierman, Hays & Handler)*

Dr. Milton D. Hassol

Professor Vsevolod Holubnychy, *Russian Area Studies Graduate Program, Hunter College, C.U.N.Y.*

Mr. Rashid Hussein, Publicist

Mr. Joseph E. Johnson, *President Emeritus, Carnegie Endowment for International Peace*

Mr. Amos Kenan, *Author*

Professor Malcolm H. Kerr, *Department of Political Science, University of California*

Mr. Zvi Kolitz, *Autor*

Mrs. Zvi Kolitz

Rabbi Baruch Korff, *Rehovoth, Mass.*

Mr. F. S. LaMagra, *Executive, International Finance*

Professor Abba P. Lerner, *Department of Economics, Queens College, C.U.N.Y; Co-Chairman, I.M.A.*

Mrs. Ida Lewis, *Publisher and Editor of* Encore *Magazine*

Mr. Julian Licht, *Engineer, Industrial Consultant*

Professor Ilse Lichtenstadter, *Center for Middle Eastern Studies, Harvard University*

Professor Sebastian B. Littauer, *Emeritus, Operations Research, Columbia University*

Mr. Charles W. Maynes, *Carnegie Endowment for International Peace*

Mr. Samuel Merlin, *Director of Institute for Mediterranean Affairs*

Mrs. Samuel Merlin

Dr. Drew Middleton, *Military Analyst,* The New York Times

Professor Hans J. Morgenthau, *City College, City University of New York*

Professor Joseph Neyer, *Department of Philosophy, Rutgers College*

Mr. Paul O'Dwyer, *Lawyer (now President of the Council of the City of New York)*

Mr. D. Ottaway, *Foreign Desk,* The Washington Post, *Washington D.C.*

Professor Raphael Patai, *Herzl Institute, New York City*

Professor Don Peretz, *Director S.W.A.N.A. Program, State University of New York at Binghamton*

Mrs. Don Peretz

Professor Amos Perlmutter, *School of Government and Public Administration, The American University, Washington, D.C.*

Professor Peter P. Remec, *Chairman, Department of Political Science, Fordham University*

Dr. Paul Riebenfeld, *Political Scientist; Board Member of I.M.A.*

Mrs. Paul Riebenfeld

Professor Benjamin Rivlin, *Political Science Department, Graduate School, City University of New York; Board Member of I.M.A.*

Dr. Joachim O. Ronall, *Head, Afro-Asian Unit, Foreign Research Division, Federal Reserve Bank of New York; Professor of Economics, Fordham University*

Mr. Maurice Rosenblatt, *Publicist*

Mr. Eric Rouleau, *Middle East Editor,* Le Monde

Mrs. Eric Rouleau

Professor Dankwart Rustow, *Graduate School, City University of New York*

Mr. Richard R. Salzmann, *Research Institute of America; Member of the Board of I.M.A.*

Mrs. Richard R. Salzmann

Professor S. Perry Schlesinger, *Columbia University*

Mr. Harry L. Selden, *Editor*

Mrs. Harry L. Selden

Mr. Leonard I. Shankman, *Financier; Treasurer of I.M.A.*

Dr. Ali Shayegan, *Fairleigh Dickinson University*

Dr. John Sherman, *Associate Professor, Department of Library Science, Queens College, C.U.N.Y.*

Mrs. John Sherman

Professor I. Robert Sinai, *City College, C.U.N.Y.*

Mrs. I. Robert Sinai, *Editor*

Mr. Allan Solomonow, *Executive Director, New Alternatives in the Middle East*

Professor John G. Stoessinger, *Acting Director, Political Affairs Division, United Nations; Member of the Board of I.M.A.*

Dr. Fouad Tawab, *Fairleigh Dickinson University*

Mr. Sidney Wallach, *Public Relations Executive*

Dr. David S. Wyman, *Professor of History, University of Massachusetts*

Professor I. W. Zartman, *Chairman, Political Science Department, New York University*

Professor Oscar Zeichner, *City College of New York*

Mr. Sidney Zion, *Journalist*

Mrs. Sidney Zion

Board of Trustees and Executive Committee Institute for Mediterranean Affairs

17

Professor Hans J. Morgenthau, New School for Social Research
Waldemar A. Nielsen

Professor Amos Perlmutter, American University

Dr. Paul Riebenfeld

Professor Benjamin Rivlin, Executive Officer, Ph. D. Program in Political
  Science, City University of New York

Richard R. Salzmann, Directing Editor, Research Institute of America

Leonard I. Shankman, Financier

Professor John G. Stoessinger, Department of Political Science, City
  University of New York

Professor Thomas B. Trombetas, Department of Political Science,
  California State College

EXECUTIVE COMMITTEE

Professor Seymour Maxwell Finger
President

Richard R. Salzmann
Chairman, Executive Committee

Professor Nasrollah S. Fatemi
Chairman of the Board

Samuel Merlin
Executive Director

Professor Abba P. Lerner
Vice-Chairman of the Board

Leonard I. Shankman
Treasurer

Peter H. Bergson
Vice-Chairman of the Board

Alfred Feiler
Secretary

Ruth Bishop
Director of Special Events

Howard Golden
Legal Counsel

Foreword

The Colloquium on the New World Balance and the Search for Peace in the Middle East was held on May 4 and 5, 1973, under the auspices of the Institute for Mediterranean Affairs. It was convened at a time when negotiation was replacing confrontation in many other trouble spots of the world; for example, in Berlin, between the two Germanies, in Vietnam, in relations of the United States with Peking, and in the détente between the Soviet Union and the United States. The question naturally came to mind . Why not in the Middle East? Could negotiation replace confrontation in the tense and dangerous relations between Israel and its Arab neighbors? What avenues might be explored? What are the obstacles and complexities?

The Institute was most fortunate in assembling a remarkable group of diplomats, scholars, and journalists to explore these questions. They provided not only a wealth of experience, knowledge, and perception, but also a wide diversity of approach. To encourage frankness, it was understood that the participants expressed their personal views only; they did not speak for their governments, their journals, nor their respective institutions of learning.

The proceedings were open and informal. They were taperecorded with the understanding that nothing would be published prior to approval by the participants of their respective texts—whether addresses or contributions to the general discussion. This report therefore contains the text of the proceedings as it was approved by the speakers. Though for understandable reasons some minor revisions were made, the report is nonetheless a faithful reflection of the proceedings. The informal and spontaneous nature of the debate was preserved.

The Institute for Mediterranean Affairs is an independent, nonprofit, educational organization established for the purpose of investigating the basic problems of the Mediterranean area—many parts of which are beset by strife and upheaval—with a view to formulating tentative options for peaceful solutions to some of the explosive situations of that region.

The Institute takes no stand, expressed nor implied, on any issues dealt with in the studies it publishes directly or through commercial publishers. Its reports and studies when produced by a panel of experts reflect the consensus of the members who made up the particular study group. When a study is prepared by one person it reflects the ideas and philosophy of the author, who is responsible both for the statements of fact and expressions of opinion. The Institute is responsible only for determining that such studies and reports should be presented to the public.

This volume is presented to the public as a contribution to the discussion of the crisis in the Middle East and as material for a better understanding of the issues confronting the big powers in the area under consideration.

Acknowledgments

The Institute wishes to express its appreciation to the Ralph Bunche Institute on the United Nations, Graduate School, City University of New York, for assistance in preparing the manuscript and in communicating with the participants. It also expresses its gratitude to the American-Israel Friendship League, Inc., 134 East 39th Street, New York City (Hon. Herbert Tenzer, President; Hon. Abraham J. Multer, Vice-President) for financial assistance in publishing this volume. It appreciates, in particular, the fact that neither organization sought to influence in any way the contents of this volume; complete responsibility therefor rests with the Colloquium participants, the Institute for Mediterranean Affairs, and the Editor.

I should like to express my deep personal appreciation to Samuel Merlin, Executive Director of the Institute, for his invaluable assistance in organizing the Colloquium. Without his superb contribution in preparing thoughtful, well-organized questionnaires and outlines in advance of the Colloquium and charting its overall shape, it is doubtful whether such a distinguished group of knowledgeable and articulate observers could have been assembled, nor would their participation have been so fruitful. I also owe a great debt of gratitude to Ruth Bishop, the Institute's Director of Special Events; her imagination, diligence, charm, and tact helped immeasurably to make the Colloquium a very special event.

21

Introduction

In October 1973, five months after the Colloquium, war broke out again in the Middle East. Had the Colloquium concerned itself with transitory matters, its significance would have been submerged by events. As I reread the proceedings, however, the opposite conclusion emerges. The tragic October war has given even more relevance, more poignancy, and more significance to the considerations, views, and proposals set forth at our sessions and recorded in this volume.

There is, first of all, the question of whether an Israeli policy relying on military strength, "buffer" territories, and an enduring status quo can bring a de facto peace. This position, still held by the "maximalists" in Israel who oppose current Israeli government policy, derives doctrinal support from the essay by Gil Carl AlRoy "Military Capabilities in the Middle East." AlRoy argues that, given the backward state of society in Egypt, Syria, and Jordan, Israel has and will retain for decades—and into the foreseeable future—a decisive military superiority. Even the October war, with its heavy cost to all parties and a disproportionately heavy cost to Israel, has not shaken many proponents of this view, who stress the fact that Israel was unquestionably winning militarily when the fighting was stopped. For them, the Yom Kippur attack proved that Arab professions of peace could not be trusted. They argue that, had Israel withdrawn from Sinai to the 1949 armistice lines, as it had after the 1956 Sinai campaign, Egypt would have been even more tempted to attack Isaeal's nearby population centers and thereby threaten its very survival as a state.

On the other hand, Merlin, Kerr, Gruen, and Finger, in their essays and interventions take issue with the thesis of enduring Israeli military superiority and stress the dangers of sitting on the status quo. They cite cases in recent history where supposedly "backward" peoples have successfully fought against more highly developed nations; for example, Korea, Vietnam, and the German invasion of the U.S.S.R. in 1941. Merlin warns: "Don't expect the Arabs to remain forever inferior in the art of modern warfare." And Hans Morgenthau states: "I would agree with those who would not bet everything upon the continuing, inevitable, and immutable Israeli superiority in the military field."

Morgenthau, in his penetrating essay on, "Big Power Confrontation in the Middle East," makes the following prophetic observation:

> For the assessment of the distribution of military power may change, and people frustrated by their enforced inactivity may delude themselves into believing that now they have a chance to win and will start another round.
> It is also possible that they will not delude themselves but that they will risk defeat rather than allow themselves to be held in this inferior position indefinitely. Because, on the basis of national passions and national pride, there are possibilities for irrational acts which people will prefer to the humiliating position of seemingly permanent military inferiority in which they find themselves today. . . . I am rather inclined to believe that since there is no possibility of a negotiated settlement, sooner or later, and perhaps rather sooner, there will be another outbreak of war.

Five months later war broke out.

The second major consideration that produced incisive essays that are highly relevant today is the role of the big powers. Morgenthau delineates the Soviet interest in "controlled tension" as a way of maintaining its influence in the Middle East, a theme Stoessinger also brings out in his essay on, "The U.N. and the Arab-Israeli Conflict." Drew Middleton, in his presentation on, "Russian Presence and Economic Interests in the Mediterranean and Indian Ocean," points to the great increase of Soviet influence in Syria and Iraq, along with a larger Soviet naval presence in the area. He also underlines the strategic importance of the dependence of Western Europe, Japan, and the United States on Middle East oil. Senator Javits surveys the interest of the Western European states in the Middle East, while Gidon Gottlieb offers thoughtful insights into the role of China and Japan in the Arab-Israeli conflict. An excellent survey of American policy is provided by Alfred L. Atherton, now the Assistant Secretary of State for Near Eastern and South Asian Affairs. It portrays the persistence, since 1967, of American efforts to bring about a negotiated settlement to the Arab-Israeli conflict, efforts in which Mr. Atherton is heavily involved today.

A third major problem highlighted at the Colloquium is the energy crisis. William Smith, in his superb analysis of, "The Energy Crisis and Its Potential Effects Upon American Policy," predicts, six months before the Arab embargo brought home the vulnerability of energy-importing countries, the long-range nature of the crisis, the hard choices faced by the Japanese, Western European, and American governments, and the vital need for an "Atlantic-Japanese oil policy." J. O. Ronall assays the political, financial, and military implications of growing Western dependence on Middle East oil. His plea for "a cohesive set of national energy policies" is no less urgent today than it was when he made it eighteen months ago. Gidon Gottlieb considers the energy problem of such great strategic importance that he raises the question as to whether Soviet-American détente has any real meaning for the United States unless it includes an understanding about energy. Soviet policies, encouraging the Arab oil embargo in the winter of 1973–74, are hardly the actions of a power interested in cooperative relations.

Also pertinent in the light of subsequent developments is the emphasis at the Colloquium on the role of the Palestinians in any settlement. Eric Rouleau, in his essay, "Peace Without the Palestinians?", stresses that there can not be an enduring peace settlement that does not provide a national existence for the Palestinians. This point is also stressed and analyzed in the opening presentation by Malcolm Kerr.

New American recognition of Palestinian interests was indicated in the Nixon-Brezhnev communiqué of 25 June 1974 at San Clemente. With regard to the Middle East, it stated :

> This settlement should be in accordance with the interests of all states in the area, be consistent with their independence and sovereignty, and should take into due account *the legitimate interests of the Palestinian people"* (Emphasis added).

The last clause is significant as the first official American acknowledgment that "the Palestinian people" constitute a distinct political factor to be considered, rather than as individual refugees. It should be noted, however, that the United States has, to date, avoided any official contact with the Palestine Liberation Organization.

A recent action of the UN General Assembly in voting to hear the leader of the Palestine Liberation Organization, setting a precedent that may have serious consequences, shows how much the political strength of their supporters has grown, and the decision of the Arab Summit Conference in Morocco in October 1974, recognizing the P.L.O. as "the sole legitimate representative of the Palestinian people on any liberated Palestinian territory," represents a new highpoint for that organization. How far they have advanced may be judged by comparing the P.L.O.'s present situation with that depicted by Eric Rouleau in this volume.

A highlight of the Colloquium was Lord Caradon's graphic personal account of the negotiation of Resolution 242, adopted by the Security Council. This provides insights not elsewhere set down in print on a resolution whose basic principles are still the only agreed hope of a negotiated settlement, even though varying interpretations of that resolution have hampered progress.

All of the aforementioned issues—a military-security approach, based on the status quo, versus negotiations; oil; the big-power factor in the Middle East; and the emerging role of the Palestinians—have become increasingly important issues in the wake of the October war. A further important development has been the growing isolation of Israel, which has therefore become increasingly dependent on the United States. The U.S., on the other hand, has made a new effort at "even-handedness," which has resulted in better American relations with the Arabs and greater American pressure on Israel to make concessions.

This naturally raises the serious question of whether improved relations between the U.S. and Arab countries will depend on American ability to press Israel into greater concessions, even if these are not reciprocated by the Arab states. Meanwhile, there are growing reports of Soviet efforts to use Middle East tension to drive a wedge between the U.S. and its allies and thus weaken NATO. Any real détente must include some understanding about the respective role of the two super powers in the Middle East, and particularly a commitment not to sabotage efforts toward a peaceful settlement through the promotion of narrow national interests.

Time may not be on the side of peace. The first result of the October war appeared to be the creation of conditions in which negotiations could go forward. Israeli overconfidence was deflated;

the Arab sense of inferiority and humiliation resulting from the 1967 war was overcome. Syria, which for six years rejected U.N. Security Council Resolution 242, has now accepted it as a basis for peace. Face-to-face negotiation between Israelis and Egyptians on the one hand and Israelis and Syrians on the other represented to first such direct negotiations in more than twenty-five years.[1] New United Nations peacekeeping forces were installed between Israeli and Egyptian forces in the Sinai and between the Israelis and the Syrians on the Golan Heights. Henry Kissinger's success in bringing about these negotiations and the disengagement of forces appeared to be leading the way, step by step, toward peaceful settlement.

The step-by-step approach is now running into serious problems. Syrian attitudes have not been promising. There was some hope for movement on the West Bank, especially after the courageous action by Prime Minister Rabin in forcibly preventing some 5,000 Israelis from settling on the West Bank. This action, taken over the strong protest of the opposition Likud party, is evidence that Rabin has been looking toward a West Bank disengagement agreement. Now, however, the designation of the P.L.O. by the Arab Summit Conference as "the sole legitimate representative of the Palestinian people," appears to have put a roadblock across further negotiations. Rabin has declared that there would be "no negotiations with the terrorist organizations."

It is understandable that Israel would not want to be party to an agreement turning control of the West Bank over to an organization that not only condones terrorists who have operated to kill non-combatant Israeli men, women, and children, but also has declared that the establishment of a unified, secular, Palestinian state would mean the end of Israel. It would not be unreasonable for Israel to look first for some evidence that the P.L.O. has disassociated itself clearly and unequivocally from terrorism, that it is prepared to have a Palestinian state alongside Israel and not as a replacement for Israel, and that the P.L.O. has the support of the West Bank Palestinians. The first two points will depend on the future actions and declarations of the P.L.O. The third might be determined by a plebiscite on the West Bank and in Gaza concerning the political future of the area. This could offer the option of a separate state or federation with Jordan. The plebiscite might be conducted by a two-member commission accepted by both Jordan and Israel, under either

[1] An excellent analysis of the evolution of Arab attitudes toward negotiations, and particularly the quiet role of Saudi Arabia, will be found in, "Arab Politics, Peace, and War," by Nadav Safran, *Orbis* 18, no. 2, Summer, 1974.

U.N. or other auspices. Another alternative might be the establishment of a United Nations strategic trust territory in the West Bank
and Gaza. Designation of the area as *strategic* would make it possible
to guarantee its demilitarization, thus assuring Israeli security, while
enabling the local population to exercise self-determination. It would
also place the trusteeship under the Security Council, not the General
Assembly; consequently, the potential Soviet and American vetoes
would protect the respective parties against any change inimical to
their vital interests.[2]

Whatever the difficulties of working toward self-determination
for the Palestinians, it would be a grave error for Israel to ignore
the problem and sit on the status quo. This issue has now became an
integral part of the overall settlement envisaged in U.N. Security
Council Resolution 242, even though that resolution makes no explicit
reference to it. And that resolution is probably the only basis on which
to build peace in the Middle East, because of its comprehensiveness
in spelling out the needs and obligations of both sides—and because
it has been accepted by both sides.

It appears evident that Israel can not have both the additional
territories and peace. Clearly, she should not withdraw from these
territories except in context of genuine peace, which would include
the negotiation of secure and recognized boundaries. But what is the
alternative to peace? While Israel can probably win another war
against her Arab neighbors, the 1973 experience shows how this has
become increasingly costly. It is certainly not a situation to be desired
in the decades ahead.

On the other side, the Arabs must be careful not to overplay their
hand. Understandably, there is renewed pride in the improved military
performance of the Egyptian and Syrian armies in 1973, even though
Israel had gained the upper hand on both fronts at the time the
fighting stopped. Moreover, the great leverage that the oil producers
now have over Western Europe and Japan may produce overconfidence. Oil money has become an increasingly important factor
in the Arab world, greatly enhancing the influence of Saudi Arabia
as well as the financial resources available to Israel's Arab neighbors.

In some ways, the present situation is comparable to May 1967
when an overconfident Nasser blockaded the Gulf of Aqaba and
threatened the annihilation of Israel. A similar error now might lead
to a similar disaster.

Above all, the Arabs and the Israelis must realize that there is

---

[2] For a fuller description of this proposal, *see* appendix.

no military solution to the problem. Israel can hardly look forward with equanimity to the prospect of being bled and drained by periodic wars. The Arabs, on the other hand, must realize that Israel will not surrender to any Arab military combination, because there is nowhere else for the Israelis to go. Moreover, they must know that the United States would not stand aside and let Israel be obliterated. In fact, the more the reality of this becomes clear, the less likely war becomes, and the more likely are they to take the hard road of negotiations.

The seriousness of the two sides in the search for peace is now being tested. The crucial element is not likely to be any magic of Henry Kissinger or Geneva but the will of the parties concerned to make peace, even at the cost of hard-to-make concessions and risks. Their actions in the coming months may well determine whether the vision of peace is a mirage or an attainable reality. While the logic of negotiation rather than conflict is evident, the tragic history of the last twenty-seven years is far from reassuring.

The New World Balance and Peace in the Middle East: Reality or Mirage?

Opening Remarks

by Seymour M. Finger

MR. FINGER. Your excellencies, ladies, and gentlemen: It is my privilege, pleasure, and honor to welcome you here on behalf of the Institute for Mediterranean Affairs.

I will be quite frank at the outset to say that the attendance for this Colloquium has considerably exceeded our expectations, not in quantity so much as quality.

I only regret that there is not room on the program for virtually all of you to speak because, as I read the list of those who are here, I find that the degree of expertise in the audience is virtually equal to that of those who are here to address you. But we are going to have time for a general discussion at the end of each session, and we certainly hope that you will feel free to join in that discussion. The agenda is quite a full one, as I think all of you will realize; because of this, I am going to be quite brief.

One other way in which I shall save time is to dispense with long introductions of the various distinguished speakers that we have. Most of them, I am sure, are already well known to you, and if I took time to mention all the books and articles they have written, this would take half the time that we have available. It is more useful, I believe, to listen to them.

Now you might ask: Why are we holding this Colloquium now

on, "The New World Balance and the Search for Peace in the Middle East?" After all, the problem has been there for almost three decades. What is there new that justifies our taking another look? There are several factors that went into our decision to invite this distinguished group to consider the matter.

First, there is a new atmosphere in the last few years in which countries that have been adversaries for decades, and even governments in divided countries that have been adversaries for decades, have now moved toward peaceful coexistence and negotiation rather than confrontation. In some cases, even cooperation has replaced the former unproductive confrontation.

We have the case of the governments of East and West Germany, which for so long did not recognize each other, now prepared to enter the United Nations together in the fall. The President of the United States has gone to Peking and to Moscow, and has developed new cooperative relationships with those two governments. First Secretary Brezhnev is expected in Washington very shortly. The Chancellor of the German Federal Republic, Willy Brandt, has been to Moscow, is shortly expecting the First Secretary of the Communist Party of the Soviet Union, and has signed treaties involving new relations with Poland and Czechoslovakia.

With so many parts of the world where, before, there was only bitter conflict and nonrecognition now moving toward negotiation rather than confrontation, one must ask : Why not the Middle East? Why should this be the only area of conflict in the world in which there has been no negotiation, whether direct or indirect? Why no attempt at communication in the Middle East?

The United States participation in the Vietnam war has been ended through negotiation. The two Koreas are talking to each other. The governments of the United States and Cuba have recently negotiated an agreement on hijacking.

Again, to use the words President Nixon used in his report to the Congress, as quoted in the (New York) *Times* this morning, we have negotiated an end to a war and made future wars less likely by improving relations with major adversaries. One again is drawn to the question : Why not in the Middle East?

Further factors that have raised this question are the growing concerns with energy and the increasing role of the Middle East, first as a supplier of energy and eventually as a major holder of dollars in the world, with all of the complications therein.

We have had in recent months the visits by King Hussein, Prime Minister Meir, and Hafez Ismael to Washington. Again we have

Mr. Nixon's statement quoted this morning in which he calls upon the Soviet Union to work independently or with the United States to make a contribution to peace in the Middle East.

We did not anticipate it at the time this meeting was scheduled, but I am sure all of you from the United Nations are aware that later this month the Security Council will be getting a report from the Secretary-General as to what has been done to implement Resolution 242. Consequently, we may expect more activity by the Security Council.

It therefore seemed to us that with so many situations that formerly appeared frozen solid giving way to thaw, to discussion, to negotiation, it is perhaps not impossible that some new ideas might come out of a forum of this type that might at long last lead the way to peace in the Middle East.

With that, I conclude these opening remarks. I shall have more to say at the end of our session.

I now have the great privilege of introducing Professor Malcolm Kerr of the University of California, our first speaker, who will discuss with us the respective positions of the Arabs and Israelis on a peace settlement.

The Respective Positions of the Arabs and Israel on a Peace Settlement

by Malcolm H. Kerr

PROFESSOR KERR. Thank you very much, Ambassador Finger. It is a pleasure to be here. When I was invited to speak on the topic of Arab and Israeli positions regarding a settlement, it seemed to me that probably the level of sophistication among our audience would be high enough that little could be gained by simply issuing a catalogue of official statements from Israel and various Arab governments in order to delineate in the simplest terms what they say their positions are. Rather, I think it would be helpful for me to try to inject a subjective note and say a bit about what strikes me as being particularly important or, for that matter, perhaps particularly misleading, in terms of positions adopted by various parties.

I noted during Ambassador Finger's introductory remarks his references to places in the world where divided countries, or previously, it had seemed, irrevocably hostile governments, have of late begun to do business with each other. He quite properly raised the question whether this could happen in the Middle East. It struck me that perhaps one difficulty in the Middle East is that we do not have two sides to a cut-and-dried issue; rather, we have a number of complications to break that model down and necessarily make the path of peacemaking much more difficult.

One of the considerations is that on the Arab side we have a number of parties that are quite autonomous from each other. We have the Palestinians who are not represented by a state or a government, but who are acknowledged by almost everyone to be a group of vital importance in the equation. We have, in addition, several Arab governments who have not always, in fact seldom, operated in real harmony on the issue of Palestine and Israel.

Furthermore, both within Israel and within Arab society at large, there have always been profound disagreements about just what course one ought to pursue, how one ought to view the adversary, what goal one should be working toward, what the most essential values are that should guide one's policy. I would simply like to try in a few moments this afternoon to clarify the ambiguities of both sides.

Despite the ambiguities on both sides and the uncertainties about their positions, we cannot, however, simplify it by saying that these ambiguities are symmetrical. Particularly if we review the positions of Israel and the Arab states, leaving aside the Palestinians, since 1967. In important respects the views and positions of some Arab governments, notably Egypt's and Jordan's, have softened on the issues, while the views in Israel have hardened. At present we have an almost ironic contrast between the debates inside the Arab world and those inside Israel. Some in the Arab world are asking themselves quietly whether they can withstand the price that they are paying for the current impasse. Can they maintain the position that they will not negotiate peace without total Israeli withdrawal to the 1967 lines as a matter of principle? Mind you, this is a debate that goes on in the most moderate circles.

The question, then, is: Can the Arabs survive the status quo? This is a question they have to ask themselves, and they do.

On the Israeli side the question seems to be the opposite, and that is: Is any obtainable settlement through negotiations better than what the status quo provides? In other words, can they afford to abandon the status quo?

So one side wonders whether it can live with it; the other side wonders whether it can live without it.

Now let me speak about the ambiguities on the Arab side. on an official level and then on a more unofficial level. Officially there is a division between those who endorse Security Council Resolution

242, especially Egypt and Jordan, and those who reject it—including the Palestinian Resistance Movement, plus a number of governments, such as Iraq, Syria, Libya, and Algeria.

I would note, however, that in recent weeks and months Syria's position has somewhat moderated, as well as in the Libyan case, because of relations between Libya and Egypt and that the union that is still formally scheduled to occur between them; Colonel Qaddafi has avoided taking direct issue with Egypt on Egypt's position toward Israel. But we do have a division over acceptance and nonacceptance of Resolution 242.

Furthermore, Egypt and Jordan have reiterated their acceptance of the principle of recognition of Israel as a sovereign state in exchange for full withdrawal. They have done this on numerous occasions and in numerous ways, the most explicit and formal being the response of the Egyptian government to the questionnaire of Ambassador Gunnar Jarring early in 1971. Also, they have intimated their receptiveness to various subsidiary arrangements, at least in principle, such as demilitarization of certain territories, the presence of U.N. forces, and so forth, as well as their willingness to sign binding contractual agreements. At the same time, both governments have continued to insist that Israeli withdrawal must be total. And while perhaps under the surface there is some flexibility on this point in the Jordanian case, there does not appear to be any so far in the Egyptian case.

Again one has the impression sometimes, from declarations out of Cairo or particularly Amman, that if it obtained favorable conditions for itself, that government might be prepared to make a seperate peace with Israel, leaving its Arab partner to fend for itself. On other occasions these implications have been very strongly denied.

Furthermore, just what rights the Egyptians and Jordanians would insist on, on behalf of Palestinians, vis-a-vis Israel, have been left undefined—and I think quite carefully so on their parts.

Both these governments, especially Egypt, see their position as involving the abandonment of major claims that they had pressed on behalf of the Palestinians before 1967. I think we should never lose sight of this element. The proffer of a tradeoff of peace for withdrawal may seem to many people, especially in Israel, as something for nothing. Israel gives something in exchange for nothing. But we have to bear in mind that from the point of view of these Arab governments, there is a considerable history to this affair before 1967 in which they saw themselves as trustees on behalf of the Palestinian cause, and in large measure it is these claims of the Palestinians before

1967 that they are now offering, in so many words, to abandon in exchange for the withdrawal of the Israelis.

I think that without this symbolic vindication by means of total Israeli withdrawal, these two Arab governments would find it very difficult to justify the formal acceptance of Israel's legitimacy to their own publics in Egypt and Jordan and in other Arab countries.

There is an unofficial level that we should consider, too, on the Arab side, and here there is room for great speculation as to just what the real significance of the stated position of Arab governments may be. Both in the case of the Jordanians and Egyptians, we want to know what lies beneath the surface of their formal acceptance of the resolution, and also, in the case of those governments that have turned their backs on the resolution or attacked it, we want to know, again, what their underlying attitudes are. Because, as we know, formally expressed policies are often stated publicly with all sorts of ambiguities underneath.

We know that the acceptance of the 242 Resolution is enunciated much more enthusiastically by Egyptian and Jordanian leaders to foreigners than to their own people. In speaking to domestic audiences, President Nasser and later President Sadat, for example, have been more inclined to stress the militant aspects of their position; the horizons of fire and seas of blood that President Nasser once spoke of in 1969; the repeated claims by President Sadat that he will have no alternative but to go back to war to try to liberate the Sinai; and particularly that in speaking to domestic audiences, Arab leaders have always tried to stress that they will not sell out the Palestinian cause.

So we have to make our own judgments whether the declared readiness for peace in exchange for evacuation is sincere or whether it is a bluff. It might be conceivably a bluff made for diplomatic purposes. It would put Israel in an awkward position, isolate her diplomatically, and let the Arabs reap the benefit of the discomfiture that Israel would incur by not agreeing to this formula of peaceable withdrawal.

Alternatively, if Israel did accept full withdrawal and peace were concluded, then she would want to know, of course, what would follow from the Arab states—Egypt and Jordan, as well as the more militant ones? Would they honor the peace? Would they consider it something to which they had a commitment in their own minds as well as on paper, or would they not?

I think that this is the question that many people have been asking, but if I may say so, it has always seemed to me in recent years that in public discussion in this country, even the hypothesis that the commitment to peace might be quite genuine and might be taken quite seriously by some Arab leaders tends to be played down considerably, and even dismissed altogether, to the point where many people who are generally knowledgeable about the Middle East are suspicious and unbelieving when one even states the fact that the Jordanian and Egyptian governments have made the public commitment that they have made.

So I would suggest that their declarations do need at least serious consideration as being plausibly genuine, even if one is to debate the matter afterwards.

Conversely, the stated position of the militant Palestinian spokesmen might need to be qualified. They state, of course, that there can be no peace with Israel, no acceptance of the existence of the Jewish state, and so forth. But I think that it does not necessarily have to be a foregone conclusion that nothing can be done to mollify the Palestinians, including the Fedayeen organizations, within the framework of a 242 settlement. I do not exclude altogether the possibility that under the surface of public militant declarations from Palestinian leaders there may be a great deal more flexibility than one tends to suspect. There may be, for example, some arrangement involving a well-organized free choice for the Palestinians between autonomy under Jordan and a separate state in Gaza and the West Bank, which would be of some interest to the more militant elements.

Nor can the views of the Fedayeen leaders be taken for granted to represent the whole of the Palestinians. After all, half of the Palestinians are living under Israeli occupation and are largely out of touch with the Fedayeen and have a variety of other attitudes, while as to many of those outside Israeli-controlled territory, one does not know what they would settle for; one only knows what their spokesmen are stating publicly.

So the important thing may be not what the Palestinians would ideally want, but what they would be willing to accept if it were offered to them.

Now let me turn to Israel for a few minutes and speak once more of ambiguities. Again there is an official level and an unofficial one. Officially the position continues to be one of insistence on negotiations as a vitally important process; negotiations, as the Israeli government has repeatedly said, without prior conditions or limited agenda; negotiations for the determination of the conclusion of peace, including the determination of frontiers. As Israel stated in her note to Ambassador Jarring in February 1971, Israel would not declare her territorial proposals in advance of negotiations, nor, however, would she contemplate a complete return to the 1967 boundaries. Pending Arab readiness to negotiate, Israel, according to her government's stated views, expects to remain in place where she is in the occupied territories or, as they are commonly termed in Israel, the *administered territories*. As the expression goes, then, Israel is waiting for the telephone to ring.

On the question of the Palestinians and their future, the Israeli government has studiously avoided formal declarations of what it believes should happen to them, although as we know the Prime Minister has stated on a number of occasions her personal opinion that no new Arab state should be created between Israel and Jordan.

The status of the occupied territories is rendered somewhat ambiguous, even on the official level, if we consider the march of time and the march of events in the occupied territories under Israeli occupation and the creation of what General Dayan likes to call *new facts*. I have in mind here the whole process of establishing Israeli settlements on the West Bank, Gaza, and elsewhere, the use of increasing numbers of unskilled Arab workmen coming in from the occupied territories each day to work in Israel, and then even little symbolic things like the use of the terms *Samaria* and *Judea* instead of a more neutral expression.

Unofficially, the stated position of the government seems to me to shield a much harder line. I have a strong impression that the thrust of Israeli thinking at the official level and in public opinion at large is much more militant than the ambiguities of official statements might suggest. This is summed up in the slogan that a square mile of territory is worth a thousand pages of Arab assurances, and in the simple judgment that the present status quo is better and yields better results for Israel than any conceivable negotiated solution could.

But these expressions refer to military security, after all. And we know that this is not all that is involved in considerations inside Israel. In addition to military questions, there are other motives to consider that tend to work in favor of leaving things as they are : some people's religious attachments to certain places; other people's considerations of the economic advantages of integration with the occupied territories; in other people's minds the hope that in due course, under continuing pressure, Arab governments will radically alter their thinking about the whole problems and undergo profound shifts in their attitudes toward negotiation with Israel.

Despite Israel's growing problems with diplomatic isolation, the size of the military budget, and so forth, she seems assured, at least for the time being, of continued American support and the Soviets' posing no particular danger.

Now we do know, after all, that there is a lively debate inside Israel. There is a very important *other side* to this whole discussion inside Israel. There are those, such as Pinhas Sapir and Arie Eliav, who have been very unhappy with the status quo, but for different reasons; Sapir arguing along ideological and moral grounds that there is something pernicious about sitting in occupation over Arabs and having the Arabs do the dirty jobs inside Israel; Mr. Eliav being concerned with the whole relationship with the Arab world in which he sees the Palestinians as an important link. I think for the moment these two gentlemen and all those who are associated with them may seem rather peripheral to the political process and the negotiating process, but there is always the open question whether future developments, within Israel, within the occupied territories, and within the Arab world, as well as the international climate, will lead to some kind of change in which these voices of dissent will perhaps become more important.

Thank you very much.

MR. FINGER. Thank you very much, Professor Kerr. I think you have done an admirable job of laying the groundwork for our discussion and responding to some parts of the question, "Why not in the Middle East?" You have made it quite clear that it is not a simple thing to accomplish.

We are going to depart slightly from the agenda in order to hear now from Dr. Drew Middleton, a military analyst with the New York *Times,* because Mr. Middleton has to be in California tomorrow.

Russian Presence and Economic Interests in the Mediterranean and the Indian Ocean

by Drew Middleton

DR. MIDDLETON. Thank you very much. My talk is mainly about the Soviet presence and the general strategic situation in the Middle East as it has developed in recent years.

I suppose in historical perspective the Soviet entry, first into the eastern Mediterranean and then into adjacent countries and seas, is as important a development as we have seen since sixty years ago or more when the German Empire decided, being at that time the greatest land power, to become the second greatest naval power.

The Soviet movement into the area began with the first shipments of arms to Egypt. They were not Soviet arms; they were done through Czechoslovakia. Today, of course, the Soviet presence still exists in Egypt, although the number has diminished from something like 16,500 to, at the last estimates I saw, about 800 technicians, military advisers, trainers of troops, and special radar and other technical people.

There is a stronger Soviet position in Syria, although by no means a stable one, a growing role in Iraq, and busy diplomacy throughout the Persian Gulf area and in the established states of the Middle East.

The reasons behind this expansion are many and varied, and they spring sometimes from the prejudices of those with whom you talk. I would suggest that on the basis of my own travels in the last ten years out there that the traditional reason for going into an area, that of economic interests—economic interests in the old sense of opening markets or winning access to raw materials—was negligible in the Soviet calculations. Perhaps we could say that interest in oil was an economic reason, but this Soviet interest took rather varied forms.

First, of course, the Soviet Union proclaims its self-sufficiency in oil, although, oddly enough, the number of Russian geological teams working in the area is now about triple what it was in the mid-sixties.

Second, the Russians may not need Middle Eastern oil now, but like everyone else, they understand the speed with which energy demands are rising in their own country, Eastern Europe, and other countries, and to some extent may become dependent on Middle Eastern oil. I am sure that they know the difficulties and the enormous cost of extracting oil and refining it from the new fields in Siberia.

Of course, for a government looking ahead, as I am sure the Soviet government does, the Middle East has another importance. We have all heard, until I am sure we are bored rigid, that the control of the Middle Eastern oil is of mounting importance to the United States, to Western Europe, and to Japan. Boring or not, this is going to be depressingly true late in this decade and into the eighties. The Russians know it as well as we do.

Obviously, they don't wield as much influence today in Iran, Kuwait, and Saudi Arabia—where the bulk of the Middle East oil reserves are located—as they might wish to do. But of course, the governments there, as governments elsewhere, can change. Indeed, as we know from our own bitter experience, great and ambitious powers often accelerate such change in small powers and find that it has not been altogether to their advantage.

However, I think we must keep in mind that if those governments were to change and to be replaced by regimes more favorable to the Soviet Union, then the Russian position, vis-à-vis the United States and Western Europe, undoubtedly would be strengthened. I would prefer, however, to look at the situation in the Persian Gulf in more detail later on.

Now I would like to move from the domain of economics and oil to the strategic implications of the Soviet move. To begin with, a great deal of ink was expended in expressing American horror at the appearance of the Russians in the Mediterranean in the late fifties. It seemed a little silly, because the Russians have been concerned with the eastern Mediterranean and with the countries of what another generation called *The Levant* for over 200 years. If you have read Tolstoy, you will remember that poignant moment in *Anna Karenina* when Bronsky is homesick, like all Russians abroad, hears the voices of Russian sailors singing, and resolves to leave the beguiling Anna and return to Saint Petersburg. The Russians were there even then.

In the second half of the twentieth century the Russian penetration, the Russian movement, has been much greater than anything that happened under the Czars. And this is explicable. First, the withdrawal of the Colonial powers, France and Britain, created a power vacuum in an area of enormous strategic importance to the Soviet Union. Then the long duel between Israel and the Arab world, punctuated by three wars, established a situation in which the Russians, by giving aid to the Arabs, could win friends throughout an increasingly important area to them. In the process of winning these friends, the Soviet Union reduced the influence of the United States in Arab countries. This we all know was in a perilous condition in any case because of American support of Israel, and this position has plainly not been improved by the events of the last five years.

The third explanation for Soviet military activity is, I think, the most important of all. In the late fifties and early sixties it became apparent to anyone who was doing any thinking on the Soviet General Staff that improvements in carrier-borne aviation in the United States Sixth Fleet in the Mediterranean and the introduction into the Mediterranean of American submarines armed with ballistic missiles radically increased the danger to the Soviet Union in either conventional or nuclear war.

Let us not forget, again, that since the end of the First World War, the Russians have regarded the eastern Mediterranean as a defensive area for them. Now suddenly this area is invaded by weapons systems of great range and destructive power. The industrial areas of the Ukraine are within range. The Americans may do anything.

Here, may I add, that this thought runs through all Soviet military writing. Since President Truman's time, the unpredictability of American actions has been dominant in that writing.

So I think it became vitally necessary to the Russians to protect this area. The most obvious form of protection was an expansion of the Black Sea Fleet to include a squadron permanently stationed in the Mediterranean as a check on the activities of the Sixth Fleet. I won't go into the details of this squadron, except to make two points: Its strength varies between fifty and sixty-five ships, combatant and noncombatant, depending on the time of the year. Its quality is extremely high—overall, I would say, higher than that of the Sixth Fleet. Almost all its combatant ships are new, designed and armed to nullify the threat posed by the Sixth Fleet: cruisers and destroyers armed with surface-to-surface missiles to engage the aircraft carriers, which carry the Americans heaviest punch and antisubmarine ships and destroyers to hunt American submarines.

For a number of reasons, some of them highly technical, which are classified until they appear in the *New York Times,* the Soviet squadron and the Sixth Fleet are in a relative balance in the Mediterranean. Of course, when you count the British, French, Italian, and other navies in the inland sea, the balance is much on the side of the NATO powers.

However, the strategic supposition that seems to be followed on the Sixth Fleet and in the Navy Department is that, in the event of war, the Soviet squadron possesses sufficient strength to effectively challenge our role in the Mediterranean.

Now let us turn to the Russian military situation in the Arab states, the Middle East. Their withdrawal from Egypt in 1972 obviously meant a shift in the area's power balances. But this shift had more effect, I submit, on the Israeli-Egyptian situation than it did on the Soviet-American relationship. What it did to the Israeli-Egyptian situation was to take away from Egypt the greater part of its ability to resist Israeli air attack. But as far as our situation vis-à-vis the Soviets, the great loss to the Russians was the air bases in Egypt, from which Soviet naval air units could watch the Sixth Fleet. Since then, surface units of the Soviet squadron have increased their activities along the Syrian coast, particularly off Latakia. They have sent an SA3—that is a SAM missile system—to Syria, and there are persistent reports that their Bear reconnaissance planes are flying from Syrian bases on surveillance missions in the eastern Mediterranean.

If this is true, then the strategic loss to the Soviet Union in the abandonment of the Egyptian bases has to some extent been made up. Whether the Soviet penetration will ever match that in Egypt in the sixties is doubtful. Syria at the moment seems to be far warier than Nasser's Egypt was over the wisdom of a mass Russian presence in their country. Iraq may be a more fertile field. In April of last year Premier Kosygin signed a treaty based roughly on the Soviet-

Egyptian model. This provided that the two nations would assist each other in strengthening their defenses and, "coordinate their positions," in the event of a threat to peace, with both countries interpreting what "threat to peace" was individually.

Thus far, the result has been a considerable increase in the flow of Soviet arms to Iraq, the introduction of a good many technicians and trainers, and the establishment of a number of SAM sites in the country, presumably as much to protect Soviet as Iraq installations.

I think we can assume that in the future the Soviet military presence in the Middle East, while perhaps less pervasive than it was in Egypt, say, five years ago, will be extremely strong; strong enough to be an important, perhaps the key factor in any thinking in Washington about aid to Israel in the event of a successful and united Arab attack.

But, of course, the whole field is widened now. The stakes have risen. We have to think, if we are thinking in strategic terms, not only of the eastern Mediterranean, but also of the Persian Gulf. The reason is the increasing dependence of the United States, Western Europe, and Japan on Middle Eastern oil. This is expected to grow in the next ten years. Most of that oil will come from Iran, Saudi Arabia, and Kuwait. The Persian Gulf is literally a military vacuum. The situation is very much like that in the eastern Mediterranean after the British and the French got out. There is no permanent foreign military power in the area.

Iran's military program at the moment promises that in two or three years, if all the weapons are delivered and the men are trained, Iran will be far more powerful than any of its neighbors. The two superpowers, the United States and the Soviet Union, obviously have very important interests in the area. Peace and friendly governments are essential to the United States if the oil is to flow and continue to flow, not only to ourselves but to our allies in Western Europe.

Instability and hostile governments would favor the Soviet Union. The easiest and perhaps the cheapest American insurance—that is, if you believe the Department of the Navy—is the presence of American naval power. At present this is on a very modest scale, a couple of old destroyers and an old tender. The Soviet Navy, although it sends missions into the Gulf—flotillas of two or three ships to show the flag—does not maintain a squadron permanently in the area. They are, as I say, a long way from their bases. Most of the ships come from Vladivostok; some have made the long trip out of the Black Sea around Africa and into the Indian Ocean; and all of the

Soviet missile-carrying submarines that we know of—I am talking about ballistic missile-carrying submarines now—come from Murmansk in northern Russia.

However, there are reports in Washington, which some people there believe, that the Soviet Union will build a naval base for Iraq under the new treaty on an island at the head of the Persian Gulf. If this is realized, then it is reasonable to assume that Soviet ships will have the use of the base and that the way will be opened to the establishment of a Russian naval force on a permanent basis in the Persian Gulf.

Before we leave the area, let us recall that there is a serious potential for instability. Border fighting between North and South Yemen has recurred throughout this century. The People's Democratic Republic of Yemen believe Saudi Arabia wants to drive a corridor through to the Indian Ocean. There has been some fighting between the People's Republic and a group of exiles and the United National Front of South Yemen, a group backed by Saudi Arabia. There is fighting going on in Dhofar, with the Popular Front for the liberation of Oman and the Arab Gulf fighting a guerrilla war against the Sultan of Oman's forces. The Sultan has the support of the United States, Britain, Iran, and, to some extent, Saudi Arabia. This support, I am afraid, is mostly verbal. The Soviet Union and China back the Popular Front.

None of this is on a large scale. It is important because fighting is taking place in an area of such vital interest to both East and West, and because it is an area in which there are political, even religious, passions that have existed for centuries.

The assessments of the strategic importance of the Indian Ocean begin, I think, on a basis that this is again a highly sensitive area for the Soviet Union. Weapons influence strategy. The American ballistic missile submarines in that area already are within range of some of the Siberian industrial sites. When the Trident submarines, with their ultra-long-range missiles, come into service late in this decade or probably early in the eighties, such ships in the Indian Ocean will command almost every important industrial area of southern Russia and Siberia. A Russian response, naturally, is progressing along the lines comparable to those in the Mediterranean ten years ago. The naval forces are generally being increased. They are not offensive forces; they are almost entirely defensive. Their function is to threaten the American ballistic missile submarines and to keep them, if possible, at the outer limit of their operational ranges.

A year ago the United States Navy moved the western boundary of the Pacific Fleet into the middle of the Indian Ocean. This was more of a paper transaction than an actual threat.

There is very little until the present naval acquisition program is completed—the end may be another seven or eight years—that the United States can do without wakening its fleet in other areas. But it raises some intriguing questions.

Does the United States intend to establish a permanent naval presence in the Indian Ocean? A subsidiary question is, obviously: Would this be politically wise? Finally, would it in fact be militarily feasible? Would we get enough out of it to compensate us for the great expenditure in money and ships and men that it would involve?

Strategy in the Middle East, therefore, embraces a great deal more than just the immediate area of The Levant, in weapons and in men. It could lead to confrontation in the eastern Mediterranean, but it could equally lead to confrontation in the Persian Gulf or in the Indian Ocean.

To the next generation the Persian Gulf may be as important in world strategy and to their futures as the English Channel and the North Sea were in the first fifty years of this century.

Thank you very much.

MR. FINGER. Thank you very much, Drew. I am very glad indeed that your assignment did not take you away from us today.

It is now my pleasure to call on a colleague from the City University of New York, Professor Gil Carl AlRoy, who will speak to us about the military capabilities in the region.

Military Capabilities in the Middle East

by Gil Carl AlRoy

ARAB-ISRAELI MILITARY DISPARITY*

PROFESSSOR ALROY. Ambassador Finger, ladies and gentlemen, the state of the military balance in the Arab-Israeli conflict is clear and simple: There is no such thing at all and most probably it never really existed even in the past. What does exist is a profound disparity that has been growing from the past. The use of the term *disparity,* rather than just *gap,* is indicated by the fact that the military capacities involved are not simply more or less of the same, but actually disparate, meaning distinct in respect to ultimate character. They are, in effect, not even comparable. One side wages modern warfare with much competence; the other has never yet been able to produce it.

It seems to me that the general and persistent conventional reference to the term *power balance* in this context is indicative of a general problem we have in the Middle East area, and that is that we suffer not so much from an inadequacy of data as from an inadequate conceptual framework. That is, we do not really need

* © Copyright 1973, 1974 Gil Carl AlRoy.

more facts but a better understanding of these facts we already possess.

Thus, the essential nature of the Arab-Israeli confrontation in the Middle East is conventionally regarded as fitting the model of ordinary conflicts, that is, disputes amenable to solution by a compromise of interests. The whole of the diplomatic process is founded on the search for the elusive formula that would fortuitously prescribe such a delicate balance of necessary concessions. The concensus of academic Orientalists goes precisely in the opposite direction. Few, if any, share the conventional assumption as to the nature of the Arab-Jewish conflict. Those who give this impression by public support of diplomatic initiatives, for instance, do not always make it clear enough that they really expect not more than another armistice to crown these efforts.

Estimating the military relationship in the Arab-Jewish conflict in the Middle East has proved to be all along a truly disastrous enterprise for nearly all concerned. Just one indication of the spectacular failure already at the beginning of the conflict is that World War II heroes, like General George Marshall and Marshal Bernard Montgomery, predicted in 1948 that the Arabs would sweep the Jews before them into the sea in a matter of days or weeks at most. All of the others did not do much better. When the first Arab-Israeli war was over, those rebuffed by the outcome wondered what had gone wrong with the world rather than with their predictions. The war was, in effect, declared a fluke and appropriate explanations emerged, the most popular citing morale, an explanation that almost all endorsed. This happens to be a particularly useful explanation: when a war is over, one can cogently assert that the winners had superior morale.

Then came the much-touted revolutionary transformation of Arab society with Nasserism and the avalanche of Soviet war material and instruction and training adding to the expectation that if the Israeli jig won't be up the next time, it certainly will prove more difficult to check Arab might. When the Arabs were overrun even faster and more decisively than before, in 1956, the new rationalization was both handy and fascinating: Anglo-French-Israeli collusion. The second trial was seen as a fluke, too, because the Arabs did not fight the Israelis but, rather, rushed back to face the real military power from the West, or so it seemed.

Undaunted by the actual experiences of two major wars and several minor engagements, the initial distortions were simply carried forward to the June days of 1967. We may have forgotten the stupendous performance of military expertise in the West in that war, so a few samples will be allowed to speak for themselves. Thus, on the B.B.C., while the war was already in progress, early news of the Arab debacle was treated as fantasy. The consensus of the British press, claiming to speak with special authority on Middle Eastern affairs, was critical of the [British] government for standing aside while Israel was being destroyed. In a summary of the B.B.C. coverage of the war, Randolph Churchill wrote: "None of the commentators realized the speed of the Israeli victory." The head of the prestigious Institute of Strategic Studies thought it would take two or three days before the result of the air battle would be known. In answer to a question, he argued that if the Israelis lost the air battle disastrously, then they could be swept into the sea. A few hours later the defense correspondent of an important journal ventured the unfortunate opinion that the Israeli claim of successful air strikes was wildly exaggerated. "If they have destroyed fifty or sixty planes, they have done rather well." On the Home Service at about the same time, the Middle East specialist of the same Institute for Strategic Studies was making similarly unfortunate predictions. "It's completely wrong to assume that the Egyptians are going to repeat the debacle of 1956." Official American military estimates, for which unsupported claims of great accurary were afterward made, appear not to have deviated from the general assumption that the Arabs had improved since 1956 at least to some extent in relation to their foes' military capacities.

The June war left a deeper impression of Israeli military power on conventional military expertise, but the tendency to dismiss the experience as "flukey" persisted. Like in 1956, it was not so much the fact of Israeli victory that surprised. What had to be explained away were its steadily rising dimensions—flatly negating the conceptual imperative of the profession. So the war was turned into a gimmick or a stroke of highly specialized skill. It was quickly said that it was merely a matter of who could catch whom with one's planes down on the ground; at most, it could be a matter of whose pilots and planes are better, which means training and access to some great power's arsenal. When Israeli superiority is confused with Phantoms and myths of invincibility, there is no real understanding of the situation. As I wrote in the Howe and Gershman anthology last year, let the Egyptians just set out to secure a bridgehead on Sinai, and the conventional wisdom will turn hysterically to visions of Israel's future demise.

What accounts for this perennially bad performance of the

military professionals and their journalistic and even some academic affiliates? There are two kinds of reasons. One is conceptual—and I will deal with that briefly—and the other deals, I think, with the Western Christendom's folklore concerning both the Muslim and the Jewish worlds. These I have expressed elsewhere as the "Orient in Flames" and the "Living Corpse" syndromes, and together they produce deep anxiety concerning the Arab East and expectations of eventual doom for the Jewish state. The "Orient in Flames" syndrome, as I like to call it, is the modern bugaboo par excellence of Western man. It is rooted in the memory of the fury of fierce Saracens breaking over the horizon like a wild storm, setting the world ablaze with elemental, savage, uncontrollable force. For many centuries the Muslim hordes indeed terrorized Christendom, and what persists is the inclination to frighten ourselves with the sheer thought of the ominous consequences of the Muslim hordes. Awesome visions quickly arise in our minds still of the East aflame bringing disaster over us all, and the terror numbs our intelligence to the point where we fail to invoke even rudimentary examination and critique of the propositions involved.

But by definition, news from the Middle East is always ominous, the situation there is always explosive. It is a measure of this frenzy that a nation there can actually expect to impose its will on us by threatening to commit military suicide, for they expect that *we* will rescue them.

As for the Israelis, I think here we carry forward from our Christian past the concept of the "Living Corpse," which simply means that no matter how secure or prosperous Jews seemed at times, the writing was always on the wall, for eventually distress and disaster were surely to be their lot. Hence, a widespread expectation that, appearances to the contrary notwithstanding, Israeli security and power are always illusory, transitory, chimerical.

The conceptual failure concerns the notion of military modernity. Once armies in the Middle East acquire the appearance of military forces in advanced industrial societies, through the acquisition of equipment and the imitation of organizational structures and action patterns, we think of them as modern armies. Hence, the basic blunder to conceive of the two opponents in the conflict there as essentially in the same generic category—in the same league, in the same race, playing the same game, as eminently comparable. One just happens to be better than the other, since it has won in the past, but the other must improve with time and, having done this substantially, will eventually crush the other with the sheer weight of its numbers and resources.

Time after time the military experts place side by side the statistical tables of manpower and material in various categories, though they know well the emptiness of the ritual, only to draw the tables out and opt for "intangibles" as spelling the difference between Israeli and Arab martial capacities. This constitutes a veritable Pandora's box of hunches, some imaginative and others less so; but for the military professional the problem essentially reduces itself to training and instruction by officers from more competent armies. Among the military in particular, the notion reigns supreme that more advanced societies can impart to more backward ones truly contemporary military capacities by this means; hence, military assistance programs all over the world; Vietnamization; Soviet efforts in Egypt, Syria, and elsewhere; and other enormous expenditures to this end in utterly poor nations.

Recently a retired American general opined in the *New York Times* that, since Soviet training seems invariably futile in Egypt, these instructors must deliberately fail in order to keep Egypt forever weak and dependent upon them.

The very idea of giving away military modernity or taking it ready-made from others remains unchallenged. Strengthened in the recent past by some loose talk among social scientists on the military as egregious modernizers in underdeveloped societies, this notion also happens to fit in well with ideas of modernization in general prevailing in the Arab world, ideas that predispose to seeking the fruits of modernity from others without really participating in it.

In reality, while they appear as modern armies, Arab forces are inherently unable to wage modern war; that is, *to sustain a war of movement on a large scale,* not just use sporadically imported weaponry. What they invariably produce are variants of premodern warfare, taking the familiar forms of small hit-and-run attacks and sedentary attrition, preferably artillery barrages from relative safety, punctuated by only fragmentary maneuvers reminiscent of those in truly modern armies. The availability of fine, sophisticated material does not compel Arab military behavior toward modernity; rather, the opposite happens: in the hands of Arab troops, the tank, the epitome of mobile warfare, turns into a more-or-less stationary piece of artillery, sometimes even ends up buried in the ground as a fixed piece. The avalanche of foreign machinery has not turned Arab armies into mechanically competent armies; rather, they are now wasters and destroyers of such machinery on a gigantic scale, and, in the process, wasters of the lives and arms of their foe, as well.

The facts themselves are well known. Only their import has not been fully grasped, because of the prevailing misconceptions of military modernity and ignorance of the anthropological and historical-sociological study of war. Works by Max Weber and Quincy Wright have probed the connection between change in society and warfare, indicating in particular the qualitative leaps in warfare, accompanying great historical-social transformations. Preliterate societies everywhere thus fail to transcend patterns of primitive warfare, characterized by the ambush and hit-and-run attack and similar sporadic acts. Arab societal warfare is almost purely primitive warfare, even including the characteristic penchant for mutilation and war cries.

Arabs also spontaneously produce the warfare pattern typical of all backward rural societies, which is *brigandage,* or *Robin Hoodism,* of which *Antara* is the romantic model and the *fidai* a later variant. The warfare of more advanced historical societies already manifests explicit tactics and discipline in larger formations engaging in stationary, protracted, and scattered hostilities. Historical warfare in modern costume and with similarly incongruous mechanical props essentially describes the wars waged by Arab contemporary armies, whether Moroccan fighting Algerian, or Egyptian fighting Yemenite, or any of them facing the Jews. Only much later, in the wake of the scientific revolution in the West, and in tandem with the industrial revolution thereafter, arose the unprecedented capacity for war of movement with great power and large scale, or modern war. Historians place the "military revolution" in the seventeenth century and even earlier. In the Middle East only the Israelis wage modern war, and do so in up-to-date manner.

The real difference in actual warfare capacities in the Arab-Israeli conflict thus spans vast changes going back several centuries in Western social development. In fact, the opposing societies stand on different sides of the scientific revolution. "In an advanced industrial country," recently wrote an Arab physicist, "not only is science sponsored as a means to national growth, but a scientific approach permeates normal life." In societies such as his own, science is viewed as alien to life. "Many circles in such countries still regard scientific activity as a form of conspicuous cultural consumption, the intellectual equivalent to adorning oneself with expensive jewelry or ostentatiously consuming large amounts of food, drink, and services.

The value of scientific production is often measured in terms of the facade of modernity which it bestows upon the society in question." He calculated that one Israeli produces about as much science as one hundred Arabs; but even this shocking figure understates the enormity of the actual disparity, for the Israelis participate in the processes of science in a creative capacity, while the Arabs do not. Not themselves engaged in the works of modernity, merely consuming its product in the form of goods, technology, and services invented and produced by others, the Arabs must start at every new level of development from scratch. "The result," wrote Bernard Lewis, "is that the disparity in scientific knowledge, technological capacity, and, therefore, of military power between the Middle East and the advanced countries of the West is greater now than a hundred and fifty years ago when the whole process of Westernization began."

The Arabs are, to paraphrase the words of J. C. Hurewitz, shooting at a moving target when trying to catch up with their Jewish foe. And, incidentally, the talk of just a "technology gap," so dear to military experts and many Arabs, is self-indulgent; for without a living, indigenous science, imported technology dies and dependence on new imports is made constant. Worse still, without it a nation can not even make rational judgments as to what to borrow abroad.

It is the consensus of my academic colleagues who have made substantial studies of the military disparity between the Israelis and the Arabs—Bell, Hurewitz, Safran, and myself—that the Arabs are not catching up and will not do so in the foreseeable future.

There now appears to be wider agreement with at least the gist of this judgment; however, in the absence of real conviction, it would be only so good as borrowed technology in a scientific vacuum. A good test may already be upon us because of the threatened implications of the latest oil problem, with the enormous wealth flowing to Arab treasuries seen as precipitating the modernization of the Arab world and as hastening the future decline of Israeli power yet even more.

The irony of the predicted oil riches is that it puts still greater means at the service of the already profound Arab compulsion to obtain ready-made the dazzling, latest products of the creativity of others. The outlook is for more Kuwaits or super-Kuwaits—futuristic environments for atavistic stagnation—for the further deepening of what the Tunisian critic, Shafiq Zaher, described as the Arab penchant for supporting and preserving backwardness with the latest achievements of the advanced societies. In real terms it is more likely to retard the necessary changes in Arab society and culture than to precipitate them. The oil riches might have a serious impact on the military situation if an entire foreign modern army could be hired for a war with Israel.

Equally ironic is the supposition that Israeli power is simply a function of American power—a widespread delusion essential to sustain Arab ideology and self-esteem and assorted needs felt abroad— ironic because the roots of Israeli power lie precisely in the imperative denial of dependence involving national destiny. It was the refusal to copy wholly from others, even down to the reproduction of their European social structure, that characterized the new Jewish community already before the establishment of British-ruled Palestine. The inclination to make do with what was available, to adapt borrowings to their own circumstances and needs, to discover everything for themselves—all this molded the new culture and naturally fashioned military affairs, also.

The familiar capacity to improvise and innovate, even in the crunch of battle, is possible only because the Israelis tamper with their own invention; they inherently grasp a military style all their own and feel comfortable with doctrines they themselves devised and weapons they created or adapted to their own needs.

Contrast this with the condition of mainly rural Muslims pressed to fit into utterly alien systems of action, replete with equipment equally alien in concept and manufacture, all originally created by others, for others' needs and circumstances. It does make a difference whether or not Israel is denied American support, for example, in the number of casualties and hardships suffered, but it is difficult to see how the essential military disparity with the Arabs can thus be affected.

Questions have been raised concerning the Israeli military preponderance : Is it conducive to peace? Can Israel force the Arabs to accept her peace terms? These are arresting questions, but badly in need of some rephrasing, since it is dubious that peace, real peace, is at all attainable. If we speak instead of an armistice, by whatever name—"peaceful agreement," a new phrase in "the battle of destiny," or some other wording—it becomes immediately obvious that some such condition has already been imposed by Israel on the Arabs, while the latter still seek to have the international community impose on Israel another kind of armistice, one more favorable to themselves.

Indeed, not for nothing does the stalemate focus on borders and withdrawals; for it is there that both sides have simply projected their essentially incompatible, fundamental positions on Jewish statehood. "If you could succeed in bringing total Israeli withdrawal about," affirms Mohammed Hasanein Heykal, in but one version of a theme pervading the Arab world, "you would have passed sentence on the entire state of Israel." On the other side, Golda Meir indicates complete agreement when saying that refusal to negotiate new borders is tantamount to refusal to live in peace.

But territory does much more than symbolize to the antagonists the integrity of their very purpose; for on it hinges the Arabs' chance of having another real go at the heart of Israel in the foreseeable future. There has been much irresponsible talk about the irrelevance of borders in the Middle East in this age of rockets and nuclear fission. Quite apart from the fact that none really acts as if this were true, when one's own security is concerned—the Soviet Union, for all its might, required huge parts of Rumania, Poland, Finland, Japan, Germany, and Czechoslovakia, plus all of Estonia, Lithuania, and Latvia, for this purpose—there is the more vital fact that the Arabs are not militarily in this advanced age at all. In it, yes; but not of it. They are still utterly unable to wage a war of movement; they still exist militarily in an age in which a rivulet, a mountain, a defended ridge constituted obstacles and challenges. The impact in space of their warfare is still only skin-deep, epidermic on land, and sporadic and desultory at sea and in the air.

The existing ceasefire lines—whatever else their political or demographic or other consequences—spell military frustration for the Arabs. For the very idea of marching from the Suez, not just a few miles, but to the heart of Israel, must bring nightmares to Arab commanders, who usually betray a pretty good awareness of the real limitations of Arab war capacities, although they must express it in a way consistent with self-esteem.

Back at the old borders, one is indeed at the heart of Israel, often without having to move at all: the great mass of the country's population and industry lies within range of ordinary artillery and even simple rifle shot. The capacity to advance several miles might then cut the country in half and nearly liquidate the resulting segments. To paraphrase a particularly appropriate saying, Muhammed can not now go to the mountain, so, with the old armistice lines restored, the mountain would literally come to Muhammed.

Incidentally, none of this is offset by demilitarization. The device of demilitarization sounds impressive only this side of the water; the Middle Eastern antagonists know only too well that not only did it not work between them, ever, but that demilitarized zones actually

engendered tension, triggering large-scale warfare within their con-
fines, even in periods between the major wars.

Finally, what is the role of Israeli military preponderance in the
persisting deadlock? Within the eastern Middle East itself, Israeli
power is so preponderant, so overwhelming, that left really alone to
face the foe, the Arabs would be crushed and there could not even
be a prayer for their cause, though assertion of defiance might occur
at great distance from the region. Even so, given the depth of their
outrage at Jewish dominion, Arab acquiescence and even formal
accommodations would not really signify legitimation, certainly not
among the literate townspeople.

Arab countervailing power comes from the outside, from the
international community, where the Arabs in turn virtually dwarf
those who crush them at home. Their numbers, resources, connections,
and lands lend them extraordinary diplomatic weight, relative to
which Israel shrinks to near insignificance. The disparity is exaggerated in the United Nations, where support is distributed, but only
publicly, collectively, and often just rhetorically. Since this and
similar forums set mild standards of sorts, the unavoidable acknowledgment of power within the region takes the form of bilateral and
often surreptitious dealings with Israel.

Thus, the Arabs get clobbered in the Middle East and recover in
the international community; they withdraw in the field and advance
once more around the table. Israel's great commanders come from
the agrarian sectors; the Arabs' from Sweden: Dayan took the Sinai,
then Hammarskjold took it back. Then Rabin took the Sinai; now
Jarring tries to take it back. While all these men are sure that they
are struggling for peace, the Israelis among them at least have no
illusion as to whose side they are really on. What seems to be happening is that while the Arabs' capacity to have their definitions of the
conflict endorsed abroad has grown, the international community's
capacity to enforce them on the Israelis has weakened. And since
both Israel's autonomous power and the Arabs' leverage abroad are
likely to grow in years to come, the outlook is one for a rather lonely
regional giant whose neighbors harass the rest of the world in growing
rage; a dismal outlook.

So, to conclude, for the time being Israel is in effect imposing its
peace on its neighbors. It is not legitimate or stable, but neither are
most situations around the world.

It seems to me that in the present circumstance the Arab side is
militarily frustrated. But it also seems to me that whether the intention
exists or not, a return to the previous position would curiously put

the Arab side in a position where even their premodern warfare could be effectively waged. Because they will then not have to move. They would be there. And the capacity to wage stationary warfare and cause casualties has never been lacking on the Arab side.

I think that both sides understand very well this proposition, and I think, therefore, much of their behavior can be understood in this light. Thank you very much.

MR. FINGER. Thank you very much, Professor AlRoy.

We are going to make one other change in our program, with your permission. We would like now to have a brief discussion on the three statements that have been made up to now.

If some of you have reactions to the statements already made, we could use the next twenty minutes in that way. This includes, of course, the right of any of the speakers to raise points with other speakers who have made statements to us today.

PROFESSOR KERR. I wondered from Professor AlRoy's last comment how he could justify it in view of all that he told us in his talk about the congenital weakness of Arab military capability. I must say that I was impressed with the shrewdness with which he analyzed the reasons and the ramifications of Arab weakness, but then at the end he said that of course if they came back to where they were in 1967, then Israel would be highly vulnerable. It seemed to me to be quite a contradiction.

PROFESSOR ALROY. The point I was trying to make in a hurry was the following : The capability that Arab military forces inherently lack is that of sustained mobility on a large scale, in a situation in which getting to the, shall I say, major part of the Israeli population and industry under the present circumstances is not just formidable—it is impossible.

If one finds oneself back at the borders of 1967, one finds that one automatically has within range of ordinary artillery and sometimes plain rifle shots an extraordinarily large proportion of Israel's heartland population.

What I said was not to indicate motivation; I merely said the capacities are such that it does not take very much even for armies practicing historical and primitive warfare to wage highly effective warfare in terms of casualties, and so forth, from this position.

What I wanted to say is that returning to the borders of 1967 is much like Muhammed not being able now to come to the mountain, so the mountain must come within the reach of Muhammed.

MR. FINGER. Professor AlRoy, I had somewhat the same question as Professor Kerr, which is: What has occurred since 1967 to make Israel so much more vulnerable than it was in 1967 when the Arabs could have used the stationary position in the same way you suggest?

PROFESSOR ALROY. I do not believe that the vulnerability has increased. If we merely project the known capacities, then we know that plain, stationary war of attrition can be waged from those lines without any need for modern military capacity. It is not necessarily a question of greater vulnerability or smaller vulnerability; we may never find out. What I am saying is that it does make a difference whether or not an army that is unable to wage modern war finds itself on top of the enemy or whether it has to go a long distance to get there. This to me seems to be the essence of the problem.

PROFESSOR GEORGE GRUEN. I was wondering whether Professor AlRoy really means to imply a congenital insufficiency on the Arab side, because historically it was the Arabs who were the transmitters of scientific method, although a more primitive scientific method, from the Greek civilization to the West, which was then in the Dark Ages. I am concerned about stereotyping national capabilities. You will recall that fifty years ago the popular image was that Jews could not farm and could not fight. The Israelis have certainly changed that stereotype.

I think we have just seen some stories about an oil university being established in Saudi Arabia. I am sure that the graduates of that university as individuals will be of a high technical calibre. I am not saying every Saudi Arabian is now on the technological level of the Israelis or the French or the Americans—but you already have a cadre of Western-trained persons who are thinking in Western terms. Certainly the American-educated Saudi oil minister's approach is very sophisticated.

My question, in other words, is: Is this an inherent gap or is it not that, as a result of training in technology over a matter of time, there can not be a process of modernization, true modernization, in certain Arab countries as it has begun at least in Turkey and various other places that have historically been non-Western?

PROFESSOR ALROY. I don't really like the term *congenital*. I don't think the problem is one of individuals. It has been demonstrated that Arab-speaking people, whether Muslims or Christians, have reached levels of excellence in science, in medicine. It is not a matter of individuals; it is a problem of culture and civilization. It is the whole society.

The subject, it seems to me, is much too complex for us to discuss in this setting. The question raised by Professor Gruen is interesting, but I don't think I can cope with it like this. It is true that many, many centuries ago individuals in the Islamic civilization acted as transmitters of Hellenistic thought to the then rather stagnant Western world. That is quite true.

What we have to talk about today, it seems to me, is the very, very shocking situation that after 150 years of Westernization in countries like Egypt, there is unbelievable dependency on other people's modern capacities. This, it seems to me, is the problem.

PROFESSOR RAPHAEL PATAI. I would like to add a comment to Dr. AlRoy's presentation, and then address a question to Dr. Kerr. I think Dr. AlRoy takes a somewhat too pessimistic view of the capacities of the Arabs in the scientific field. Taking a long-range approach to this issue, let us imagine that this meeting is taking place not today, but a thousand years ago: the leaders in every scientific field at that time were Arabs. There is no congenital or historical reason why this leadership role should not be again at least approached by them.

The first sign that there is a movement in this direction is that in recent years there have arisen more and more Arab critics of the Arab situation with regard to science. Just recently I read an Arabic book by Dr. Hāmid Ammār, entitled *The Building of Man,* in which the author criticizes with extreme sharpness precisely this lack of scientific attitude among the Arabs.

I think one can observe generally that whenever such a criticism occurs or arises, it is followed by an attempt to remedy the situation criticized. In other words, I think that we may be just now at the very beginning of a period when the Arabs will again enter more actively into scientific endeavors. I think that the threefold debacle they suffered at the hands of Israel is certainly an additional impetus propelling them in that direction.

This is my comment.

Now my question to Dr. Kerr is this: He spoke about Egypt and I understand him as saying that he takes seriously the intention of the Egyptians to make peace with Israel in case Israel withdraws to the pre-1967 boundaries. At the same time, he emphasized that when it comes to the statements, pronouncements, and threats of the Palestinian Arabs, those should not be quite taken at face value, because it is very easily possible that they are merely statements for external use and that in reality the Palestinians will be satisfied with less than liquidating Israel. On what basis do you give greater credit to Egyptian statements and lesser credit to Palestinian Arab statements?

PROFESSOR KERR. I thank Professor Patai for his question, but if you recall I tried to stress in my talk the ambiguities on the part of all parties, including the Egyptians, including the Palestinians, including the Israelis. I simply tried to underscore the point that to dismiss Egyptian professions of interest in a peaceful settlement out of hand, to the extent that these professions are even completely overlooked in many quarters, seems to me rather simplistic, and that if we had the time to devote a full afternoon's discussion to what lies under the surface of Egpytian declarations and intentions, I think that perhaps the point could be established that at least there is something there of some consequence at the very minimum in terms of serious interest.

On the Palestinian side, I simply would like to suggest that again you can not take things at face value. I do not take the Egyptian leaders' statements at face value, neither to their domestic public nor to the international public. But on the Fedayeen's part, I think we have to take into account that after having suffered one frustration and defeat after another, both at the hands of Israel and at the hands of a number of Arab governments, it would be rather surprising if the Palestinians had not had a practical tactical, or strategic thought about how to move politically in the next twenty-five years. I think that they have.

MR. FINGER. Mr. Bergson had his hand up earlier, and then Ambassador Doron had asked to speak.

MR. BERGSON. I would just like to ask two questions of Professor AlRoy, without taking a stand on his fascinating, provocative remarks.

One, would he dare project any kind of a date, with respect to the present imbalance or disparity, be it ten years, fifty years, two thousand years, assuming your thesis is right, that we are heading, no matter how slow a curve, into a position where Israel's neighbors, commonly referred to as Arab, would achieve that degree of modern civilization, scientific development, for which one can arrive at immoral modern warfare?

The second question is: What is the consequence politically, assuming the military analysis of your thesis, if it were realized, if the military experts stopped making their flimsy analyses and assumed your analysis, Professor; would this encourage a real state of understanding and peace??

PROFESSOR ALROY. The Middle East has produced many prophets, and I am not going to join them.

It seems to me, from a practical point of view—in view of the fact that the Israelis are in effect already in a nuclear age themselves—

that if in our lifetime, and sooner perhaps, that moment arrives, then the issue has already been closed. It seems to me that, in military terms, we can close the door, for all practical purposes.

As far as the other question is concerned, I believe that the outrage felt by most Arabs—and I know there are variations among people we call *Arabs*—the sense of outrage particularly among the Sunni Arabs nearby, and the very existence of Jewish dominion, no matter what its shape—I think it is so profound, it is so deep, that with their characteristic capacity for self-delusion, there will always be on the horizon some future event that they will see as rectifying this cosmic injustice. Whether it is the future Taiwanization of Israel or the oil crisis or the turning of the *sabras* against the founders' ideals or the "normalization" of the Jews, however they see it; I do not believe that a sharp realization of their military shortcomings will produce much of a change in that respect. As a matter of fact, I feel that Arab military commanders and many other Arabs, not military specialists, have always known very well what their limitations are, and they express them in words consistent with self-respect.

But you see what they do with it? They are using that very limited military capacity in order to obtain leverage within the international community to produce the results that they can not produce with'n their limited military capacity. It seems to me that is the impor*-nt thing.

MR. BERGSON. May I have one additional statement. Could you give an indication of how Israel, as the clearly stronger power, should behave in comparison to how the obviously weaker opponent, as you have defined them, should be, and I would appreciate if you would say how your analysis should affect a line of behavior and future behavior from the obviously superior Israel militarily.

PROFESSOR ALROY. I want to tell you that in my many years of concern in Middle Eastern affairs, involving a long residence in the area itself, I made one important discovery that I would like to enunciate here. I have discovered that the Jews are not good Methodists and the Arabs are not good Presbyterians. The Arabs are Arabs, and the Jews are Jews, and they both have their hang-ups. And no amount of preaching here in the name of reason is going to make the slightest imprint on anybody.

MR. FINGER. I won't certify that that is an answer, but I do want to go on to further discussion.

I have two speakers, Ambassador Doron of the Israeli Mission and Mahmoud M. Osman of the Egyptian Mission, and I hope I won't be misunderstood if I make a plea that we do not repeat the Security Council debates.

AMBASSADOR DORON. Mr. Chairman, when you opened this meeting today, you started by enumerating a number of situations in which solutions have been found or solutions had been approached by means of the process of negotiations in one form or another. Then you concluded your opening remarks by asking the question : Why not in the Middle East?

I was hoping that Professor Kerr would try to provide an answer to this. His assessment that the situation there is complicated was, I am sure, not intended as an answer and obviously it is not, because especially when the situation is complicated, no effort should be left untried to achieve some kind of solution or at least progress toward a solution.

Professor Kerr seemed to have been impressed by some kind of a weakening or softening in the Arab position, and especially in their reply to the letter of Dr. Jarring of 8 February 1971.

It seems that the use for the first time ever—when I say "ever," I mean at least since 1947—of the word *peace* or *peace arrangement* or *agreement* or *peace settlement* in that reply caught the headlines of the press. But none of the conditions that hedged in this *peace* or *peace agreement,* and none of the subsequent statements, or even the conditions contained in the same letter of reply, were used. Just as the Israeli repetition, day in and day out, of our wanting to reach peace, of our quest for peace, makes no headlines any more, because it is not new. It is a thing that we have been saying for the last twenty-six years at least.

The thing to remember is this : that within a few days of that very same letter in reply to Dr. Jarring, where the word *peace* or the words *peace agreement* were mentioned for the first time, Egyptian leaders and the leader of Libya and authoritative writers in the press of Egypt made it quite clear what they really meant.

First of all, the distinction was drawn between some kind of third-class peace arrangement, Salaam, which means peace but not that kind of peace, not the kind of peace that you and I and everybody else understand when one speaks of peace. What was not given in the letter was the English equivalent for another word in Arabic, which is *sulh, conciliation,* actually, *forgiveness,* and again it is a word, interestingly enough, that is very close to the Hebrew *Seliha,* which is *forgiveness.* After all, the languages have the same root. So that it was not the real conciliation, a true peace, but just some kind of a "little arrangement," that the Egyptians had in mind.

In fact, within a few days after that, there was an article by Mohammed Hassanein Heykal that made quite clear what they meant: "Yes, as the first step to regain our territories lost in 1967 we will make some kind of peace, agreement, or arrangement. The next step, the next stage, will be to put an end to the State of Israel." But this, of course, did not catch the headlines, and it apparently is not taught at some universities. Since then there have been so many other similar statements.

Today is the 4th of May. Well, three days ago President Sadat of Egypt made another speech that held out very little hope of any kind of peace settlement.

On the other hand, we indeed are intransigent. We are intransigent in the sense that twenty-six years ago we said we were prepared to negotiate a peace, and today are still in exactly the same position. We are prepared to negotiate a peace without any peace conditions. We really want peace.

MR. OSMAN. I want to address myself first to some of the remarks stated by Professor Kerr. As to what he referred to, as far as the Arab-Israeli crisis is concerned, I must say that, as comprehensive as was the exposition he gave us this afternoon, it is regrettable, however, that he stated what he thinks is the fact, that the Resolution 242 was not adequately covered in the local press, which he interprets as a forbidding circumstance. I can assure Professor Kerr that the full text of Resolution 242 was published in the domestic press of Egypt, as well as throughout the entire Arab world.

However, suppose, just hypothetically speaking, that this resolution had not received its due coverage in the domestic press, I want to remind him that we are, after all, working within the framework of the United Nations. Does this mean that unless a resolution adopted by the Security Council unanimously finds adequate coverage in the domestic papers, no matter in Egypt or in Jordan or anywhere else in the areas of conflict around the world, does this mean that this resolution is null and void?

May I allude to what has just been said by the representative of Israel. He indulged in the literal translation of the word *peace*. I, of course, disagree with him totally. He is totally mistaken, because the word *peace* has one and one only interpretation and that is *Salaam*. It has nothing to do with what he called *sulh*. It has nothing to do with what he called *conciliation*. Salaam means *Salaam*. However, when we accepted 242, we were addressing the permanent members of the Security Council as well as the nonpermanent ones. We were even addressing the international community embodied in the United Nations.

So the permanent members know exactly what Egypt is after. The nonpermanent members know exactly what we are after. And we don't have to deviate from the real endeavor exerted by Egypt since 1967, which nobody can dispute now, that after six years have elapsed since the occupation of Egypt in Sinai, the Golan Heights, and the entire West Bank of Jordan, nobody disputes the genuine and candid desire of Egypt for peace.

If the representative of Israel is talking about the ways of solving this problem by emphasizing the element or the variable of negotiations, he better than anybody else knows that it was Israel who obstructed the way for negotiations by repeating now and again, everyday, systematically, that Sharm-el-Sheik is not subject to negotiations, that Jerusalem is not negotiable, that the Golan Heights are out of the negotiation realm.

If all of these areas are not negotiable, how then can we even think of getting into this process of negotiation?

Now I would like to address myself for a while to Professor AlRoy. Actually I am at a loss as to what he has said. He was juggling between religion, military competence, oil technology, and all kinds of knowledge that he assumes that he knows. Apparently he has been in this area. Unfortunately I regret the fact that he has been talking for almost fifteen or twenty minutes about war and not a single mention in all that he has told us this afternoon about the prospects of peace in the area.

I want to ask him a direct question, and I anticipate from him a direct answer: Does he by any chance maintain that the prospects of peace in the area are only and solely based and established on annexation of other's lands or not? Does he, in other words, assume that annexing lands, changing their demographic physical construction, is conducive to peace? Does he consecrate or preach occupation as a device for peace or not? I thank you.

MR. FINGER. Thank you. I would like to exercise a chairman's prerogative to postpone further discussion until we have heard from our next three speakers. No one will be cut off.

In defense of those who have spoken, I must say that I did not expect Professor Kerr to provide the entire answer to the question: "Why not the Middle East?" We will have a day and a half, and we will have done well to have approached the answer in that time. But his statement, I thought, did provide useful background. In defense of Professor AlRoy, he was asked to speak about the military balance in the region. This, I think, explains why he addressed military subjects.

I would like to go back to our presentation of papers, because we have with us a most distinguished professor of international relations, Dr. Hans Morgenthau, and it is a great privilege to hear from him.

Big Power Confrontations in the Middle East

by Hans J. Morgenthau

DR. MORGENTHAU. Mr. Chairman, ladies and gentlemen, the conflict in the Middle East operates on three different levels: the level of great power confrontation, the level of the local governmnts in conflict, and the level of popular movements uncontrolled by any government.

Those three levels are, on the one hand, distinct; on the other hand, of course, they operate upon each other and they do so in an ascending level of complexity.

So we start with what is relatively simple and we will end with what is relatively complex.

The confrontation of the great powers is, of course, a mere outgrowth of the commitment of the United States to Israel and the commitment of the Soviet Union to the Arabs.

Those commitments differ in intensity. In fact, the commitment of the United States to Israel, at least for the time being, is unqualified, in a sense total, while the commitment of the Soviet Union to the Arab states is ambiguous and by no means total.

The Soviet Union has a rather low opinion of Arab military potential, and there has existed a considerable amount of friction

69

between the Soviet Union and certain Arab states. The expulsion of the so-called Russian technicians from Egypt on the initiative of the Egyptian government is, of course, a measure of the tension that has existed between the two states, for the expulsion of the Russians greatly weakens the military and political position of Egypt. Thus, Egypt would not have taken this drastic step if there had not been very serious differences of opinion and policy as well as a general resentment between the two governments.

This resentment and this difference in positions and policies as well as objectives is clearly demonstrated by the kind of military aid that the Soviet Union has given Egypt. It has given lavishly, up to the point at which the Egyptians can not win a war, while the United States has given lavishly to Israel up to the point at which Israel can not be defeated.

So we have here an imbalance, which is extremely reassuring to the Israelis and extremely frustrating to the Arabs. But this is essentially the position of the two superpowers facing each other in the Middle East. Neither of them is interested in war and both, in different ways, are interested in the status quo. Neither is interested in the disappearance of Israel. For if Israel were to disappear tomorrow, viewed from the perspective of the Soviet Union, the Soviet Union would lose the main lever it has in the Arab world. Since there is no love lost between the Arab world and the Soviet Union, once Israel disappears, the inevitable present dependence of the Arab states upon the Soviet Union would necessarily disappear, too, and there would be a break or at least a great lessening of ties between the Arabs and the Soviet Union.

So the Soviet Union has an interest in what has generally been called *controlled tension* in the Middle East, while the United States has an interest in a peaceful settlement of any kind that preserves the survival of Israel.

On the local level, there exists an impasse that can not be resolved under present circumstances. It seems to me to be idle to talk about peace per se and for both sides to claim their peaceful intentions. Obviously no statesman in his senses would like to go to war if he can get what he wants by peaceful means.

The real issue is not the dedication to peace on one or the other or both sides, but the real issue is the substantive one: first, of the survival of Israel, and second, what are to be the conditions for that survival?

So Israel says that the precondition for the survival is, for instance, the control of the Golan Heights, the demilitarization of Sinai, and the control of the Straits of Tiran.

Egypt, on the other hand, says the occupation of the territories that fell into the hands of the Israelis in consequence of the war of 1967 is the main obstacle to peace. Every inch of Arab territory occupied by Israel in consequence of the war of 1967 must be returned to Egypt.

The two claims are obviously incompatible. These claims are very similar in their incompatibility to the one that baffled, at least for a moment, so wise a ruler as King Solomon; he tried to solve the issue by dividing the baby. The baby has already been divided in the Middle East, and obviously it can not be divided again. The very division of the baby—of the territory—is unacceptable to both sides.

So you have here a conflict that in the terms in which it is posed seems to me to be resistant to any kind of peaceful solution.

I have heard here a discussion of the relative military capabilities of Israel and the Arab states. Whatever the long-range possibilities may be, and I would agree with those who would not bet everything upon the continuing, inevitable, and immutable Israeli superiority in the military field. But certainly at present there is nobody as far as I can remember who does not believe that if a full-scale war would break out tomorrow in the Middle East, without foreign intervention, Israel would win it, which seems to me also the main reason why no war has broken out.

What the future will hold in this respect is anybody's guess. I do not believe in the congenital inferiority of one nation to the other, nor do I believe in the inevitable congenital superiority of one nation over the other.

I remember very vividly a speech I heard in 1937 given by a statesman of considerable stature by the name of Winston Churchill, who said in Paris that the only thing that stood between civilization and barbarism was the French army. If he had been right, obviously barbarism would have triumphed.

So, to conclude from a particular distribution of military power that this particular distribution is a kind of permanent attribute of nations, something congenital, congenitally connected with the nature of the nation itself, seems to me to be bad metaphysics, and I would rather not argue on that basis.

But certainly at present and for the immediate future the military advantage of Israel seems to be obvious, especially in terms of the negative reaction of its Arab neighbors, and it is this advantage that thus far has preserved the peace in the Middle East.

This foundation of peace in the Middle East is obviously a rather fragile and precarious thing, for the assessment of the distribution of military power may change, and people frustrated by their enforced inactivity may delude themselves into believing that now they have a chance to win and will start another round.

It is also possible that they will not delude themselves but that they will risk defeat rather than allow themselves to be held in this inferior position indefinitely. National passions and national pride provide possibilities for irrational acts, which people will prefer to the humiliating position of seemingly permanent military inferiority in which they find themselves today.

So I would not want to conclude from the fact that since 1967 there has been, in a manner of speaking, peace in the Middle East, and that in recent years since the armistice agreement there has been a rather complete cessation of organized military activities on both sides of the lines of demarcation, that this situation will last indefinitely. I am rather inclined to believe that since there is no possibility of a negotiated settlement, sooner or later, and perhaps rather sooner, there will be another outbreak of war.

I remember a week before the outbreak of the war of 1967, I gave a speech in Chicago in which I made exactly this point. I don't expect that I will be proven right within a week, but I am afraid that the present peaceful situation is unstable and is not likely to last indefinitely.

This brings me to the third level on which the conflict in the Middle East is fought out, and that is the level of popular movements, that is to say, of Palestinian organizations that, profoundly dissatisfied with the status quo, are willing to try to change it at any cost to themselves. Nobody can say what the future importance of those organizations is likely to be within the Arab states, how much pressure they are capable of exerting upon the different governments, but most certainly those governments can not pursue whatever policies they would prefer to pursue, without regard to this intangible, inchoate ferment that exists within their own populations.

So you have pressures on all sides of the line of military demarcation. You have the pressure to which the Arab governments are exposed from within, which makes me think it is intolerable for them to countenance indefinitely the status quo in the Middle East. And you have the pressure from without those governments, from below, inchoate, passionate, irrational, but determined, which is another factor that puts the preservation of peace in the Middle East into question.

Finally, let me say that as the different Arab governments have great difficulties in controlling those popular movements threatening peace, so the two superpowers, deeply involved in the affairs of the

Middle East, have very limited ability to control their respective clients. If the United States, for instance, in the interest of oil supplies, were to stop identifying itself with Israel tomorrow in terms of policies and supply of funds, there is no doubt in my mind that Israel would not by one iota change its policies; it would simply reorganize its national priorities and try to stand militarily and politically on its own feet. Egypt has already shown the Soviet Union to what extent it is willing to forego temporary military and political advantages in order to maintain its own national posture.

So you have here, indeed, a complex situation that grows more complex as one proceeds from the surface phenomena, which are easily identifiable and definable, to the more profound secular movements that are inchoate, incalculable and, for this very reason, perhaps more important than the others. Thank you very much.

MR. FINGER. Thank you, Professor Morgenthau. I understand Senator Javits has arrived. We are very fortunate indeed to have Senator Javits here to talk to us about Western Europe and the tensions in the Middle East. He has had many involvements in Western Europe, he is very knowledgeable in that area as well as the Middle East, and I will not attempt even a brief catalogue of his accomplishments and qualifications, which are very well known to all of you. It is a great privilege to have the Honorable Jacob K. Javits speak to us at this time.

Western Europe and the Tensions in the Middle East

by Jacob Javits

SENATOR JAVITS. Thank you very much, Mr. Ambassador. I am sorry to give the management such a hard time, but I found it very difficult to get here exactly as scheduled. I am very pleased that Professor Morgenthau took over.

I came today because I was deeply interested in hearing as well as making whatever slight contribution I could to the thinking upon this subject, because all of us are deeply concerned with points of entry to what can be a better situation in the Middle East area. And Europe conceivably could be a point of entry. Discouraging as it may seem, considering the history of Europe's past relations with the Middle Eastern struggle, and one can not be categoric about Europe per se, but the dominant note in Europe seems to have been rather hard on Israel and very unusually soft on the Arab states.

Since the time that the German Federal Republic paid its debt of conscience to Israel, almost a billion dollars in reparations, Israel has not got much comfort out of Europe, except perhaps in the trade field. They have not done too badly with respect to trade in their relationships with European Common Market. But at the UN and in diplomatic affairs and certainly in military backing, it has been pretty sterile.

One may credit this to the fact that the last twenty-five years have seen Europe, as it were, catching up. Strange to say that, for it is the most mature area of the world politically, but the shock of World War II and the occupation of Europe during that time, which so many of us are inclined to forget, could easily destroy any civilization, and, indeed, had, if anything, a remarkably sparing effect upon European civilization.

So it is not surprising that in roughly that whole period of time, once the abortive effort in 1957 took place, the Suez debacle, Anglo-French debacle, which was more an effort to save what they considered to be an absolutely indispensable passage through the Suez Canal, Europe has pretty much left the influence of the West in the affairs of the Middle East to the United States. The United States has carried that burden, I think, extraordinarily well.

I heard Dr. Morgenthau say, I think very properly, that he speaks of a very heavy reliance of Israel upon the United States in respect to its policy. But I believe that now we are at the stage where perhaps in the next two decades—and I have no illusions about timing here— you might get some more stable conditions, which could lead to some modus vivendi that might be called *peace* in that area of the world. I think Europe can play a very helpful part, and I believe that this is almost required of Europe and will be the outcome of stern necessity: that stern necessity, of course, is the energy crisis in which Europe is very much more vulnerable than the United States and in many ways much more vulnerable than Japan.

Though Japan has no energy supplies at all except for what it imports, and we don't believe it has any formidable reserves, Japan does have a great area for oil exploration near it and is not in any ultimate sense as dependent on the Middle East as Europe is. Japan is working very hard in Indonesia, which is known to have enormous reserves of oil, and in other aspects of possibilities of supply. While she still depends to the extent of ninety percent on the Middle East, a seemingly greater dependence than Europe, my own study of the situation would indicate that she is less likely to be politically motivated respecting the Middle East than Europe, even in respect to energy. She has got the resources to buy it, she does not have any previous colonial history with the Arab states, and she does have this tremendous potential right at or near her door in the Indonesian archipelago.

But Europe is very much at hazard in the Middle East, and

therefore I believe that you will see the emergcnce of a very real relationship of Europe to that area. In addition, there have already been agreements between the European Common Market and the nations of northern Africa respecting an association between the two, which we call *specialized preferences* and which in an economic and international economic sense we are in great disapproval of. Indeed, as I think the Ambassador (Finger) knows, because we worked on it when I was a general delegate at the U.N., we are going to try very hard to eliminate the special preferences and try to work out generalized preferences with the developing world. But in the meantime, Europe does have this special economic relationship with north Africa as well as with other countries south of the Sahara.

So here are two respects in which European policy must more and more consider what is happening in the Middle East.

There are still other aspects that lead me toward that view. The United States is now reviewing, obviously, after Dr. Kissinger's speech, its whole relationship to the security of Europe as it relates to the security of the Atlantic and the security of the United States. For a very long time Europe has overlooked the vulnerability of European security in the Mediterranean, and for a very long time it has without question accepted the American Sixth Fleet as really a NATO instrument, because it assured the security of Europe, first in respect to the Russian fleet, which is in the same area, and second in whatever might happen in that very unstable situation.

The United States in connection with its review of its relationship to security in Europe is undoubtedly going to review its relationship to security in the Mediterranean. I believe that we should insist that Europe play a greater role in the Mediterranean naval establishment if there is to continue to be one on the major scale that we have had it there up to now, and that that will be one of the elements that may represent another way to carry on burden-sharing in respect to that particular operation, which is a very expensive one for the United States.

I think that Europe is beginning to reconsider whether American self-interest is so great or is so unmanageable as to require the United States to man all the ramparts that it has manned and is manning. I don't wish to indicate by that any doubt on my part as to the absolute indivisibility of Atlantic and American security or Mediterranean and European and American security. But nonetheless within that context, and considering the growing concern of the United States about balance of payments problems, largely attributable to our security posture throughout the world, there is bound to be reconsideration of this whole issue.

So I think it is fair to say that sooner or later, and not too long from now, there will be a much greater European military presence in the Mediterranean than there is today.

Finally, and very important, great efforts are being made to give some sense of stability and order to the Middle East, especially in respect to the Persian Gulf states. There are great problems between Iraq and Iran, to take one example. But that does not seem to me to represent nearly the big issue that monetary affairs represent. The Arab states are going to acquire fantastic amounts of foreign exchange, both from Europe and the United States. When I say fantastic, I am talking now in terms not of billions but of tens of billions. Let us hope not hundreds of billions. But even tens of billions are pretty formidable when they are floating and in the hands of very few powerful people who have shown no compunction about using their funds in whatever way it suited them, either for economic reconciliation or economic war or real war or subversion, materially and adversely affecting world exchange markets and currency stability, and so forth. A fourth reason, because of the enormous impact upon the world monetary situation, Europe has to get involved.

So I don't think it can be doubted at all that in the next few years you will see a much greater involvement by Europe in the resolution of the Middle East situation than we have up to now.

The grave question is: How will that participation, which is inevitable—and indeed, in my opinion, not only inevitable but desirable because this is very much a partnership venture we are engaged in—how is it going to work? And I will just take a minute, if I may, Mr. Ambassador, on that.

If it goes the way of United Nations Security Council resolutions in the most recent past, it is going to work very badly. Because the Europeans have certainly shown every disposition, notwithstanding the rhetoric, to assume that Israel was expendable. I may be rather cruel, but nonetheless that is the gist of their policy. I do not believe the United States will accept that policy, and I believe the policy is disastrous for any hope of redeeming the Middle East from its benighted condition of misery as well as ignorance, and therefore that, if there isn't a change, there will be a disaster, a cataclysm in terms of the strategic nature of the territory involved and many other considerations.

So I believe that the policy of the United States will now have to be directed toward reaching a much better understanding and accommodation with Europe in respect to Middle East policies. One of the big problems for the Atlantic Alliance is going to be a much more intelligent rationalization and harmonization of alliance policy respecting the Middle East, which will have to be alliance policy under the circumstances I have just outlined rather than a European or a U.S. policy.

We may have to give something, and Israel may have to give something. The question is, how vital and how critical will be what has to be given? There again the United States will be the formidable factor in the equation.

So I see, in summary, a trying period during the next two years in Middle East policy when Europe will properly and necessarily wish to assert itself. At the same time, the United States will wish to accommodate Europe by all means—I feel that that is very important and inevitable—but the U.S. will not wish to see the policy that the U.S. has pursued go down the drain to the great harm of what the Arabs think is their great enemy, Israel. But that will turn out, perhaps long after I and many of the rest of us are gone, to be the only thing that redeemed them from the darkness in which they have lived for centuries. The United States' influence and the United States' policy will be the saving grace in that situation.

I am not pessimistic. I am optimistic. But I believe that we must understand what is going to be at stake and how much will depend upon the United States in respect to Middle East policy in these next years. Thank you.

MR. FINGER. Thank you very much, Senator. I am constantly amazed by the extent to which you can grasp the political, national, military, and so many other aspects of the problem and at the same time lead a busy life as a senator.

Now I should like to introduce another man whose virtuosity amazes me, Dr. John Stoessinger, who is a professor and at the same time the Acting Director of the Political Affairs Division in the United Nations Secretariat. He is also the author of some remarkably fine books in the area of international relations.

The United Nations and the Arab-Israeli Conflict

by John G. Stoessinger

DR. STOESSINGER. Thank you very much, Mr. Chairman. Since the general subject of the United Nations' role in the Middle East has been covered extensively in published material,* I shall address myself briefly to one aspect that I consider particularly significant at this time: the widening spectrum of discord among the five powers that make up the veto-wielding members of the Security Council. Perhaps what prevents a United Nations' solution to the conflict more than anything else is simply the fact that each of these five permanent members of the Security Council has a very different perception of the problem and a very different idea on how it should be resolved.

Professor Morgenthau has already explained the positions of the great powers, also. So let me simply sketch vignettes to prove the basic points of my thesis: that it is the disparity among these five powers, in addition to the impasse between Israel and her Arab neighbors as such, that makes the solution even more difficult than it already is.

* *See,* for example, "The Arab-Israeli Problem and the United Nations," Appendix of this volume.

The Soviet position in the Middle East at this point, above all, is to entrench the Soviet interest, to maintain and secure the Soviet foothold in the Middle East. At this point the Soviet Union is no longer a revolutionary power trying to gain a foothold in the Middle East. It is, as the Chinese have pointed out time and time again, an establishment power with already well-entrenched interests in the Middle East, and it is the maintenance of these interests that the Soviet Union, above all, is committed to maintain.

Toward this overriding end, the Soviet Union wishes to strengthen the Arab states, but not beyond the point of military confrontation with Israel, for fear, of course, of risking another humiliation of the 1967 kind.

Similarly, what may surprise some people is that the Soviet Union is not interested in the destruction of Israel, for the simple reason that if Israel were destroyed, then the Arab states would no longer need the protection of the Soviet Union. This is precisely what the Soviet Union knows. For this reason, it wishes to weaken Israel short of destruction, strengthen the Arab states short of military victory, and hence in this uneasy, no peace-no war situation—in which one is strengthened and the other weakened—to attain the overall, paramount objective of the Soviet quest; namely, the permanent presence of the Soviet Union in the Middle East.

United States' objectives in the area are far more ambiguous, far less clear. One could say, I suppose, that the United States is committed in the Middle East in at least three different directions that vacillate constantly, which sometimes get in each other's way. It is almost as if this nation juggled three balls, which have a way of sometimes falling out of its hands.

There is first the commitment to some of the Arab kingdoms, recently enhanced because of the growing energy crisis, which you are going to discuss. There have even been some rumors, which I can not substantiate, that the recent American abstention from the last Security Council resolution—rather than a veto, which had been cast several months before—may have been sparked by fears of the United States not to antagonize Arab states because of the growing energy crisis—this is something that I can not substantiate, but one hears it time and time again. At any rate, this is definitely one source of commitment.

Another source is a commitment to some of the other Arab states, because many American Arab strategists make the point that the basic reason why the Russians are in the Middle East is that the United States backs Israel and therefore the best way for the United

States to improve relations with the Arab states is to relax and untie itself from Israel. As a result of this, there is a residual commitment to other Arab states. Then there is the commitment to Israel for various reasons, including the powerful domestic voting bloc.

These are, then, a number of conflicting considerations that put any candidate for elective office in this country in a very difficult position.

There is always the problem of the Jewish vote. There is, on the other hand, the pressures on a President by the Pentagon and by Arabists in the State Department that militates in still another direction. Therefore, any President finds himself frequently in a kind of existential squeeze among these three mutually exclusive considerations, and that explains the extraordinary ambiguity and, if you will, the vacillation that the United States and the Middle East are guilty of, which contrasts very sharply with the clarity of the Soviet position and also its ruthlessness.

The position of Britain at this point is perhaps the least difficult to explain, largely because Britain is on its way out of the Middle East. The author of the famous Resolution 242, which is so ambiguous as to be almost meaningless at this point, was Lord Caradon. It was the only resolution acceptable to all, which still hopefully may be resuscitated some day. I understand that Lord Caradon will talk to you, and it may be interesting to find out what he thinks of its present status. At any rate, at this point Britain finds itself in the Olympian position of arbitrator, fairly equidistant from both sides. France, however, has shifted and, in fact, continues to find herself, under the Pompidou regime, fairly close to the Arab position, again for reasons of her own national interest. There are mainly three reasons: first, to erase the bitter memories of the Suez fiasco, where France found herself on the side of Israel and Britain; second, possibly to erase the memories of the Algerian War, when France fought the Moslems; and third, to become the Arab bridge to the West, now that France is one of the leading major Western states on good terms with the Arabs—if the Arabs become tired or suspicious of their alliance with the Soviets, they might wish to walk back to the West, and then France might become the bridge and thus garner concomitant prestige for herself.

There was some thought during the recent election that France might shift somewhat, but, because of the reelection of the Gaulist Party, at this point there seems to be little change in sight.

Finally, there is the Chinese position, which is way out in left field. For the first time in their participation in the Middle East conflict, the Palestinians have got themselves a great power sponsor, namely, China, which has widened the spectrum of discord even further. I don't believe that the Chinese commitment to the Palestinians is racial or even ideological. It is fundamentally to be seen in the Machiavellian context of a triangular configuration among China, Russia, and the United States. What China fears most, in my opinion, is the possibility of a collusion between the two superpower-establishment nations. What she fears is a compromise between them that would divide up the Middle East between them and leave China out in the cold. It is that suspicion, that fear, which makes China back that entity which is dead set against a compromise solution, and that happens to be the Palestinian group.

I sketched these vignettes for you briefly, ladies and gentlemen, because there is no such thing in the Middle East at this point as a United Nations as an independent entity. The only way you can discuss the United Nations in the Middle East at this point—and the Middle East is the last remaining point of Cold War global confrontation remaining with us today—is to look at it as a disparate group of large states. Each has its own national interest to follow, which it places above a solution to the conflict. As a result, the Middle East tends to get lost in the shuffle. That, I believe, is the only fair and objective way of looking at it.

I think the only hope in the Security Council in that sense, perhaps, is what may be what the Chinese fear most: some kind of compromise solution between the Soviet Union and the United States. This may take an initiative for a more concerted effort by the Security Council to bring about, perhaps, some hopes for an ultimate breakthrough toward a solution in the area. Thank you very much.

MR. FINGER. Thank you very much. I am especially grateful for your reminder to all of us that the United Nations is not a magic wand, but only what the member states make it. Also, your series of vignettes was very helpful to our understanding. I now call on Professor Joseph Dunnor of Yeshiva University.

PROFESSOR DUNNOR. I agree with Professor AlRoy's strategic assessment of that portion of the Middle East which comprises the Arab states bordering the Eastern Mediterranean and Israel as of today, 4 May 1973. But I would like to bring to your attention that any major change in the military technology of Israel's Arab neighbors might nullify this assessment. Moreover, if Israel were to return all the territories gained by it in the June 1967 war—all of Golan, all of Sinai, East Jerusalem, the West Bank, and Gaza—Israel's Arab neighbors would need no new or more sophisticated weapons. They could organize another, and again another round with what we have come to call *conventional arms*. Like before June 1967, Israel's population centers would remain the open targets of Arab snipers equipped with machine guns or just plain rifles.

I have my doubts about the validity of Professor Morgenthau's thesis, reiterated here, according to which the Soviet Union wants the survival of Israel in order to hold up Israel as a kind of bogeyman whose existence allegedly compels the Arab states to ally themselves with the U.S.S.R. as their protector. First, I see no reason why the Arab states should fear the state of Israel, which has no interest whatever in making war on them. Let us not forget that whatever territorial expansion Israel achieved since the U.N. partition of Palestine in November 1947 was caused by Arab unwillingness to accept a Jewish statehood in the Middle East and that the three wars imposed by the Arab states on Israel forced Israel to seek more defensible borders than those originally allocated to Israel by the U.N. As far as the Soviets are concerned, I believe that their position will, in the final analysis, depend on the military strength of the U.S.A. and the willingness or lack of willingness of this country to aid Israel militarily, politically, and economically. To a considerable extent, Soviet policy in the Middle East will also be influenced by what the People's Republic of China will do in that region. I am convinced that in the spring of 1967, the Red Chinese appeals to the Arabs to start "a war of liberation,' coupled with the denunciation of the Soviet Union as a coconspirator with the U.S.A. prompted the Soviets to demonstrate to the Arab world that only they, and not the Maoists, could be counted on as the true protagonists of the Arab states and the Palestine-Arab guerrilla forces. What would happen if the leading Arab states should follow the example of Iraq or the People's Republic of Yemen and accept Communist regimes? In view of their social structures and autocratic traditions, there is no guarantee that they won't become willing satellites of either the Soviet Union or Red China. In that event, for sure, the Soviet Union would have no further need of the Israeli bogeyman and could easily decide not only to truncate and weaken Israel, which is present-day Soviet policy, but also to destroy Israel altogether.

I wish I could be as sanguine about the role of the United States as an invariably reliable ally of Israel as the former speakers. There is, no doubt, the fact that in a democratic America no American administration can completely disregard the sympathies that Israel enjoys not only among the close to six million American Jews, but also among the millions of American non-Jews as well.

But the administrations of the U.S.A. are also influenced by the claims of a very powerful oil lobby that has always been clearly pro-Arab; in the months to come, the oil issue will be of special significance, as Senator Javits rightly remarked a few minutes ago. If we also consider the global strategic interests of this country, the best that Israel can expect from the U.S.A. in terms of realpolitik is what has been labeled *even-handedness*: a policy of appeasing the Arabs without surrendering the very existence of Israel.

I, for one, would prefer if, beyond the scope of political and military strategy, we would address ourselves here to the moral issue that so far has been completely neglected. The Arabs have vast, largely underpopulated territories at their disposal—not to speak of the tremendous wealth of such oil-producing states as Saudi Arabia, Kuwait, Libya, and Iraq, whose governments could have solved the Palestine-Arab refugee problem long ago. The Arabs do not need the few thousand square miles of Israel to preserve their Arab-Islamic civilization and to live secure, peaceful lives. For the Jews, Israel, sanctioned by Jewish history and prophetic Judaism, constitutes the only place in which they can overcome the sufferings of 1,900 years of dispersion and persecution. For the Jews, Israel is the only country in which they can cultivate their cultural heritage without being forced to make continuous concessions to the religions and cultures of the non-Jewish majorities in all other lands on this earth. Should we not devote some time to a serious consideration of the moral rights of the Jews of Israel to a secure existence and to consider how this could be brought about?

MR. FINGER. I now call on Professor Gidon Gottlieb.

PROFESSOR GOTTLIEB. Mr. Ambassador, we have had some brilliant statements this afternoon; we have had one by Professor Morgenthau that leads us to the conclusion, which I share, that the outbreak of fighting sometime soon should not surprise anyone. Indeed, the probability of such an event should weigh seriously on our minds.

But in the process of developing his argument, Professor Morgenthau suggested that the confrontation between the big powers in the Middle East was the outgrowth, a side effect, of the commitment of the United States to Israel and the Soviet Union to Egypt.

By presenting the confrontation argument as an outgrowth, one does build in remedies. If only the Soviet Union could back off from backing the Arab states to the extent it does and if only the United States could moderate its support of Israel, then the confrontation between the two superpowers would lessen. This is something that, I suspect, we may wish to hear his views on a bit further.

Indeed, it has been argued that nothing could exacerbate the relations between the United States and the Soviet Union more than a U.S. attempt to return to more even-handed policies, as the term goes, and, therefore, to take advantage of the difficulties the Soviet Union has encountered in Egypt.

This would presumably be directly contrary to the spirit of the Moscow agreement reached between Mr. Nixon and Mr. Brezhnev. It would suggest, indeed, that the confrontation between the two superpowers is at this time moderated by their incompatible policies with regard to the Middle East conflict. Any radical change in U.S. orientation or in Soviet orientation could throw the relationship between the two superpowers out of balance.

Perhaps further, if we look at an area where Israel is not present, namely, the Gulf, and we see the confrontation between Iraq and Iran, to which allusion has been made, and if we see the military moves involving Iraq and Kuwait, and the relative positions of the superpowers in this regard, it might lead us to the conclusion that the difficulties the U.S. and the Soviet Union face are *not* directly related to the Arab-Israeli conflict or to their espousal of particular clients.

Moreover, shouldn't we, in considering the U.S. interest in the area, pay closer attention to the Nixon Doctrine, such as it may be, in the sense that the United States has used—and I use the word *used* with apology—Israel to check hegemonial attempts by Syria or perhaps by the Soviet Union through Syria? I have in mind the intervention in 1971, for example, of the Syrian invasion of Jordan. The United States may also be "using" Iran to restrain any Iraqi move against Kuwait, with or without the blessing of the Soviet Union. If that seems to be the pattern, then presumably the stability of the American interest in maintaining its commitment to Iran, Israel, and other countries similarly situated, is somewhat independent of the dimensions of the Jewish vote or of moral intangibles.

If that should be the case, then are we not really led to a further potential conclusion: that if the United States and the Soviet Union would like, at this point, to consolidate the détente between them, it is entirely unavoidable to link—it is a terrible, dirty word—the Middle East *problem,* at least as far as energy is concerned, to the question of European security, to the question of SALT II, to the question of mutual-balanced force reductions, and to the other major questions outstanding between the Soviet Union and the United

States? We already see the framework of the Atlantic Alliance threatened and a divergence of U.S. and European policies. We already see that the instability which the Middle East could breed in superpower relationships could threaten the fabric of the détente. In that sense, I certainly hope Professor Morgenthau could tell us something more in support of his viewpoint.

MR. FINGER. Thank you. I assume that Professor Morgenthau would be willing to comment. But may I first call on Dr. Richard Ovinnikov, the deputy permanent representative of the Soviet Union. Since so many references have been made to Soviet policy, it might be well to hear from someone who represents the Soviet government.

DR. OVINNIKOV. Thank you. I will reserve my right to a substantial contribution to a later stage in the debate. What I do want to say is the following: our debate as a whole at this stage already puzzles me. It puzzles me, first of all, that one of the speakers here, a supposedly impartial international servant, takes sides, takes biased positions, and uses, to paraphrase, ruthless descriptions.

This is, in my mind, a minor question in the present context, although I think it is an important one in a different context.

But what really puzzles me is why the very basis of the discussion is as follows: Could outside powers afford a settlement in the Middle East at all? Why, with the whole basis of the Middle East, is it not how outside powers could *contribute* to the peaceful settlement in the Middle East? This, I submit, is the more relevant basis.

Lastly, I have listened with attention to the presentation of Professor Morgenthau. His thesis is that the two superpowers are interested in keeping a status quo in the area. Moreover, he said that as far as the Soviet Union is concerned, this country is interested in a controlled tension there, and the United States is interested in a peaceful solution there.

I am not going to engage, at this stage, in a substantive debate, so I have a practical question addressed to Professor Morgenthau: If your thesis is correct—you are aware, of course, of the association that existed as recently as a year ago in the form of consultation among the permanent members of the Security Council on the Middle East—then why has it been the United States and not the Soviet Union who put an end to those consultations? If your thesis is right, then why does the Soviet Union continue to put forward suggestions in favor of resumption of those consultations and why does the United States oppose them?

MR. FINGER. Thank you, Dr. Ovinnikov. If I may make just one comment: it seems to me that the position that you have expressed, that the big outside powers can not only afford a settlement, but should also contribute toward it, is one that the American government has certainly expressed as its viewpoint; and I am sure it will be very helpful if the Soviet government joins in the same sort of search.

If I may, I will call first on Dr. Stoessinger and then Dr. Morgenthau to reply to some of the comments that have been made.

DR. STOESSINGER. Thank you. First, I should like to emphasize the point that whatever I said here today is not said in my official capacity. It is after five o'clock. But it is said in my personal capacity. That is point one.

Point two, however, is this: I did not single out the Soviet Union for any attack here today. The basic point I made—and this is precisely a point that should be made from the United Nations' vantage point—is that each of the five permanent members of the Security Council has placed its own narrowly defined, selfish interests above the quest for a solution to the Middle East problem. That applies to all of them equally and is not meant to be as a single attack upon any one member, whether the Soviet Union or anybody else. I want to make this absolutely clear.

If someone from outer space could appear and would suggest a solution for the Middle East, I think he might suggest the best solution might be for all the five powers of the Security Council who are inextricably involved in the Middle East problem to disappear and to leave the Middle East to the obscurity that it enjoyed for two thousand years. That, I believe, might be the solution. But that, alas, is not to be.

It is true, however, that since each of these five members has applied its own narrowly defined national interest above the quest for an objective solution, such a solution has consequently eluded us; and all of them, I believe, are guilty of that, and it is precisely that someone from the United Nations ought to make that point after hours. Thank you very much.

DR. MORGENTHAU. Let me address myself first to the suggestion of Professor Gottlieb. I think his point is well taken, if the United States tomorrow were to withdraw its protection from Israel and pursue a policy conducive to closer relations with the Arab states, it would come into direct competition with the Soviet Union. From the Soviet point of view, the commitment of the United States to Israel must be extremely welcome, for it precludes any normal relations with most of the Arab states. It leaves the field free for the Soviet Union to expand its influence. So the Soviet Union appears today as the protector of the Arab states, in a way comparable to the appearance of the United States as the protector of Israel. If the United States were to give up this position, it would come into direct competition with the Soviet Union, a situation that the Soviet Union can not favor.

I am somewhat at a loss to respond to the Soviet representative, because I have difficulty in understanding his argument. The point I was trying to make was that both the United States *and* the Soviet Union have convergent interests in the Middle East in that *neither* is interested in a new outbreak of war.

Furthermore, the United States is probably not even interested in the present status quo. The United States would probably be delighted if Israel were to accept the Security Council resolution to withdraw to the boundaries of 1967. But since Israel is not willing to do so, the United States is not willing to use pressure upon Israel.

So I have not tried to assess the peaceful contentions of the two superpowers and give the United States a particularly good mark over the Soviet Union. I think both superpowers are interested in peace, but are unable to control the tensions, the local tensions, developing into a resumption of war.

PROFESSOR SINAI. I agree with almost everything that Professor AlRoy said about the Arab military capability at the present moment, except that I would go further and state that the main reason for the lack of peace or the absence of possibilities for accommodation between Israel and the Arab states springs from the fact that the Arab world is involved in a series of multiple crises.

First of all, the Arab world has not been able to respond to the challenge of modernization. Modernization should not be confused with or should not be treated as synonymous with mere economic growth, with mere spread of education, or even with the spread of scientific education or the mere importation of technology; but modernization demands a revolution in the basic structures of a society. If a society is not capable, first of all, of committing itself to the goals of modernization, which the Arab world has not, if a society is incapable of revolutionizing not merely its social structure, its political structure, its political institutions, and, above all, its mentality, ethos, and approach to the world, then that society is incapable of producing the demonic forces of modernity. Modernity requires the emergence of a class of entrepreneurs. These entrepreneurs are economic revolutionaries, they are economic Napoleons; that is, innovators, innovational personalities. And these innovational personalities have to be present not merely in the economic sphere, but also in all the spheres of society. These are precisely what the Arab world has not been able to engender. The Arab world is not premodern. There are very few premodern societies left in the present world. The Arab world is a transitional world; it is a world that has felt the impact of modernity, where the forces of modernity have been at work upon it for about 200 years. But these forces of modernity have only served to further undermine, erode, dissolve, and corrode the old traditional order in which the Arabs have lived for centuries.

I want to take issue with my friend, Professor Morgenthau, when he said that no society is congenitally incapable of developing. But some societies, because of all kinds of historical factors, once they enter a period of decay, are incapable of escaping from that process of decay. The Arab world, I believe, is in a proces of decay and it has not been able to release the forces of regeneration or rejuvenation that are required for the development of modern societies.

Not only is the Arab world in the process of decay, but India, for example, is also in the process of decay. Many other transitional societies are in the process of decay. In Southeast Asia, they have only reached the level that Europe attained in the fourteenth and fifteenth centuries.

Some societies, for example, Haitian society, have probably reached such a level of degeneration that no force will be able to rejuvenate it, that no force will be able to save it. I believe that is also true of the Arab world.

The Arab world, therefore, lives in two or more worlds without belonging to any one of them. They don't belong to the traditional world. They do not belong to the modern world, because essentially they do not want to modernize. They do not live and are not capable of living in the modern world. Therefore, they are caught between these two worlds and they live the lives of social schizophrenics.

On the other hand, there is Israel, the only society that has been modernized by some of the processes that I have described.

Israel is a modern society becoming stronger every day. The gap between Israel and the Arab world is growing daily. Israel is becoming the strongest power in the Middle East, and we know what power does. Power is also corrupting. And there are certain elements of the arrogance of power that have already appeared in Israel. But that is another matter. In any case, Israel is the dynamic growing power with which the Arab world can not deal. That is why its protestations—the Arab protestations of peace— are absolutely meaningless; they are worthless, for one day they want peace, the next day they want the destruction of Israel. Because the Arabs do not know where they are, who they are, or where they are traveling.

I would just like to make one more comment about the great powers. I recently had a very interesting discussion with a Soviet intellectual who said that Russia's involvement in the Middle East and with the Arab states was on a par with America's involvement in Vietnam, except that they have not committed the ultimate folly of sending in 500,000 Russian soldiers, who would probably melt in the sun of the Middle East. Russia's involvement with the Arab states is an involvement that springs from Russian imperial interests and Russia's imperial interests in this case do not even serve Russia's real national interests, but are merely the result of its having been caught in a trap of its own devising from which it can not escape. The other powers who want to become involved in the Middle East are fated to face exactly the same result, and that is to become involved with decadent dissolving societies, which is to invite disaster for themselves and disaster for their clients.

MR. FINGER. I have at least five people who want to speak. General Burns had asked for the floor, and then we will call on the others in turn.

GENERAL BURNS. Thank you very much, Mr. Chairman. It is in connection with a suggestion made by Professor Gottlieb that I would like to pose a question. As I understand what he said, it was that it would be possible for the United States to rely, to some extent, on Israel and Israel's territory for maintaining her strategic position and base of her armed forces in the Eastern Mediterranean, and also to rely on Iran for bases and support in the Persian Gulf.

I don't wish to argue about the position of Iran, but I would feel they are probably more interested in preserving an independent status than in becoming allied with the United States in this respect.

But my understanding has been throughout that, while the Arabs have in their propaganda statements frequently accused the United States of wishing to use Israel for this purpose, the policy of the Israeli government has generally been to avoid any such complications and to stand independent in this respect. Possibly the representative of Israel here might say that my view is wrong, and perhaps you will wish to make some further comments on the matter.

MR. FINGER. Did you wish to speak?

MR. RASHID HUSSEIN. My name is Rashid Hussein and I am a Palestinian. I thought on many times today that we were celebrating the anniversary of Israel when the doctor here spoke or we were talking about things that really did not belong to the main problem of the Middle East : the Palestinians. We were talking about oil, we were talking about the Soviet Union, about the United States, and about China. But no one touched the root of the whole problem of the Middle East. This is just a comment.

A question to the Israeli representative : I lived in Israel seventeen years. I came out feeling that Israel does not want peace because peace is bad for Israel. You know that and I know that and everyone who studies Israel knows that it is bad for Israel. The more war you have, the more tension you have, the more money, the better off you are.

I want to ask you, when you spoke about the borders, you said all the time, "we want secure borders." OK. Suppose I agree with you. What are secure boundaries? When the Golan Heights were in the hands of Syria, you said it was essential for us to occupy it, as you do now, because there are new settlements in the valley. Now you are building new settlements on the Jordan River and you again say that. You are building new settlements on the Golan Heights. So are you going to apply for Damascus for secure borders? Now you are in the Suez and you are very close to Cairo and you are again building settlements there. What are you going to settle? The other side of the canal to have secure boundaries?

That is all.

DR. TAWAB. It seems to me that the three speakers who talked about military aspects were under the influence of the idols that were formulated by the British philosopher, Francis Bacon—namely, the idols of the tribe that make the person believe what pleases him and disbelieve what displeases him. Under such an influence, the person finds it easy to look for conforming evidence and to disregard or to avoid any evidence that seems to disprove it. This actually was the content of the talk that we heard about the disparity between the Arabs and the Israelis and about the military superiority of the Israelis over the Arabs for a considerable amount of time. It seems that they think of superiority as a natural factor that the Israelis have inherited. Superiority is cultural and the Arabs, like other human beings, can acquire any cultural element or cultural trait—namely, modern science and technology. Since the inception of Israel in the area of the Middle East, the Arabs have been in continuous progress to acquire modern science and technology. In fact, they have at this time more educated people with graduate degrees than Israel has in number. This will be reflected, I am sure, if they are faced with a new challenge. So, their conclusion : that not only will the military disparity not be bridged in the near future, but also that the Arabs will not be able to catch up to the military superiority of the Israelis and therefore they should not waste their time as long as they are starting from scratch—lacks the scientific outlook.

With regard to what they said, that the Arabs were unable to face the reality because peace has already been achieved by Israel, also lacks scientific outlook. Peace can only be achieved through understanding, which can only be realized through building bridges of understanding between the two cultures. Behind any conflict there is a cultural conflict and the two sides have to recognize the fact that they have different ideologies. However, they should not build walls, but they must build bridges of understanding. The President of the United States was very clear on this point when he visited the old wall in China and stated the following:

> We have to recognize that we have different ideologies. We should not build walls—on the other hand, we have to build bridges—bridges of understanding—and this is what my visit is; the first step to establish this understanding.

It seems to me that the Colloquium should embark on spelling out the positive aspects that, in my opinion, will be the real foundation and the productive contribution to this area that has been in this conflict for three decades.

With regard to the point that the previous speakers highlighted, that the neighboring countries have to accept the fact that Israel has to keep secure boundaries and not to return all the territories captured in 1967, this does not conform with the history of the people living in this particular area. In fact, the bordering countries witnessed occupation, not only from Israel as a small country, but also from certain super powers, and they, at last, succeeded in liberating their territories. This is actually the case of Egypt and Syria. Egypt will not give up the occupied Sinai to any power, including the super powers. I would like to assure the Colloquium that Egypt is not worried about recapturing its Sinai—it will do so either by peace or by force, if necessary, because this is the history of Egypt. By the same token, Syria will not give up its Golan Heights—it will take its territory because this is the history of Syria. So, we are left with one alternative, which is the objective of this Colloquium: to find out positive ways and means in order to build bridges of understanding between the two cultures. This, in my opinion, is the only way to achieve a just peace in this area; my hope is for every participant to avoid negative aspects and to embark on the positive aspects.

Thank you, Ambassador Finger.

DR. RIEBENFELD. Professor Morgenthau, in mentioning the different layers of the Middle East conflict, also made the point that they operate upon each other, in ascending order. Indeed, contrary to former expectations, there is at this moment no great-power confrontation in the Middle East, at least not on the Suez Canal. However, I believe that the main reason for this has nothing to do with the Middle East, but is connected with the European Security Conference that the Russians were seeking. Since the Soviet position in Egypt was not only a threat to Israel, but also to the Europeans —or a threat to their southern flank—Russian withdrawal from Egypt facilitated the convening of the Security Conference.

Then there is the relationship between the conflict among the states of the region and the conflict of their populations; for example, between the Jews and the Arabs of Palestine. It seems clear to me that there can not be an Arab-Israeli peace without a discussion of the Palestinian problem. The Arab states feel that the question of boundaries and of peace with Israel in principle are linked with this as a matter of honor. They do not want to appear as having sold out their Palestinian brethren. Whenever a move was made in that direction—and it seems that President Nasser, in August 1970, may have been ready to move toward an agreement without taking much account of the Palestinians—the Palestinians not only made their position felt, but they also caused a reaction in the Arab world, especially inside Egypt and Jordan, that forced a change of policy by those governments.

The other day, when reading the minutes of the recent Security Council meeting, I was struck with something that was said by Ambassador Baroody representing Saudi Arabia. They were words spoken from the heart when he said that Arab youth were inflamed. "Rightly or wrongly they are on the side of the Palestinians. What can we people of my generation do? Can we tell them 'to hell with you'? They will send us to hell. This is the truth."

Of course, his solution to the Palestinian problem was that Zionists should cease to be Zionists, the State of Israel should cease to be a Jewish State, should become the Palestinian's so-called democratic state, and so forth. This dilemma will certainly not be solved by a Palestinian nationality arising from the self-destruction of the State of Israel.

On the other hand, to deal with the question of the Arab people of Palestine is a vital issue, indeed. It is vital for the Arab states, especially those who wish to stay in the Western camp. It is vital for American policy because the Palestinian issue is used inside the Arab countries for the purpose of anti-Western demagoguery. But the only way to solve the Palestine problem is to tell the truth at last.

Since we are here in an academic and diplomatic circle, I think it is true to say that much of the Palestinian issue is due to demagoguery and exaggeration. The Palestinian issue has been manipulated as a weapon against Israel, mainly. But much of it is also due to ignorance. And on this point I accuse the community of scholars, including Jewish scholars, and those experts who are interested in the conduct of American policy and of Israeli policy.

I suggest that we separate the question of fact and law from the question of policy. It may be true that from the point of view of immediate expediency, it does not recommend itself to weaken the Hashemite regime in Jordan and to question the Jordanization of the Palestinians in Jordan. On the other hand, out of consideration for the Hashemite regime that they prefer, both American policy and Israeli policy have put themselves—in the eyes of a large part of world opinion that is interested in questions of national liberation, self-determination, and so on—into a position that is not only damaging, but which also does not correspond to the true facts of the problem.

The Palestinians in Jordan are not 40 percent or 50 percent of the population, but nearly 80 percent. It is also widely unknown that Jordan was a part of Palestine until 1946 and not until 1922, as is so often stated. Even sixty percent of the Jordanian army consists today of Palestinian units.

From the point of view of American diplomacy—or perhaps I should say of American, Israeli, and Jordanian diplomacy—the key question is how to give Jordan an official Palestinian identity without the overthrow of the regime of King Hussein? No one in the West or in Israel would prefer the rule in Jordan of the Palestinian militants, who do not really represent the Arab people of Palestine, to that of Hussein. On the other hand, it is impossible ever to come to grips with the problem of Jewish self-determination and Palestinian-Arab self-determination, unless the deformation of the Palestinian problem is corrected.

The Arabs say that there took place between the wars a basic change in Palestine as a result of the Balfour Declaration. This is correct. I do not know to what degree the Balfour Declaration was decisive for Jewish settlement, but, during the period of the Mandate, Palestine was demographically deformed, from an Arab viewpoint, by Jewish development. But there took place, during the period of the Mandate, another deformation, a geographical one, that took away eighty percent of Palestine from the context of the Palestinian problem. There is the key.

There is absolutely no reason why Jordan should not be considered a part of Palestine, just because, in 1946, Mr. Bevin wanted to create a difficult situation for the Anglo-American Committee of Enquiry by reducing the area of the Palestine Mandate. He wanted to aggravate the conflict by showing how little room there was for Jewish immigration. Trans-Jordan became independent in May 1946. Just because it had been independent for nine months prior to February 1947 when the Palestine Mandate was submitted to the U.N. for adjudication, that does not mean that it was not a part of Palestine. The story even has been invented that there existed a separate "Mandate of Trans-Jordan." That is simply not true.

You will find that nobody has bothered to define what Palestine is. That is where the Palestinians are most guilty. Yasir Arafat in November 1971, after the defeat of the Fedayeen in Jordan, said in an interview with Eric Rouleau when asked what he thought of a state on the West Bank, that the land of the Palestinians extended to both sides of the Jordan, in spite of all artificial boundaries that were created. This shows that the militant leaders know the situation well. For tactical reasons, to maintain the thrust and dynamism of their anti-Israel propaganda, based on the legend of national homelessness, they restrained from changing the status of Jordan. But in the rest of Palestine, the Jews have built their nation-state. The militants may have fallen between two stools. They will not be able to build a Palestinian state on the ruins of Israel. On the other hand, I doubt whether today they can take over Jordan. They are paying heavily for posing as revolutionaries.

I do maintain—and this was just as true before 1967—that American diplomacy has never come to grips with the fact that the settlement of the Palestinian problem between Jews and Arabs has always lain within the sphere of United States policy. In spite of all the intervention of Russia in the Middle East, at the moment of the firmest hold that the Russians had in the area, the solution of the Palestinian problem lay within historic Palestine, for example, in an agreement that would identify Jordan as a part of Palestine.

The other day, Professor Yigael Yadin said in an interview in London that he, for one, would not mind seeing Yasir Arafat replacing Hussein in Amman, since the Palestine problem has become such a powerful propraganda issue and was even undermining the morale of certain elements in Israel who do not know enough about the history of Zionism. This is an extreme viewpoint so far not widely shared in Israel. I think it is a sound view. I just do not believe that it is necessary to maintain the regime of King Hussein in Jordan on the basis or at the risk of acquiring a reputation of injustice, brutality, and ruthlessness. This is all simply not true. There is enough room in the Palestine of the League of Nations Mandate for all the Arabs and the Jews of Palestine. Jordan is the Palestinian Arab nation-state just as Israel is the Palestinian Jewish nation-state.

How Hussein can come to an agreement with the Palestinians and how his government can be made representative of the Arab people of Palestine may be a difficult problem—certainly more difficult now than it was in 1967—but United States policy has to address itself to this question.

Now one last point. It is simply not correct that the Russian position in the Arab world has rested upon their support of the Arabs against Israel or upon Western support for Israel. We all know that, before the 1967 war, President Nasser for a long time considered his relationship to Israel as a side issue. He called himself an *anti-Imperialist* and was anti-American because he realized that the United States not only stood in the way of Israel's destruction, but that it also stood in the way of his taking over Jordan, Saudi Arabia, and the Gulf sheikdoms. If Israel were to disappear—the imminent key issue—we could be sure that the other issues of the inter-Arab conflict would come to the forefront again and would be exploited by whomever feels he is in a position to exploit them.

MR. FINGER. I now call on Dr. John Stoessinger.

DR. STOESSINGER. One concluding word about the role of the U.N. in this, ladies and gentlemen. I have always felt that one key to resuscitating the United Nations is not through structural changes or weighted voting devices or other scholastic techniques, but simply through a commitment by the member states to bring their problems to the United Nations at an earlier point in time. I think the Middle East is a very good case in point, where member states wait until the last moment or even beyond and bring their problem only when it has become virtually intolerable, thus making the United Nations a receiver of bankruptcy. Then they proceed to blame the United Nations in addition for being bankrupt.

It was in that sense that the British dumped Palestine on the U.N., that the Belgians dumped the Congo, and that Greece and Turkey dumped Cyprus. I believe the larger point to be made here, with particular reference to the Middle East, is that one way of giving the United Nations a more meaningful role to play is to bring it into the conflict at an earlier point in time.

Lord Caradon put this very well once when he said that there is nothing wrong with the United Nations except its membership. Thank you.

(End of first session.)

Demography, Economics, and Technology and the Middle East Conflict

by Abba P. Lerner

MR. SAMUEL MERLIN. Ladies and gentlemen, the man who will preside at this morning's session is Professor Abba Lerner, a world-renowned economist and author of several books, and cochairman of the Institute for Mediterranean Affairs.

MR. ABBA LERNER. Good morning, everybody. I am scheduled to speak on Demography, Economics, and Technology and the Middle East Conflict, and I shall begin by speaking about none of these; not demography, not economics, not technology, not even the Middle East conflict. I want to begin by recalling something that I heard a little while ago about Ireland. It was in a talk by Conor Cruse O'Brien reviewing some books about Ireland. He spoke about Irish republicanism as a view of Irish history enshrined in the Proclamation of 1916, which called for the complete independence of all Ireland from England. This notion has had quite a place in government offices and schools and young minds have been encouraged to approach it in a spirit of uncritical veneration analogous to that of the Declaration of Independence in America's cause. There is an important difference. The American war of independence is generally accepted as being now over, while no one adhering to the Irish republican ideology is likely to concede that Ireland's struggle for independence against Britain is over. Inherent is the fact that the official ideology that the state enjoined on the young is an ideology to which the state does not in practice adhere and whose consistent adherents it finds itself obliged to punish. The sense of Irish history lies in breaking the connection with England. O'Brien concluded: "While Ireland holds these bones—the bones of the patriot dead— Ireland unfree shall never be at peace."

I am quoting this because it reminds of the kind of thing we were talking about part of the time yesterday. The attitude of the Arabs to the existence of Israel is similar to the attitudes of the Irish to the existence of a nonunited Irish republic, without which they feel they are not free, and that end is an objective to which they are devoted—but not officially; therefore, the Irish government has to try to punish the Irish patriots just as Jordan and Lebanon have to punish their patriots.

I think this ideological thing is the center of the whole trouble, and I think I must repeat something that I said in this very hall at a previous meeting of this same organization several years ago. Not long after the Six-Day War, my wife and I got several very intelligent Arab students at the University of California at Berkeley to discuss with us what kind of peace could come about in the Middle East. I tried very hard, and with surprising success, to get them to put aside various reasons they gave why the Arab countries could not make peace with Israel. I got them to suppose for a moment, just for the sake of argument, that Israel does not want to capture the whole of the Middle East, to agree that they were not really concerned about Israel having some nationalistic (which they called *racist*) ideology, and that Israel's development need not mean the economic destruction of all the Middle East. I got them to withdraw all these objections that they had put forward, and to admit that they were not being realistic. But finally we were left with one thing that could not be removed. It was very, very simple. They don't want Israel to be there. Everything else is dragged in only as a more respectable justification. This was the essential proposition that remained after all the unrealistic justifications had been discussed. This is where my very successful discussion ended without any success.

Therefore, peace is impossible, and yet we have what to many, for most purposes, is peace in Israel. War, the absence of peace, to my mind is largely the danger of getting killed, and at the moment there is less danger of this in Israel than in New York. There is peace, what Dayan and others have called *de facto peace*.

Our discussion last time was concerned with other meanings of the word *peace*. Maybe I should borrow something from the technique of the semanticists and talk about Peace I and Peace II and Peace III. Peace I is what we have now in Israel. People go to work regularly, they are not afraid of being shot or mugged or bombed for the time being, and the Arabs are also benefiting not only from peace, but also from free trade, movement, work, and development in Israel. That is Peace I.

But what we often talk about is Peace II, that is, where there is a formal agreement on recognized and guaranteed boundaries of the kind that exist between the United States and Canada or the United States and Mexico. This, of course, is not a guarantee of permanent peace. Wars have broken out many times even when there was Peace II.

I suppose the ideal is Peace III, when we will beat our swords into plowshares and study war no more.

I think there is much too much consideration of Peace II. Mr. AlRoy spoke to us yesterday about the growing disparity between the military power of Israel and the Arabs and how Israel's military superiority is likely to last for a very long time. I suspect myself of being too willing to accept this belief, but I am held back by the fear of succumbing to wishful thinking. I remember what happened in this country at the time of the Sputnik when the changing conditions caused us to do something about it. I recall the stupidity of all the people mentioned by Mr. AlRoy who did not believe that the Jews would fight, and the widely prevalent belief that Jews don't know how to fight. It could be that some of the same kind of error is present in our present evaluation of the military potential of the Arabs.

We heard an even stronger proposition from Mr. Sinai who said that the Arabs were not merely backward in the sense of being unscientific. As a matter of fact, he said they had lost their way in the desert and would never get out of it again. This is certainly something that I don't think we can depend upon.

Mr. Kerr spoke about symmetrical ambiguities and of how the Israelis may be tougher than they say and the Egyptians softer than they say. I liked his formulation very much—how the Arabs can not afford to wait and how the Israelis can not afford not to wait. But where this puts us I don't know. It gives us neither stability nor instability; and if there is neither stability nor instability, we have to consider it to be instability.

Professor Morgenthau told us also about the world balance related to Peace II. He explained to us how the Middle East is stabilized by the Soviet Union wanting to help the Arabs but not to the point where they would win, and the United States helping Israel to the point where she will not lose; so there is neither win nor lose. Again, this is neither stability nor instability.

I enjoyed his impression very much of controlled tension desired by the Soviet Union and of peaceful settlement desired by the United States, but I remember how, in response to an Arab who was upset by this, he pointed out that both statements really mean very much the same thing: that both powers want the present condition to continue.

Mr. Gottlieb turned this thing neatly around. Instead of the Soviet Union and the United States stabilizing the Middle East, he saw the Middle East stabilizing the relationship between the Soviet Union and the United States. The danger is of America turning to competing with Russia for the favor of the Arabs.

Mr. Middleton saw the United States and the Soviet Union sparring around in several power vacuums in the Middle East, in the Persian Gulf, and in the Indian Ocean. Mr. Burns turned away even from the Middle East and from the U.S.S.R. to say that Israel, like Iran, does not want to be convulsed and concerned with racism. Both countries are really more concerned with independence.

Mr. Stoessinger completed this expansion of our topic by talking about the United Nations, of how, having been captured by the Arabs, it has become impotent, and how nothing is wrong with the United Nations except its members. And I remember very sadly that when I was a young man this is what we said about what we called the *League of British Nations*. It was fine except for its members. I would hope that this is not too bad an omen.

I come back to Peace I, which is really the important one, and the dangers to it. The only speaker who really stressed it was Dr. Morgenthau, who spoke about the third level of the conflict. The first or highest level was that between the superpowers. The second level is that between Israel and the Arab states, and the third level is the popular movement. The third is what seems to me the most important thing here. Egypt and Syria talk about peace or not peace, and whether they can afford to wait, and the Fedayeen talk about a secular, democratic, non-Zionist Arab state. But the Arabs in Israel do not talk much. As far as we can tell, they have two thoughts. In the first place, they would rather be under (or in) Jordan than under Israel. In the second place, whether in Israel or in Jordan, they would like to continue to enjoy the higher standards of living and of trade and other benefits they have gained under Israel. I think the second thought is more stable, but the first thought is part of the ideology of which I was reminded in hearing about Ireland.

But what has been happening all the time is that while we are still so staggered with the way Israel won the war, we are paying insufficient attention to the way in which Israel is winning the peace in the development of Israel and of the occupied territories. Israel has been an example of a tremendous rate of economic development. The West Bank has even been more so. Whereas Israel has been growing at about ten percent per annum, the West Bank has been growing at about nineteen percent. This has established conditions that would seem to be likely to last for a long time. The danger that I see is a danger from certain trends in Israeli policy, not from Russia, not from the United States certainly, not even from Egypt or Lebanon or Syria. The danger is from policies that may spoil the winning of the peace. These dangerous policies derive from : (a) a fear that the possible integration of the Arabs with Israel would spoil some people's idea of a Jewish state; and (b) too great a concentration on the formal *de jure* Peace II, at the expense of hampering the strengthening of the *de facto* Peace I. This is the actual peace that is being enjoyed and that could continue to be enjoyed for quite a long time no matter what progress or lack of progress there may be or what prognostications there may be about long-term future *de jure* peace. The danger is that important contributions to consolidating the *de facto* peace would be prevented for fear of their interfering with negotiations with Egypt or with Syria.

Of course, it is desirable that there should be a peace settlement between the countries of the Middle East, but I do not see it coming about for quite a long time for the basic ideological reasons that I have stated. Some leaders in Israel feel that we must not do anything that would hurt the possibilities of negotiation, even though this might damage the existing state of affairs. This inevitably reminds me of Aesop's dog who dropped his piece of meat into the water in an attempt to get at its reflection. What is being threatened by such leaders is an interruption or a spoiling of the peaceful development, the result of which has been that, although we have violence now from the Fedayeen in Lebanon, as we had in Jordan, we don't have it in Israel. We don't have a Vietnam in Israel, because there is unprecedented prosperity among the Arabs in the occupied areas and because Arabs are earning much more when they go to work in Israel. There is not the economic basis for dissatisfaction that could be the greatest danger to Israel's *internal* security, and that would also greatly increase the *external* dangers.

The kinds of things that I have been hinting at are, for example, the attempts to put limits on the employment of Arabs in Israel by calling this *exploitation*—as if we were doing harm to them even though it is perfectly clear that everybody is benefiting from it. Stress is laid upon the fact that the per capita income in Israel is many times that of the Arabs, as if that were a good reason for not allowing them to rise from where they are. It reminds me very much of the concern of Mr. Chavez who, in his zeal for equality, is trying to prevent Mexicans from improving their condition by coming to work in the United States.

Before attending this conference, I was at another conference bearing a title even more closely related to what I am talking about. It was organized by American Professors for Peace in the Middle East and attended mostly by economists. Some of the participants there were thinking of reasons for preventing the Arab economic development under Israel from going too far. There seemed to be a far of Israel being flooded by Arabs, with more and more Arabs coming in from all over the Middle East into Jordan and from Jordan into Israel, and Israel will find itself with perhaps millions of them in a short time. Then there was the calculation of differences between private cost and social cost in that the employer of an Arab does not pay the cost of the social services that have to go with it, and therefore he should pay for them via a tax on Arab workers in Israel.

All these are ways of preventing the winning of the peace, establishing feelings of discrimination greater than they really are. There will be some discrimination in any case because of differences in background, in education, in training, and so on, that lead to prejudices. But these are minor compared to the dangers of policies that would destroy Peace I in the hope of this doing something more toward getting Peace II.

This leads me back to the title of my talk. It is demography that is important. Not the demography of the hundred million Arabs, more or less. but of the one or two million Arabs, perhaps, in the immediate area. Technology, economics, and development have established a state of affairs that makes it impossible for the Arabs to go back to a pre-Israel condition. It leads to something that I don't know whether to call *Peace I* or *Peace II*, but the general outlines of any possible settlement have taken a definite shape. There can not be a single state because this will satisfy neither the Jewish nor the Arab aspirations for their national state. They have different cultures that they want, and are still entitled, to carry out separately. But there can not be an *economic* division. We will not be able to ask the Arabs with any kind of free will to go back to a lower standard of living, to lower wages, to a smaller area, once they have learned to move toward a more developed life. This means that there would have to be a Palestinian entity (perhaps absorbing Jordan rather than being absorbed by Jordan), and an Israeli entity with some arrangements for security. Everybody whom I heard making sense about this sees the same kind of picture. We do not see it happening for quite some time because of ideology. The only thing to do now is to continue to develop the economic integration as far as possible, to make use of the connections between Gaza and the West Bank and between the West Bank and Jordan, so there will not be a *factes accomplis* of a kind that prevent Peace II, but an established *de facto* Peace I that will serve until we can get Peace II accomplished formally, if at all, in some distant future. Thank you.

MR. SAMUEL MERLIN. The discussion now is on oil, and the first speaker is Mr. William D. Smith, oil specialist of the *New York Times*.

The Energy Crisis and the Middle East

by William D. Smith

MR. WILLIAM D. SMITH. I think I should start by saying that President Nixon's long awaited energy message that was delivered a few weeks back was too late before it was even delivered. To have been effective, it should have been President Johnson's energy message and have been delivered about six years ago. I am not, although I work for the *New York Times* in this case, trying to shift the blame for possible future brownouts, blackouts, and rationing from Republican to Democratic shoulders. Rather, I am trying to point out that the nation's energy situation is such that possibly there are no short-term solutions available that will guarantee America's protection from some unpleasant changes in their style of living.

Quite simply, the United States, for a variety of reasons, does not have sufficient supplies of the right sources of energy available at the right places. Yet paradoxically the United States has the resources to be basically self-sufficient. However, even a massive effort probably can not develop them adequately much before 1980. What exists, therefore, is a growing shortage of energy that is available or acceptable in terms of price, environmental considerations, geographical and political positions, or technological capabilities.

What I am saying here is that we have the energy but we do not have it where we want it; what we have, we can not use.

There would appear to be four basic solutions to the American energy dilemma: sharply increasing oil and gas imports, greater exploration and production from domestic sources, development of alternate energy sources, and conservation.

Upon closer examination, each of these escape routes has its pitfalls. Increased imports bring with them dependence upon foreign sources, possibly unreliable foreign sources, as well as massive and unacceptable increases in our balance of payment deficit.

Greater domestic exploration carries an almost certain rider of higher prices as well as environmental hazards.

Alternate sources of energy, often touted as panaceas, are either unproven, very costly, or too far in the future to solve the immediate problems; thus, the person you meet at a cocktail party who says, "Hey, we have oil shale." Well, we have oil shale but it is a long time down the pike, and I wouldn't want to drive my car with what it produces.

Then there are conservation programs, everyone's darling. If applied strictly, it would possibly or probably be unacceptable to a democratic country. You are not going to tell most persons who drive their car to New York City that they can not. If you do, you will have a lot of difficulty convincing them that you will be elected the next time around. If conservation is applied in a very loose fashion, it is almost meaningless.

Thus, when all is said and done, there is a good chance that even a wise combination of the four approaches to the American energy problem will not allow the nation to escape unscathed from its self-imposed energy dilemma. What the United States needs most over the next ten years is probably good luck. The country has arrived at this unenviable and unnecessary state through a combination of growing energy demand, declining reserves, new environmental awareness, poorly conceived laws, horrendous planning, lack of foresight, and blatant waste of irreplaceable resources. It is enough to make us wonder how we ever got a man on the moon. In fact, someone remarked, if you look at the energy situation, we should have a rocket going to the sun right now with no one knowing and no one caring.

Although almost unbelievable, the United States' energy situation is still somewhat understandable. America grew up and became a superstate on a diet of cheap, plentiful, indigenous energy resources. With six percent of the world's population, the United States accounts for almost thirty-three percent of the world's energy consumption. That is a heck of an appetite! This ready supply of energy has played a major role in making America the world's largest industrial complex and in giving its citizens, even its poorer ones—this is something that should be remembered, even its poorer ones— a standard of creature comforts unrivaled in history. From New York to San Franciso, the average American is a profligate user of natural resources. With regard to energy, he floods his home with light even when no one is in. In fact, the police tell you to leave your lights on to prevent robberies. He heats his home until it is oven hot, as any person who comes from England will tell you, and drives a gas-devouring monster for a pack of cigarettes rather than walk a block. In Texas women carry full--length mink coats in August to watch a baseball game in an air-conditioned stadium. If you have been to Houston, you know that is not an exaggeration. And then, of course, there are the electric toothbrushes, combs, tie racks, and hair dryers. I haven't been able to figure out why you need an electric tie rack, but they advertise it. And while we are at it, today we all took an elevator to the second floor of this building when it would have been a lot better for our hearts as well as the energy situation if we had walked up.

If we are to believe the majority of experts, some of these creature comforts may have to go and, for the ones that remain, a higher price will have to be paid. Rationing is a probability—it has already started—it is not a possibility.

This vast storehouse of coal, oil, and gas that we had in the past and that catered to our creature comforts also allowed the United States an unequaled foreign policy independence, for America alone of all the major industrial countries in the free world was self-sufficient in energy. We are no longer, and to this extent America's control over her own destiny is being circumscribed. Now only China and the Soviet Union of the major world powers remain totally independent of foreign control over energy needs. The rest of the world, including the United States, will have to depend to a greater or lesser degree on the Middle East and north Africa to bridge the gap between domestic supplies and growing demand. These same Middle Eastern nations in the years to come, in return for their oil, will receive an unprecedented influx of marks, yen, dollars, and other currencies, making the area before the turn of the decade a major factor in world monetary affairs as well as a master of the world's energy lifelines.

This realization prompted Britain's prestigious International

Institute for Strategic Studies to warn recently that "the threat of the burgeoning power and changing tactics of the Middle East oil-producing countries seemed to overshadow almost all military threats to North America, Europe, and Japan." It may be an exaggeration but an interesting comment from a group like that.

The situation has been put quite starkly by Senator Henry M. Jackson of Washington (State), whom many people consider the most informed and unbiased man in the capitol, who sees energy matters as the most difficult problem facing the nation today, either internationally or domestically.

To Americans who everyday are told they must face up to another crisis—the urban, the racial, the monetary, inflation, employment, the Middle East—the placing of energy at the top of the hit parade may be an overstatement, yet a strong case could be made for its preeminence, for if the nation's energy house is not put in order, many of the other problems will be unsolvable.

In a way energy is the lifeblood of American civilization. The monetary, inflationary environment and employment problems will be pretty hard to solve if the energy system that runs the economy is out of order, and urban and racial woes obviously will be forgotten if the economy is falling apart.

The effect on world political stability of a staggering, stumbling, energy-short America can be envisioned by all of us here. All of what I say may still be somewhat of an exaggeration, but even if half of the implications are true, we are in a very interesting time in our history. Yet generations of energy abundance have conditioned the average American to apathy or disbelief in the possibility that anything but unlimited supplies of energy would forever be his lot.

Part of the confusion is not just the ignorance of the American population or the apathy, but because there are several energy crises, not just one. I use the word *crisis* in the advised sense. There has been a lot of argument about whether there is or is not an energy crisis. If anyone goes to the dictionary, he would find that there should be no argument at all, because the first definition of *crisis* means a vital time when vital decisions should be made: I think this would meet that criticism, no matter how you want to view the future.

The problems of the United States are one part of the overall, world energy crisis. They differ from the rest of the world. While in both cases solutions must be viewed in short-, intermediate-, and long-range terms, the interlocking nature of the world energy system makes some ideal short-term solution disastrous for the long-term.

Actions that might be beneficial to the United States could well be unsettling for other nations. For mankind as a whole, the basic danger lies, at the earliest, well into the next century when man has consumed most of the earth's storehouse of usable fossil fuels. Alternate sources of energy, such as solar or nuclear energy, will have to be found and perfected; or the human race could well return to the caves. For the United States, the most pressing problems are short-term and we have already begun to experience them in the form of blackouts, brownouts, and shortages of natural gas, fuel oil, and gasoline. The situation could get worse before it bets better.

A major part of the short-term problem is logistical, in that there appears to be little chance over the next few years that we can build enough refineries, create ports, and find and develop oil fields to avoid the shortages that seem to face us. It takes three years to build a refinery. None are presently planned. We have a shortage of refining capacity in the United States. That is a heck of a good job of planning by someone. It takes five years to build a port. You mention a port to anyone on the eastern seabord and they go beserk, but we need them if we are going to import oil. It takes five years to develop an oil field, eight to ten years for a nuclear plant. This is the sort of timing we are facing and doing nothing about it at the moment, while the President delivered his energy message in Congress.

A good friend of mine, John Lichtblau, head of the Petroleum Research Foundation, commented rather dramatically, "If an oil field as large as Prudo Bay in Alaska, the largest ever discovered in the history of North America, were found tomorrow in New Jersey, it would be a big help, but the United States would still have an energy problem for the rest of the decade."

Among most informed people there is no longer debate on whether there is or is not an energy crisis. Even Senator William Proxmire of Wisconsin, long and still a staunch opponent of the oil industry, admits that there is a problem now.

Debate has shifted to questions of how severe the problem is, the best methods to remedy the situation, and most vociferously where to place the blame for present and future difficulties. As we all know, when you don't know an answer, it is best to find whom you can put the blame on. The oil industry lays a large portion of the blame to environmentalists for *unreasonable*—that is their word—delay in the delivery of oil from the North Slope, the blocking of needed refineries, drilling, and nuclear plant siting. The oil industry probably has a point. Others blame the oil industry. They charge that the crisis is a device to get higher prices. The critics of the industry have a point. The massive multimillion dollar advertising campaign in recent months by the oil industry and utilities makes it appear that even though the industry may not have orchestrated the energy crisis, it is certainly playing background music to its own advantage.

There would seem to be, however, enough blame to go around, with the oil industry, consumer advocates, environmentalists, and John Q. Public, who wastes more energy in a day than the Japanese consume in a day, all deserving a fair share of the blame. I think if we all examine what we do every day and, say, some of the silly things we do with energy, we could realize that certain easy things could be done to help us out of the situation—not entirely out of the situation, but at least an inch ahead.

The one thing that everyone seems to agree upon is that the chief culprit is the government, the United States government, which through the years as a result of pressures from various groups as well as lack of foresight failed to create a stable, well-thought-out energy program for the nation. Instead, what has passed for a national energy policy has been a jerry-built, Rube-Goldberg system that has crumbled under both internal and external pressures. Each attempt to patch it up in recent years has resulted in another segment coming unexpectedly unglued.

There were forty-four federal agencies involved in making energy decisions in the past. Now, that is a barrel of bureaucracy that would be tough to beat on any item. This has not been changed any by President Nixon's energy message. Expectations that President Nixon's energy message would offer an instant cure for the malady were never too strong in any quarters. If anything, the message has been less portentous than even the minimal hopes.

The reasons for the energy message not having too much in content are understandable. It is a complex subject, there are too many sources of input, too many interests that have to be thrown a crumb in order to make the program politically digestible to the majority, if not appetizing to the very many.

A problem, though, that would seem to be less understandable would be the people who became the top advisers on the energy message. In the beginning, a man named Akins* from the State Department submitted what he thought should be contained in the energy message. Mr. Akins, if reports are to be believed, received

---

* James E. Akins, former Director of the Office of Fuels and Energy, Department of State; now U.S. Ambassador to Saudi Arabia. Author of: "The Oil Crisis; This Time the Wolf Is Here," *Foreign Affairs* 51, no. 3 (April 1973).

nothing but abuse. Instead, the final decisions were turned over to President Nixon's three chief aides: George P. Schultz, the ubiquitous Henry Kissinger, and the late-lamented John D. Ehrlichman. None of these three knew a damn thing about energy. They are very bright men but they did not know anything. Right behind them was another key figure, Charles J. DiBono, who was brought in in February as a special consultant. His expertise was with the Center for Naval Analysis. He know as much about energy as we do: he put gas in his car. Next in the chain of command was Earl Butz, Secretary of Agriculture and Counsel for Natural Resources, and then came William Simon, an investment banker. This was the energy team that finally made the decision. Beneath this, of course, was the whole great strength of the United States Interior Department and other agencies. Yet I think it should be questioned not just in energy but in all other areas whether bringing in uninformed people to make the final decisions results in objectivity or ignorance. And we do this not just in energy matters, but also in many other matters as well.

The energy problem has become a political issue in the United States. Indeed, activists, including some consumer and environmentalist groups, are showing signs of making energy a rallying point, a sort of peace-time Vietnam. Their reasoning is that it will be here for a long time and is a high-profile issue as well. In the realm of establishment politics, congressmen and senators are aligning themselves on the various sides of the energy issue. While ten years ago only legislators from the oil states took a deep interest in energy matters, now almost every congressman feels obliged to speak out on the subject. Local government officials also feel duty bound to become experts. With governors, mayors, and even city councilmen getting into the act, the room is open for the demagogue to get in; innocent demagogues, but you hear some pretty foolish things being said by some apparently bright people.

The energy crisis has also created a new form of schizophrenia in certain political circles. Politicians who have long been advocating elimination of all import restrictions on energy products are starting to worry about what effect increasing American dependence on Arab oil will have on the United States' relationship with Israel. While on the other hand, certain oil-state congressmen who for many years considered oil imports close to treason are now very near advocating massive import programs.

How serious is the energy situation? Every expert has his own opinion. Optimists view the situation at worst as involving some minor dislocations over the short-term resulting in occasional blackouts and brownouts. Pessimists give events a far more dire forecast. None see a darker future than Edwin C. Barbe, a professor of electrical engineering at the University of West Virginia, who is writing a book on the subject. He told me over the phone that one day—the day of Sunday, July 4, 1976, the 200th birthday of the United States of America—will dawn on a nation not in celebration, but one that will see it desperately trying to save itself from the crush of a collapsing economy because of the shortage of energy. He envisions an unemployment rate of 22.6 percent, with twenty-one million unemployed people walking the streets looking for work, food, coal, oil, and fuel. Auto traffic will be almost at a standstill with twenty-one million cars unable to move and all for lack of gasoline. Some twenty million homes will be without oil or gas, and heating and cooking will be done again by coal. Electricity will be turned off for hours at a time every day, and a million companies from manufacturing plants to barber shops will have gone out of business.

The position of most experts hopefully falls toward the optimistic side. The advent of even the most optimistic circumstances, however, will put a slight crimp in the average American's life-style. What exactly is the state of America's and the world's energy resources? Mankind has used more energy in the last thirty years than he has consumed in all history prior to 1940. The apex of this energy orgy is yet to come, according to many experts. World energy consumption is expected to double between 1970 and 1980, increasing from an equivalent of eighty-seven million barrels of crude oil a day to around 150 million barrels a day as population grows and less industrialized nations strive to develop.

Energy consumption in America doubled between 1950 and 1970 and is expected to approximately double again during the period 1970 to 1985, increasing from the equivalent of about 31.8 million barrels of crude oil a day to sixty-two million barrels of crude oil a day. Most of the figures are from industry sources and their perspective can therefore be considered one-sided. The trend, however, would appear inescapable based simply on population growth and aspirations of the have-nots in our society. Rigid conservation programs can reduce growth, but can not turn back the clock.

On the supply side, the United States, to quote John G. McLean, Chairman of the Continental Oil Company and head of the National Petroleum Council, an industry group, "has basic energy materials to meet our needs for at least 200 years at present levels of consumption." That is not bad. The National Petroleum Council estimates reserves of recoverable oil at about 350 billion barrels, a quantity sufficient to cover present demand for sixty-five years. Potential recoverable natural gas is estimated at 1.2 quadrillion cubic feet, sufficient to heat present levels of demand for more than fifty years. The Bureau of Mines indicated coal reserves at almost 400 billion short tons, equal to 700 years' supply. The Atomic Energy Commission conservatively estimates uranium reserves at one million tons, enough to cover present total electrical power needs for twenty-five years.

This is all well and good, but there is a huge step between potential reserves and presently available fuel. Covering the distance takes time, money and technology, and thus the short-term outlook is nowhere near as sanguine.

The most critical problem facing the country is natural gas, which currently provides one-third of the nation's energy. Over the last three years, schools and factories in various sections of the country have been closed for limited periods of time because of shortages. The Federal Power Commission reports that curtailment of natural gas by suppliers to customers with firm contracts increased during 1971, and in the first three months of 1972 increased sharply. These statistics do not include natural gas cutoffs to customers under interruptible contracts, as well as the denial of natural gas to new customers.

Coal would appear to be the most obvious answer to the nation's energy problems. It is by far our most abundant source of fossil fuel with several hundred year's potential supply, but as stated by Mr. S. David Freeman, head of the Ford Foundation Energy Study, "The trouble with coal is two things, you can't mine it and you can't burn it." And I think that pretty well says it all. Coal, for all it potential, is a difficult fuel. Obtaining it means deep mining or strip mining, both objectionable; the first because of the human hazards, the second because of the environmental depredation. Consuming the coal carries its own environmental threat, since much of the coal is high in sulphur content and burning it emits high pollutants into the air. Coal's third drawback is that it is expensive and difficult to transport.

The solutions coming from things thermal, solar, and shale are all something in the future, therefore leaving atomic energy—and atomic energy takes time to develop as well—and that can only mean electrical needs, not other fuel needs. When all is said and done, oil, the mainstay of the American energy diet, supplying forty-four percent of the total demand at present, will have to shoulder an even greater load in the future. Oil is the energy jack-of-all-trades, it is the swing fuel capable of running huge electrical generators or powering the family car. Just as important, it is easily transported and can be used in hundreds of products from gasoline to plastic. Because of these factors, oil is expected to be carrying more than fifty percent of America's energy load by 1980. Yet though the oil must carry the load, domestic production no longer has the capability. The United States exhausted its spare production capacity in 1970 and will probably never again be able to meet its oil needs from domestic resources. Output from domestic resources can be improved by various methods. If and when environmental objections to off-shore drilling are met, this opens up a vast potential petroleum harvest. The North Slope of Alaska will add about two or three million barrels a day when it is finally brought to market. Yet these additions will probably only be able to make up for declining production in Texas and Oklahoma, and most experts believe that American production will never exceed twelve million barrels a day again. On the other hand, this year's demand alone will exceed seventeen million barrels a day. By 1980 the United States demand will be around twenty-four million barrels, according to the State Department. The gap between domestic supply and demand is obvious and growing. It can be cut back by unexpected domestic discoveries or by conservation programs, but the trend can not be reversed.

Only one option is available in the short term: increased importation of oil from foreign sources. Whether this is good or bad is debatable, but it is a fact. It has already begun. In 1965 the United States imported 2.5 million barrels a day or about twenty percent of its demand with all but two percent coming from Venezuela or Canada. Imports which inched up to twenty-three percent by 1970, jumped to twenty-seven percent last year, and this year will be about thirty-five percent of total demand. By 1980 the United States could be dependent upon foreign sources for between forty and sixty percent of its oil. Thus, at the turn of the decade, thirty percent of the country's total energy demands, not just oil, would come from beyond its borders.

Several years ago in *Foreign Policy* magazine, Walter Levy warned that no nation can be considered a world power if it is dependent upon the goodwill of others for its energy needs. This can be debated. It is still an interesting comment. The United States is presently entering upon such a critical period, and the others on whose goodwill the United States may well have to depend are almost certainly the Arabs—the people in the world who, with the possible exception of the North Vietnamese, have the most virulent dislike of the United States and its policies. Unlike North Vietnam, however, the Arabs have something we want and need. The publisher of the *Middle East Economic Survey* commented : "The United States could get up and walk out of Vietnam any time it felt like it. I do not believe you can do this in the Middle East."

Let me just point out a few other aspects you will hear in cocktail-party conversation. One is that we can get our oil in other places if indeed we have to import this much. The other places usually mentioned are Canada and Venezuela. Venezuela has been supplying the world with oil, principally the United States, for half a century and its production has peaked. New reserves are hard to find and costly. In addition, there is growing support in Venezuela and around the other oil-producing nations for the theories of former oil minister Juan Perez Alfonso, who advocates production cutbacks to maximize profit rather than volume and preserve the nation's resources for the future.

Canada, once considered the United States' ace in the energy hole, has become a great deal more reluctant card. Although the potential for major discoveries exists in the Canadian Arctic, they would take time to develop. Canada does not now have the productive capacity to meet the near-term demand. For the long-term, the concept of continental energy policy, once appealing to many in the Canadian governmental circles, is now looked upon with disfavor. The Canadians are saying for the record, anyway, that they may not have enough energy supplies for their own needs. In addition, and this should be remembered, the attitude of the Canadian government as well as considerable portions of its population have become considerably less friendly to the United States in recent years.

The oil provinces of the North Sea, Nigeria, Indonesia, and the South China Sea are additions to the world's oil supply but not an alternative to the Middle East. The North Sea will supply only about fifteen percent of Europe's requirements by 1980. The South China Sea, despite the canard floated by certain peace groups in the United States that it has more oil than the Middle East. is just now an exploratory province. Nobody knows what it has. and in the next ten years there is no chance the South China Sea will provide anything for anyone other than minimal amounts maybe for the Japanese nearby.

The failure to discover a substitute for Middle East oil, it should be noted and remembered, is not from lack of trying, for in recent years eigthy-five percent of the new exploration activities of the oil companies have been outside the Middle East. America's dependence on foreign energy sources comes at a time when the balance of power

in the international oil trade has decidedly shifted to the producing
nations after having resided with the oil companies, and thus with the
consuming nations, since the inception of the international oil trade
in the early part of this century. The vehicle for this total shift has
been the Organization of Petroleum Exporting Countries, O.P.E.C.
During the sixties the balance of power remained with the companies,
strained only by the Arab-Israeli war of 1967. Then a combination
of events, some planned, others accidental, dramatically turned the
tables. A quick rundown of this: The Suez Canal was closed as a
result of the Arab-Israeli hostilities, making supplies from the Persian
Gulf less accessible and forcing tanker rates to an all-time high.
Civil war in that area caused disruption. The trans-Arabian pipeline
was damaged in Syria. While all this was happening, Europe had
become increasingly dependent for a lot of its oil upon friendly
old King Idris in Libya. He was replaced by less friendly Colonel
Qaddafi—Colonel Qaddafi, a young man, knowing nothing about
oil but not being so stupid as not to realize Europe's dependence
upon Libya's North African sources because of the canal's closing
and the tanker shortage, requested an increase in payments for his
country's oil. The oil companies, with that great native shrewdness
they have shown on many occasions, replied with what some observers
now consider an insulting small price improvement. Colonel Qaddafi,
again showing his calm nature, became enraged, cut back production,
and within no time the companies had capitulated to terms far
greater than observers thought the colonel would have taken earlier.
It was by far the greatest victory ever won by an oil-producing
country, and its shock waves went out to all the other producing
nations. What was won by young revolutionary colonels had to be
exceeded by shahs and kings, so that even greater payments were
to be obtained by O.P.E.C. in Teheran in 1971. Since then the companies have been whipsawed back and forth, and the consumer with
them, with ever higher settlements culminating for the moment with
the participation agreement earlier this year giving the Persian-Gulf
producing companies a twenty-five percent interest in existing concessions. The oil companies, once masters, are now on the way to
becoming servants, a servitude that is not viewed with much pleasure
by the consuming countries' governments. Although the severity of
the change in relations of the companies is denied by the companies,
Sir Eric Drake, Chairman of the British Petroleum Company, has
gone so far as to call the companies now *tax-collecting agencies*.

From Qaddafi's triumph to the present, the oil-producing countries
have increased their per barrel revenues by almost 100 percent. By

1980 the governments in the area will have an annual income of sixty-three billion dollars from oil, according to the State Department figures. Mr. Akins from the State Department points out that the cumulative payment of O.P.E.C. companies is even more staggering, probably reaching 210 billion between now and 1980. The government's official estimate of expenditures for this period will be well under one hundred billion by these Arab nations, leaving more than one hundred billion in capital accumulations to be put to whatever uses they feel like.

I think certain clichés about Arabs and oil should possibly be reconsidered. The first is that the Arabs can not drink their oil. As they accumulate more money, they may not be able to drink their oil, but they can certainly drink champagne from their bank accounts. The usual answer to this—

PROFESSOR GRUEN. Not in Libya, Qaddafi won't allow it.

MR. SMITH. I know that, but a lot of them go to Rome for a little action, as you know. The counter to this usually is, well, they don't have unity, Murray Adelman's theme. The producers' O.P.E.C. is working now. Has any great unity on the part of the consuming nations been demonstrated? Do the Japanese love us so much as to cut off their oil supplies, especially after what we have been doing on the monetary scene? The unity of the consuming nations is far less than the unity of the producing nations. So, willing away O.P.E.C.'s strength is interesting and perhaps a worthwhile thing to attempt but I wouldn't bank on it.

The third and somewhat interesting point, because it goes back to what I heard in yesterday's debate, is about the capabilities of the producing nations, not just Arab, but Iranian, Indonesian, and Venezuelan. Sheik Ahmed Zaki Yamani, for those people who have not met him, is a highly sophisticated graduate of Harvard International Law School. Facing him at the debate table over which way the world is going on its energy policy, you have for the oil companies' side a collection of engineers whose skills I think are certainly less than Qaddafi's. The producing nations put their top skills in the oil industry, and while I know many people and have made many friends in the oil industry, it would be very hard to maintain that the consuming nations, the United States, Britain, put their top people in the oil industry. Therefore, the skill equation would lie on the part of the producers, and this should be considered.

Of course, caught in the middle is the United States' relationship to Israel and how this concerns our energy matters. Will all the good friends in Congress be around when the farmer in Minnesota does not have heating oil at thirty below? I think it is a question that should be asked. Will this pressure create a decisiveness in the American political scene stemming from the energy crisis? So I think that many of the lasting or the long-standing equations on the Middle East should be reconsidered in light of what the energy crisis could mean to the United States and the world politically as well as practically. Thank you.

MR. SELDEN. May I, before we leave, just go back for a moment to the first of Mr. Smith's clichés. It was a little glib, I think, to say that if the Arabs can not drink oil, they can drink champagne. I am concerned about the transition. If the United States is not buying Middle East oil, to whom are they selling it? You can not buy a lot of champagne with rubles. I doubt that Tiffany is interested in rubles. If Japan were to be able to take up the slack, what would be the ramifications of our relations with Japan if we were completely cut off from that source of supply? I don't think we can quite dismiss so easily the question of what the Arabs will do with their oil if we did not buy it.

MR. LERNER. Thank you. I must now ask Mr. Ronall to continue the talks and then we will have some discussion afterwards. Mr. Ronall is the head of the Afro-Asian unit, foreign research division, Federal Reserve Bank of New York.

The Energy Crisis and Its Potential Effects upon American Policy

by Joachim O. Ronall

DR. RONALL. Ladies and gentlemen, in listening to the speakers yesterday and this morning, particularly my predecessor Mr. Smith, it occurred to me that if my memory serves me right, each and every one of the speakers mentioned oil and energy in connection with the Middle East.

We have heard reference to the differentiation between an energy *crisis* and an energy *problem*. There is to my mind a difference and I would like to state at the outset that I do not believe that in the United States we have an energy crisis, but we do have an energy problem. There is no doubt about it. The problem is the outcome of an increasing imbalance between domestic energy supply and demand. The dimensions of this imbalance have been widely publicized and no longer come as a shock. In addition, the main policy options are likewise well known : more emphasis on domestic supplies, more imports, and restraints on demand growth. The difficulty begins when we want to transform any of these options, or a mixture of them, into a practicable policy.

119

At this point we have to distinguish between the short-term and the long-term aspects of the energy problem in the United States. For the short term, as it has been correctly pointed out, our policy options are limited : more intensive exploration and exploitation of our domestic resources would be expensive, would require time, and the time requirement would also include the use of the reserves in the Alaskan North Slope and could lead to dislocation in industries where energy cost is an important part of total cost. Therefore, unless the United States is prepared to introduce some form of rationing —through pricing or otherwise—we will, over the short term, have to increase imports. If current United States' policies and trends continue, oil imports will increase from 4.7 million barrels per day in 1972 to 11 million barrels per day in 1980. Oil represents 75 percent of all energy used in the United States.

I have said that our energy problem is the result of a growing imbalance between supply and demand. There seems to be consensus about the projections for demand growth, but disagreement, if not uncertainty, marks the projections of energy supply. I have the impression that most of the generally accepted demand projections originate with the industry and may therefore be in need of bias correction.

Factors such as zero population growth, antiwaste consciousness, and ecological considerations may not have been adequately taken into account by the demand projectors. Most analyses do not appear to consider the possibilities of price elasticities—that is, that sharp increases in prices may retard increases in demand. The general assumption, usually implicit, is that energy demand is quite inelastic, on the argument that energy is such a basic need that price rises will not adversely affect impact consumption. However, with the anticipated sharp rise in energy prices—and oil in this respect is only one of the energy sources, of course—and the increasing popular sensitivity to waste and pollution, it is likely that we will see some moderation of increases in energy use by households resulting from better insulation, wider use of storm windows, fluorescent lighting, and appliances with improved energy efficiencies. The same will in all likelihood occur in business use of energy. For example, Alcoa recently announced a new process for making aluminium that requires thirty percent less electricity—a notable achievement since aluminium requires more energy per unit of output than any other United States industry. However, to whatever correction the demand projection may be subjected, for the short term higher oil imports seem inevitable. Because of the size of the known reserves and the time required for developing new oil and other energy sources, most of these additional imports will have to come from the Middle East, north Africa, and possibly west Africa where Nigeria's production is rapidly increasing. This new situation is, of course, creating a series of problems.

After a lengthy period of relative stability and constant production increases of about eight percent per year, oil prices during the last three years began to climb persistently, mainly due to deliberate action on the part of the major producing countries. The Organization of Petroleum Exporting Countries, O.P.E.C., through a series of concerted operations and in the absence of a unified stance among the major consumer countries, has decolonized oil and forced up crude oil prices about fifty percent during the three-year period that ended December 1972. Further increases are probably in the making due to present international uncertainties. Besides forcing up prices, O.P.E.C. members have reduced the reliability of supplies. Kuwait and Libya have cut back production because of apprehensions over reserves nearing exhaustion. Additional cutbacks may be effected if producer countries begin to think—as a result of the continuing monetary uncertainty—that "oil in the ground may be worth more than money in the bank." Also, some of the Middle Eastern and North African countries have come to be regarded as insecure sources of supply because of their having threatened to interrupt shipments. Whether these threats and the concomitant risk of interruption are real or exaggerated is difficult to assess. But the fact remains that the United States is becoming increasingly vulnerable to oil being used as a political weapon. The threat is being taken seriously by the Administration and will probably influence policy formulation for some time to come.

Another set of problems arises out of the financial implications of increased imports on the balance of payments of both producing and importing countries. While the importers will have to allocate increasing funds to oil imports, the producers simultaneously will accumulate funds to an extent to which few of them have an adequate capacity to productively handle. The remaining accumulation and their use on the international money and capital markets are likely to create problems.

The significance of Middle Eastern imports rises if we take into account that the Western Hemisphere's oil production potential, over the short run, appears reduced despite the new reserves in Alaska and Ecuador. At the same time, the flexibility of the oil companies to shift supply sources has been curtailed due to their declining strength in the international oil-power constellation. That leads us back to the Middle East and North Africa on which, as already noted, the United States will have to depend, during the foreseeable future, for an increasing part of its crude oil imports, notwithstanding promising Atlantic coast offshore explorations and shortages in the United States of adequate discharging facilities and refining capacity.

All Arab countries in the Middle East, except Saudi Arabia, have at one time or another threatened to withhold oil from the Western buyers, and even Saudi Arabia most recently has linked United States' policy in the Middle East with the availability of more oil. These threats, as mentioned before, are taken seriously by the Administration, but apparently for political and economic reasons rather than for reasons of national security. Military opinion seems to agree that in the event of a nuclear war, continued crude supplies are irrelevant since refining and transportation capacity would be much more affected. In the event of a conventional war, military needs could be met from domestic sources. However, the interruption of supplies to Western Europe and Japan may pose a more difficult problem. So much for military contingencies.

More important seems the possibility of a political oil embargo. Here we have to distinguish several options. A total embargo of all oil supplies would require the full cooperation of all major producer countries, a rather unlikely event. But a collective total embargo is not the only possibility. Any embargo imposed by a combination of several major producers would severely affect Western Europe and Japan, where there is little domestic production, and the absence of contingency planning could lead to serious predicaments for these countries. But even without interference with the physical flow of oil, O.P.E.C. members have, as we have seen during the past three years, a considerable economic leverage.

One does not have to elaborate on the many possibilities that the present situation offers. The point is that the concentration of world oil reserves in an area of political volatility carries risks to those depending on that oil. The difficulty is a proper assessment of these risks. Recent writings by James E. Atkins, Charles L. Schultz, and M. A. Adelman confirm the divergent views on the subject.

Under the circumstances, the formulation of an Atlantic-Japanese oil policy and its possible implementation through the O.E.C.D. (Organization for Economic Cooperation and Development) oil committee has been suggested. The principal topics to be dealt with in such a policy formulation have been tentatively summarized as follows :

1. Review energy demand and supply including refining and transportation facilities; program for maximum diversification

2. Program research for additional energy resources and the feasibility of their use; review present energy technology

3. Review present oil-import arrangements by consumer countries through purchases, concessions, or service contracts

4. Program for stockpiling, rationing, and equitable sharing of availabilities in case of emergencies

5. Review and coordinate economic development programs for developing countries

6. Review prices, costs, and balance-of-payments effects of oil exports, including government revenues in producer and consumer countries, effects on world trade, money and capital markets, and financial cooperation.

7. Review the dependencies of producer countries on Western industrial and agricultural production, military equipment, technical know-how, and continuously assess the mutual interdependence as well as the availability in cases of oil supply, trade, and finance emergencies.

From this description of the energy scenario over the short run, it is evident that the main issue arising from Middle Eastern oil is likely to be economic rather than political. The relevant point here is that the recent sharp price increases for crude oil do not reflect a physical shortage of oil, but rather a joint action by the oil-producing countries for whom the oil companies—according to Professor Adelman—have become tax collectors to the tune of about $15 billion in 1972, with more of the same to come.

Is dependence on imported oil inevitable for the United States? Or is this prospect one of several options depending on the policies that the Administration will devise? We said that during the short run increased imports seem indeed inevitable since trends in proven reserves in the Western Hemisphere are discouraging. But proven reserves of oil and gas are a restrictive measure. They refer to the amount of fossil fuel in the ground that can be recovered in the future under present economic and technological conditions. In formulating policies one has to take into account probable and known reserves of oil and gas, and also of shale and coal. In addition—which may be of much greater importance—we will have to investigate, much more intensively than in the past, other energy sources besides fossil fuels, for example, nuclear, solar, and hydrogen power. Some of the technology used in these fields today seems to border on science, but it would be a mistake to underestimate our capacity for technological innovation.

Energy problems can not be discussed without mentioning the

rising public concern with ecological issues. This concern at present handicaps development of future energy supplies from all sources. Prophets of doom abound, but one of the reasons for their proliferation may be the fact that theoretically much is known about the interaction between energy and the environment, but little about the empirical relationship between energy sources and environmental quality. The prophecies of doom seem plausible when one realizes that the use of any primary source of energy produces some environmental damage. What we do not know is: how much? The problem is therefore twofold: first, to arrive at more precise measurements of the ecological effects of energy production and use, and second, to determine, how shall the choice be made between more energy and a cleaner environment?

It seems therefore urgent to formulate a cohesive set of national energy policies. To shape and to carry out such policies will require much study of policy options and their implications. This does not mean that the overhauling of present policies should be postponed until research has answered all the questions. That time may never come. What it does mean is that major efforts should be concentrated to reduce critical areas of ignorance.

To come back to our initial question: whether the United States faces an energy crisis? The few points that we have been able to touch on in this presentation suggest that increased imports of traditional energy sources are inevitable over the short run. Over the long run, the answer depends on us, on the United States. As long as present policies are left as they are, the set of disturbing elements that has emerged during the last few years could conceivably bring about a basic change in the country's hitherto favorable energy position. But this does not need to happen. There exists an abundance of energy sources in this country that could be used to maintain the country's energy balance, if we are able to devise national policies adequate to the situation.

It seems therefore permissible to state in summing up that under the prospect of such development, the energy problem in the United States may not be of very long duration. By the same token, the concentration of about seventy percent of the world's oil resources in the hands of a small number of countries may decline in economic and political significance in a not too distant future.

MR. LERNER. I am very much tempted to start a discussion on this subject. I am always tempted by a major problem such as this, even more so now, but I can not do so because we have two more people to speak and I will leave the discussion until after that.

The next speaker will be Professor Gidon Gottlieb, School of Law, New York University, who will speak on China and Japan and the Arab-Israeli conflict.

China and Japan
and the Arab-Israeli Conflict

by Gidon Gottlieb

PROFESSOR GOTTLIEB. Ladies and gentlemen; allow me to consider first the point raised by General Burns at the end of the discussion period yesterday. It involves the role of the Nixon Doctrine and the perception of the role that Iran and Israel might play with regard to the Middle East situation. I did not at any time wish to suggest that either Iran or Israel, or for that matter Turkey or Saudi Arabia, were willingly going to become the tool of any of the superpowers. Rather, the kind of cooperation that had developed between Israel and the United States during the Syrian invasion of Jordan may still bear heavily in the mind of the policyplanners in Washington. This cooperation was recently described with a great deal of eloquence by Mr. Henry Brandon in *Foreign Policy* magazine, in an apparently well-informed account. Perhaps *parallel interest* is a more accurate term than *cooperation,* the parallel interests of the United States and Israel, the United States and Iran, the United States and Turkey, the United States and Saudi Arabia. These parallel interests are a very useful introduction to the discussion of the roles of Japan and of China in the Middle East.

CHINA

Japan and China share a common characteristic with regard to the Middle East : both states are very deeply affected by events in the area, but they are both unable significantly to influence the destiny of the area. There is a disparity between the magnitude of their interests and the means at their disposal to safeguard these interests, and that leads to a certain tension in their posture.

As far as China is concerned, I think it is fair to say that this tension has led the P.R.C. to adopt a rather strident policy directed primarily, as they quaintly put it, at "one or two superpowers." As far as Japan is concerned, this tension has led them to adopt perhaps the lowest profile foreign policy of any major power on any major issue affecting it. It is the lowest profile on record. How does that situation look from Peking? It is often suggested that ideological considerations weigh heavily on Chinese minds. It is easy to cite the support of China for the Palestinian movement. for the Popular Front for the Liberation of the Arab Gulf, and alleged Chinese support for the Eritrean Liberation Front. The posture of the Chinese government with regard to all revolutionary movements in the broad area has made many headlines, but it is questionable whether it tells us much about the general character of Chinese policies. Indeed, it is as easy to balance this image of China as a friend of revolutionaries with the competing image of a China that has been tightening and improving its relationship with "progressive" regimes like those in Spain and in Greece, that has sent a delegation to the "proletarian" feast of Persepolis, where more crowned heads came together than at any time since the coronation of Queen Elizabeth II, and where Chinese envoys consorted with Vice-President Agnew and President Podgorny, very poor company by their standards.

If we look for the interests of China at this time, we may perhaps be guided best by what they have said about and how they have perceived the conflict that has most directly threatened them in the last few years : I refer to the conflict in the Indian subcontinent. I quote here from the statements of Ambassador Huang Hua in the Security Council at the time of the Indo-Pakistan War. He vehemently denounced Soviet policy in the Indian subcontinent, and charged that the armed aggression by the Indian government against Pakistan was being carried out with the connivance, support, and shielding of the Soviet Union:

> To put it bluntly, in supporting India and its provoking of armed conflict with Pakistan, the purpose of the Soviet government is to take advantage of India's inevitable dependence on the Soviet Union in the war and to control the Indo-Pakistan subcontinent and the Indian Ocean and to expand its sphere of influence so as to compete with another superpower for world hegemony. This is exactly the same tactic it has used in the Middle East question.

He went on to state in the debate:

> The secure boundaries of the Soviet Union have all of a sudden been extended to the Indo-Pakistan subcontinent and Indian Ocean. The aim of the Soviet leaders is to gain control over the subcontinent, to encircle China, and to strengthen its position in contending with the other superpower for world hegemony. What the Soviet leaders of today are frantically seeking is the establishment of a great empire which the old Czars craved after but were unable to realize, a great empire controlling the whole Eurasian continent.

These statements by the Ambassador of China should be given weight if only because their rhetoric reflects the text of the communiqué issued at the conclusion of the visit of President Nixon to Peking with the Shanghai toast. The concern with hegemony, the concern with preventing any power from achieving hegemony in the Pacific-Asia region, seem to direct both Chinese and American policy. The theme of the encirclement of China explains how they view their position on their western frontiers. Current attempts to weaken West Pakistan further, to encourage, for example, the secession of Baluchi tribesmen, to encourage local dissidents in the west, can not but run directly counter to Peking's interests. Recent incidents, such as the reported discovery of arms for Baluchi rebels in the hands of Iraqui diplomats in Pakistan, would immediately lend themselves to a conspiracy theory suggesting that the Soviet Union may be behind the plots. We should not underestimate China's direct security interests in West Central Asia, and I do not mean just an interest in the export of revolution or the export of Chinese ideology. What I have in mind is the Chinese view of their own immediate security interests.

Events in Afghanistan, events in Iran, events in the Gulf states have an impact on Pakistan's destiny and on China's own fears of encirclement. It should be recalled that China has a common border with Afghanistan, (however small it is), and that Chinese security interests in the Gulf area are not any more improbable than the Soviet Union's professed security interests in the Mediterranean. Both powers have an interest in the area and it appears that Iran and the Gulf are becoming a focal point of competition between the Soviet Union and China, not to speak of the direct concerns of the United States, Western Europe, and Japan.

We can therefore direct attention to two dimensions of Chinese concern: their fear of encirclement, and their related dedication to the defense of Pakistan's integrity and of Iranian security.

The recent development of ties between China and Iran, the great and exquisite delicacy they have put in the reception of the sister of the Shah of Iran, the courtly statements published in the Chinese press that are reminiscent of the *London Times Court Circular,* all these do suggest that China is by no means prepared to neglect her state interests in Central West Asia.

On top of these comes the acute Chinese concern with any possibility of Soviet-American entente. The Chinese have been making no secret of their desire to see Western Europe remain strong, of their desire to see NATO remain effective. They thus welcomed Britain's entry into the Common Market. They were not happy with Chancellor Willy Brandt's political approach. They have suggested both by the pattern of diplomatic relations established and by their overt pronouncements that they would like to see tension and pressure remain on the Soviet Union in the West, if only in order to decrease the weight of massed Soviet forces along their own borders. The concept of lighting as many points of tension as possible on the western side of the Soviet Union is easy to grasp. It seems to be an approach that the Chinese government is pursuing at this time.

From Peking's viewpoint, the Middle East conflict serves as a method for exacerbating a focal point of discord between the Soviet Union and the United States. It is related to the energy problem. If we take recent statements of the Chinese, we can see that they are concerned with the Soviet role as suppliers of energy to Western Europe and with their potential role as suppliers of energy to Japan. In a recent documented study by Robert Abel, it is reported the Soviet Bloc will import about twenty million tons of crude oil per annum by 1975, and that the communist countries will be exporting at that time some twenty-five million tons of oil to the West. Italy is already receiving seventy percent of her oil supplies from communist countries. That is a position of tremendous influence for the Soviet Union, which must not be to the liking of Premier Chou. It is clear to the Chinese that Western Europe is less likely to pursue an abrasive policy vis-à-vis the Russians when the oil resources of Western Europe are exposed to Soviet displeasure. China was herself once dependent on Soviet oil imports. With the growing Sino-Soviet feud, Moscow stopped deliveries and China had to turn elsewhere. The Chinese then relied primarily on imports from Rumania and Albania, a very long supply line with the Suez Canal closed. The awareness of the political use of the oil weapon to stabilize relationships between the U.S.S.R., Europe, and Japan preoccupies the Chinese, whose concern is heightened with talk of an accommodation between the Soviet Union and Japan tied to the joint exploration for Siberian oil. Such proposals are casting a shadow over the fresh reconciliation between China and Japan. China does not welcome the Soviets becoming suppliers of oil to Western countries and to Japan. It would limit potential reliance on those very same countries in efforts to divert Soviet pressure away from Chinese borders.

China makes no secret of its policy. In the U.N. Assembly in his inaugural address, the Chinese representative said, "The Chinese government and people resolutely support the struggles unfolded by the petroleum-exporting countries in Asia, Africa, and Latin America, as well as in various regional and specialized organizations to protect their national rights," and so forth. China displays a keen awareness of the use of the oil weapon on the stability of international politics. For China, Middle East oil plays a crucial role in regard both to their policy of reconciliation with Japan, in regard to their policy of maintaining focal points of tension alight in the West, and with regard to their policy of preserving their own direct security interests in the West Central Asian area.

It is true that with all these considerable interests at stake, China is not able to do very much about them, and recent testimony before the House Subcommittee on the Middle East suggests that the Chinese have now given up playing a direct military role in the area. There was talk of Chinese military presence and aid to West Pakistan. There was evidence about their role in Tanzania. But their support for the Palestinians seems to be primarily verbal, and they are not translating eloquent statements into effective material aid on any large scale. Significantly, even in relation to Jordan, the Chinese government has changed its tune. While it was vehement in its condemnation of King Hussein in the wake of the civil war, the Chinese government has now softened its criticism of the Jordanian kingdom and hardly any reference to Jordan can be found in the *Peking Review*. Strikingly, if you look at the recent index to the

Peking Review, one country that is not even mentioned is Jordan, quite a change from the year 1971.

JAPAN

In connection with Japan, it is necessary to focus on the overwhelming Japanese dependence on Mideast oil. It is so overwhelming and so well known that it is right to restate it. In 1968, which was four years ago, of 152 million metric tons of oil that Japan did import, 132 million came from the Mideast. Japan has reached the position of complete dependence on Mideast oil that is now forecast by pessimists for the United States for the year 1985. The Japanese are there now. In 1980 Japanese reliance on oil imports as a percentage of their total energy supply, not just oil, is estimated to range between seventy-five and eighty percent. Iran, Kuwait, and Saudi Arabia are, and are likely to remain, Japan's principal suppliers. By 1975 Japan will be consuming an amount equal to one-half of the total output of Mideast oil fields. The security of these oil supplies is therefore a matter of the most acute concern for the Japanese. Even though Professor Adelman, to whom so much reference has already been made, suggested this can be cured to a large degree by sophisticated storage devices, it seems that the Japanese remain as nervous as they ever were even though they are pushing forward their attempts to develop alternative oil-supply sources, in the China Sea, offshore Korea, and on the continental shelf where they are already running into rival Chinese claims. They are prospecting in Sumatra, in Indonesia, and they look with a great deal of hope to the Alaska oil fields.

These are the facts of Japanese dependence. They can not be overdramatized. They have led to a very, very deep concern on all Mideast matters. The seating of China in the United Nations has had an interesting impact on the policies of Japan. Japan had at one time desired to remain neutral and evenhanded in all matters pertaining to the Arab-Israeli conflict. She tried to make the world forget her Axis connections, and was much concerned with her World War II image. At this time we see a constant, delicate, and persistent erosion in the Japanese policy of evenhandedness. The Lod massacre took Japan out of her hiding corner on Mideast policy and made her position very visible. It braked but did not stop the cautious drift of Japanese diplomacy toward the majority pro-Arab position of the General Assembly. Japan is less preoccupied now with her image as an Axis power. She fears that Arab boycott policies would be more effective on Japanese industry than on European and American concerns. In 1967, on the very sensitive issue to Japan of freedom of navigation in the international Straits of Tiran, Japan chose to avoid entanglement in the proposed maritime naval task force that was going to sail up the Straits, and preferred not to uphold the principle of free navigation so necessary for her independence and oil trade, if that meant displeasing the Arabs.

There is little to suggest that it would be in Japan's interest to raise her profile in Mideast matters. Her drift toward the position of the pro-Arab Assembly majority is likely to continue.

Significantly, there is much more now being written about Chinese policies and interests in the Middle East than about Japanese policies and interests. China is more appealing to researchers and scholars than Japan. It is quite unfortunate that so little serious work is being done on Japanese policy in the area.

CONCLUSIONS

If we wanted to draw some conclusions, I think we should do that separately with regard to China and Japan. As for China, it seems that her rapprochement to the United States, her reconciliation with Japan, her response to the Soviet-backed Indian intervention in East Pakistan, reflect the new realities in the post-Vietnam world. Nothing symbolizes this better than the parallel votes of China and the United States during the India-Pakistan crisis, or the parallel movement of Chinese forces north of the Himalayas and of the carrier *Enterprise* from Vietnam to the Bay of Bengal. This seems to be the pattern, the pursuit of parallel policies in the area, and those parallel policies may extend to West Central Asia.

Second, China's support for a continuation of the armed struggle by the Arab peoples against Israel, which is vehement and explicit, is motivated by a fusion of ideological and diplomatic concerns. Her sensitivity to Third World positions may have restrained her from an explicit denunciation of Resolution 242, even though that denunciation was left up to Albania. China will probably continue to vote with Algeria, Libya, and Syria on issues bearing on the Arab-Israeli conflict.

Focal points of tension between Washington and Moscow could not but assist Peking in her attempts to create American-backed counterweights to Soviet pressures in the Far East.

More important, China's impact in the Middle East must not be overrated, nor must Japan's impact for that matter. China still is essentially a developing country and China's representatives point this out winningly every time they have an opportunity to do so. China is not a superpower. She is technologically weaker than either of the superpowers or Japan. She did not play a military role in the India-Pakistan War. Her ties with the countries bordering on the Soviet Union are diplomatic, not military. She has been trying to tie a ribbon of good relations with countries encircling the Soviet Union, but that is a ribbon of diplomatic relations, not military alliances. The degree of military and other aid that China can give to liberation movements is negligible, and it is unlikely that she will put support for liberation movements ahead of state to state interests.

China's maritime interests in the Middle East are likely to focus on the Persian Gulf states, (Iran, Iraq), as well as on the states bordering on the Gulf, which are of much more consequence to China than the more remote Middle East conflict between Israel and the Arab states.

The awareness in both Moscow and Washington that China may encourage limited conflicts between them continues to strengthen prospects for some limited United States-Soviet understanding on the mideast. It does nourish hopes for some measure of agreement between Mr. Brezhnev and Nixon when they next meet. China's interest in Soviet-American tensions, in keeping the superpowers apart, is one of the principal factors working for accommodation between Washington and Moscow.

Finally, there are strong reasons for assuming that China may aspire eventually to the role of an arbiter in a global balance-of-power system rather than that of a catalyst in a tacit anti-Soviet entente. But she may have no option in the matter, especially if President Nixon and Mr. Brezhnev remain determined to reach an understanding on the continuation of détente.

From China's perspective her Middle East policy is limited both in terms of her capabilities and her sense of priorities. It does lead, however, to some questions regarding the role of the United States, and I would like to conclude with these.

POSTSCRIPT: DÉTENTE AND THE MIDDLE EAST

In the first place there is no doubt that the Sino-Soviet rivalry puts the Soviet Union into a dilemma: on the one hand, how to avoid the creation of those tensions in the Mideast between Moscow and Washington that are precisely those that China would welcome; on the other hand, how to prevent the United States from continuing to shake and weaken the hold that the Soviet Union has managed to acquire in Arab states.

Second, the Arab-Israel conflict is helping the Soviet Union to drive a wedge into the Atlantic Alliance, as far as the Arab-Israel conflict is concerned. That wedge is of concern for the global posture of the United States.

Third is Soviet oil policies. The purchase of Arab oil on the one hand and the sale of energy to Europe and eventually to Japan on the other could become—I don't say it does or that it is intended to—an instrument for the Finlandization of dependent powers. It could help the Soviets slow down the reconciliation between Peking and Tokyo. That is again a matter of tremendous global concern.

Next, the potential impact of a suicidal Egyptian attack on Israel, the impact of such an attack on United States-Soviet détente is hard to calculate. It is hard to suggest at what point the Soviet Union may feel forced to come to the aid of the Arab states and what this would do to the prospects for the trade arrangements and other agreements to be negotiated between the United States and the Soviets. The tightrope act of the superpowers in the Middle East, the Soviet tightrope act and the American tightrope act, could be blown out of control by irrational moves in the area, and that is a matter of concern for leaders in Moscow and in Washington who put détente at the head of their priorities.

Further, would an American effort—and to this we already alluded yesterday—to win back the good graces of Egypt and the Arab world at the expense of Israel not constitute a violation of the Moscow agreement of last spring? Indeed, Mr. Sisco has suggested on a number of occasions that the United States will not take advantage of a difficulty that the other superpower may run into in the area, and the failure of the United States to respond more generously to Egypt's expulsion of Soviet personnel is in large measure attributable, it is said, to the spirit of the Moscow communiqué.

The most important immediate question that the United States must decide concerns the link between energy and détente: The talk of the energy crisis this morning, the emphasis given to it, the impact it has already had on relations between the United States and Europe, the impact it is likely to have on the relationship between the United States and Japan and those between China and Japan, do raise the question whether it is possible to have a lasting détente with the Soviet Union unless the energy problem is dealt with in an agreed manner, not only between the Atlantic partners, not only between the Japanese and the United States, but also between the Soviet Union and the United States. In other words, should the United States insist on a linkage of the Middle East issues and the other issues outstanding for settlement between Moscow and Washington; can the energy issue, the Middle East issue, be left out of negotiations on European security, mutually balanced force reduction, SALT II, or has the energy problem now acquired such salience that the energy problems will have to be negotiated alongside the other ingredients in a global package deal?

If the answer is yes, and if there is an awareness that the United States and the Soviet Union should jointly insist on moves toward a settlement in the Middle East, on a process of negotiations between Egypt and Israel, then other questions arise. Should the United States bring its influence, not pressure—you know, Mr. Sisco designates a difference between *influence* and *pressure*—should the United States bring its influence to bear on Israel once this process of negotiation has started? He alluded to such *influence* after the process will have begun on "Meet the Press" recently—should a process of negotiation be set in motion in an arena in which China would be able to interfere with settlement efforts? That is a question of great importance at a time when the Security Council is engaged in a review of Middle East policies.

It would seem that for the détente between the Soviet Union and the United States to be effective and lasting, for it to be more than a makeshift arrangement likely to collapse with the first winds of crisis in the Mideast or elsewhere, it would seem that a genuine effort should be made by both the United States and the Soviet Union to get such process of negotiations under way, and that the last place they should do that is in the Security Council where the Chinese would have an opportunity to impede the process.

Last, one sentence, a comment about the recent Egyptian position, and I feel I would really like to differ with the interpretation that Professor Kerr gave of the Egyptian position yesterday. I agree with him that the Egyptian position was very flexible, as recently as about four, five months ago. At that time there were indications and statements made that Egypt would indeed be extremely flexible on all issues save the retention of sovereignty over every inch of Egyptian soil. Egypt, it was said, would be forthcoming and willing to negotiate arrangements that would be responsive to Israeli security interests. Now, in his March 24th speech, President Sadat has dispelled that notion and has indicated very clearly that the attempt to reconcile Israeli security interests with Egyptian sovereignty is bound to fail because Egypt will not be willing under any guise to limit Egyptian sovereignty through overt or concealed security arrangements other than the stationing of a U.N. force.

It appears that the hardening of the Egyptian position, the shift in the Egyptian strategy, may have more to do with the threat that Egyptian diplomats may be wielding over the United States-Soviet détente than with the prospect of a military victory. At this time one can wonder whether for Mr. Sadat, resumption of hostilities in the Middle East would not play the same role on the global scale that the Jackson Amendment plays in the United States. In the very way that the Jackson Amendment is designed to exercise a veto or to exact a price for the resumption of trade negotiations between the United States and the Soviet Union, in the same way the threat of a military outbreak is designed to work as a veto that Egypt would wield over any efforts to deepen the entente between the two superpowers.

All these arguments should militate toward a more profound understanding between the two superpowers, an understanding that should be left to them and only to them, if only because not all the other major powers are at this time committed to the concept of a Middle East settlement. Such an understanding, if it does indeed come, would have to be limited by existing United States' commitments to Israel and Soviet commitments to Egypt. It would suggest that all that such an understanding could lead to is the initiation of a process of negotiation rather than the dictation of terms. But even such a limited understanding would be a very considerable move forward. How it can be done and when it can be done, whether before or after Mr. Brezhnev's visit, we don't know; but it certainly appears to be one of the acute questions they will have to decide. Thank you.

MR. LERNER. Thank you, Professor Gottlieb. Now we will listen to Professor Lichtenstadter, of Harvard University on religion as a cultural and political factor in the Middle East—past and present.

Religion as a Cultural and Political Factor in the Middle East—Past and Present

by Ilse Lichtenstadter

PROFESSOR LICHTENSTADTER. The topic of my paper is the role that religion played in the course of millennia in the region that we now call the Near and Middle East, not just as a religious and cultural factor, but also in its political impact. One might think religion and politics to be incompatible, but in the history of the Near and Middle East, from time immemorial, religion and the state idea were closely allied. They were in fact interchangeable, almost identical.

In ancient Egypt, the king was god and god was the king, and the land itself was linked to king and god. In Assyria and Babylonia, the same relationship between kingship and deity prevailed, and in ancient Iran god and the ruler were closely related. Persepolis, which was mentioned in this meeting rather ironically in a previous paper, actually represented this identity of the god and the ruler. The king received the homage of his people as the representative of the god, as can be seen to this day in the friezes that show the procession of people under the king's rule who present their tribute to the king and through him to the god.

137

In ancient Israel we have the same close connection between religion and the ruler. The king of Israel was guided by God. He had to be obedient to His will, he had to carry out His commandments; and therefore, the connection between the deity and the state was established. This relationship continued also in ancient south Arabia, the region that includes today's Hadramawt and Yemen and the Emirates. The king or the priest ruled and regulated everyday life as well as the religious activities of the country. In the north, the region now comprising Sa'ûdî Arabia, Muhammed, the Prophet of Islam, continued in the same vein, in so far as he was conscious of having been called by God to reveal God's word to his people. The Koran to the Muslims is the word of God, while Muhammed is His mouthpiece.

Though the religious ideas conveyed through the Koran to the Arab people would be an interesting topic, I shall concentrate here on the development of the state idea in Islam through the centuries. Though there were many other religions in the area both in classical and in modern times, since its birth Islam was the dominant religion and the one that shaped the fate and the thought processes of that area most distinctly and most emphatically.

In Muhammed's own time what one may call the *political aspect*, by way of simplification, of Islam became very strong. Even before his emigration to Medinah, the Prophet tried to bring about a change in the orientation of the Arabs from the tribal to an all-inclusive allegiance. Separatism was dominant in pre-Islamic Arabia. Though sometimes a tribe would become allied with other tribes, the real allegiance of the pre-Islamic Arab was to his tribe, his loyalty was to his tribe, his security was within his own tribe. If he failed to honor his obligations, if he committed a crime within his own tribe, he became an outlaw. His life was without security, everybody's hand was against his, he was entirely on his own.

Muhammed, consciously or subconsciously—that, of course, is a moot question—aimed at and achieved intertribal alliances in Mecca. He created brotherhood among people who were adherents of his faith, but did not belong to the same tribe or clan. The classical Arabic sources, for example, the *Biography of the Prophet,* list the names of these "brothers"; through this act, he created loyalty among people who were not blood relatives, a feeling hitherto unknown in Arabia. The Prophet's emigration (*Hijrah*) to Medinah changed the situation, since he was leaving his own native group and was settling in an alien environment. He was called to Medinah because his ability to unify nonrelated groups, proven in Mecca, had become known in Medinah. That oasis (called *Yathrib* in pre-Islamic times) was in dire need of an outstanding and at the same time impartial personality who would be able to restore peace within that strife-torn community and among its many feuding components. Muhammed, after a short stay in the city, achieved peace and unity by an amazing contract between himself as the representative of Allah and the various groups of Medinah. He called the newly established community the *ummat al-Islâm, community of Islam,* which was to be under his leadership as the Messenger of Allâh.

A striking factor in this contract was that several Jewish tribes were included in this *ummah*. Three great Jewish tribes with their various subtribes and their clients were accepted with their right to retain their own religion and the exercise of their own faith was confirmed. I believe this to be the first document establishing religious freedom in the history of mankind.

It is a common assertion that in Medinah Muhammed changed from being a prophet to being a politician. This assertion is at least doubtful; to express it more strongly, it should be denied. From the very first moment when he felt God's call to him, to the last day of his prophetic activity, Muhammed was aware of being under Divine Command to bring a Divine Message to his people. God asked him to lead his people away from Ignorance, for example, ignorance of the one and only God, to His worship. The apparent difference in Medinah was due to the fact that there he had to guide a large community composed of many elements. There were three groups: (1) the native people of Yathrib who themselves were split into two big tribes, the Aus and the Khazraj, with their respective clients, (2) the so-called Muhâjirûn, Meccans who had emigrated with Muhammed to Medinah, and (3) the Jews who, however, gradually became his adversaries. As the leader of the community, he had to deal with certain aspects of everyday life, had to promulgate laws and regulations, and had to make decisions in disputes; he presented these to the *ummah* as Divine Commandments, as revelations from God.

Throughout his life he remained sincerely convinced that even the most commonplace decisions were divinely inspired. Thus the Koran abolished limitless marriage, restraining men to four women; it contains regulations regarding the Fast and the Pilgrimage, forbids usury and drinking of wine. All of these laws and regulations were given in the name of Allah as His revelations.

However, as a basis for the development of Islam after Muhammed's death, the Muslims could refer only to the Koran. To give the ever-expanding community of Islam, which grew through the conversion of many people from various religious, cultural, and ethnic backgrounds, a unified law and an Islamic way of life, the Koran alone was not enough; the Muslims found a way, unique in the history of religious and cultural development, to establish a norm of Islamic behavior : they used the Prophet's alleged ideas and habits as the norm by which to regulate Islamic religious and social attitudes.

By projecting back into Muhammed's time the problems of the post-Muhammed era, the Muslim scholars decided them in a way they felt would have been acceptable to the Prophet or that would have been his own decisions, if he had been confronted with these problems during his life. To state a very complex problem concisely : the so-called sunnah of the Prophet (for example, his "way") is an abbreviated expression for the fact that the post-Muhammed *contemporary* decisions were made on the basis of *alleged* actions, commands, or prohibitions of the Prophet. The terms *sunnah* and *hadîth,* "tale," are commonly used to indicate this procedure.

Through the conquest—not "by fire and the sword," but by the force of an overwhelming idea—the Muslim empire comprised people of different backgrounds, ideas, customs, languages, and historical memories. These divergent components were unified by the religious ideas of Islam; and by the end of the first century of the Hijrah a *Muslim* community emerged consisting of Arabs, Iranians, converts from Judaism and Christianity, and other religious sects, including nonmonotheistic ones. From the very beginning, the one factor that molded this heterogeneous empire into a community was Islam.

The unifying process was checked by antagonistic factors, especially through Iranian nationalism. The Iranians, aware of their ethnic difference, tried to counteract the Arabization that went hand-in-hand with Islamization, by emphasizing their own Iranian heritage, the finest literary expression of which is in the Iranian national epos, the *Shah Nameh.*

At the same time a great Muslim literature developed. The term *Muslim* is used advisedly, because, although this literature was written in the Arabic language, its leading exponents were mostly non-Arabs, mainly Iranians, whether their work was concerned with religious and philosophical problems or with the sciences.

In modern times, a new factor arose, namely, the well-known intrusion of the West into the Near and Middle East. In particular, the higher and educated classes showed great willingness to accept Western influence. The Khedive Muhammad 'Alî was instrumental in bringing Western knowledge, above all Western science, into Egypt, his main reason being his desire to enable his country to stand up against the military powers of the West.

There were, however, other factors that worked against modern-ization and Westernization. The leader in this countermovement was al-Afghânî, who tried to use Islam, the religion common to many Eastern people, to agitate against Western supremacy and to unify the Muslims of the Near and Middle East, of Indonesia, and of East and Southeast Asia under the banner of Islam to put an end to the domination of the West over the East.

Pan-Islamism did not work, for the nationalistic and chauvinistic forces in the Muslim nations were too strong. Nor did Pan-Arabism work, which was tried after the failure of Pan-Islamism, for the ancient particularistic tendencies of the various Arab nations were still effective. Their historical memory, rooted in the differences of their ancient history, had dominated their development of their special interests throughout the centuries; as a result, neither Pan-Islamism nor Pan-Arabism succeeded in creating an efficient unity.

In the religious sphere, the famous head of the Azhar in Cairo, Sheikh Muhammad 'Abduh, a disciple and friend of al-Afghânî, tried to adapt the tenets of Islam to modern ideas and sought to reconcile Koranic philosophy with modern scientific insights. This approach is still continuing, but neither Muhammad 'Abduh nor his disciples fully succeeded. The result of their endeavor was an apology for the Koran rather than an acceptance of modern scientific ideas.

In the framework of our present discussion, the relationship between Islam and Judaism, and Arabs and Jews must be dealt with. It is well known that during the Middle Ages there was close coopera-tion among Jewish and Christian and Muslim scholars in all fields of scholarship : the sciences, medicine, astronomy, and also philosophy. Except for rare times when the relationship between Jews and Mus-lims became somewhat disturbed, they lived peacefully together. In the Middle Ages, citizenship in Western Europe in the so-called Holy Roman Empire was possible only to those who belonged to the Church; likewise, the only way in which a non-Muslim could be a citizen of the Muslim empire was through the institution of the *dhimmah, protection,* an attempt to integrate non-Muslims as *dhimmîs* into the Muslim empire as its citizens.

All my lectures in groups like this that are concerned with the Arab-Israel conflict aim at calling for mutual understanding, for cooperation and conciliation between Jews and Arabs. Judaism and Islam never confronted each other as enemies. They have much in common intellectually, religiously, emotionally; they share the com-mon Semitic heritage. What is needed now, however, is a deeper understanding of their inner motivations and emotions, and not superficial reactions and judgments, but a meeting of the minds and the hearts in order to put an end to war and hatred and bloodshed. We should understand each other, and meet with each other, not just the intellectuals and the leaders, nor the politicians, but also the ordinary people as well. By living with Arabs and Muslims, by visiting their lands again and again, I know that we can understand each other, and work together for a common aim : peace.

MR. LERNER. It is time for us to close. I wish I could participate in the discussion, but I think what I will do instead is to close the meeting immediately and ask you all to be here at two o'clock this afternoon.

(End of second session.)

American Strategic
and Economic Interests in the Area

by Amos Perlmutter

MR. FINGER. Your Excellencies, ladies and gentlemen, we now begin
the third session of our colloquium, and it is our privilege to hear
from Professor Amos Perlmutter.

PROFESSOR PERLMUTTER. Thank you.

I have been asked to do a very modest task—to assess American
strategic and economic interests in the Middle East. One can take at
least three aproaches to the analysis of American strategic interests.
One can, of course, take an intellectual approach, which most
professors of political science take when they are not in the government. When they are in the government, they may change some of
their conceptions. I have reread some articles written a while ago
by a very famous professor from Harvard (Kissinger), and what he
has written about foreign diplomacy in 1954 would certainly not
apply to 1973.

Another approach that one could take is the political approach.
We usually talk about politicians being pragmatic, hard-headed, and
so forth, or people who usually get to know about a crisis at the

last moment and have to make the decision on the spot, if possible.

The third approach, which is the easiest of all, is the professional; in other words, the diplomatic services' approach or the approach of those who are exclusively engaged in foreign-policy analysis and work in their daily routine.

I would say that on the whole there is an alliance, sometimes canny and sometimes uncanny, between professionals on the one hand and intellectuals on the other hand. Seldom is there an alliance between professionals, intellectuals, and politicians, and I think it is very healthy. Take your choice in history to discover whether it is or it is not.

Since I would like to discuss, from an intellectual point of view, the professional position in the Middle East, I would like to say something about professionals in general and then the American diplomatic professional position in the last twenty-five years in the Middle East; then we can assess it together. I am not a great admirer of professionals—not among professors, not among the military, and not among the diplomats. I am not talking about the unusually talented members in each profession, but I am talking about each profession as a whole.

There is one thing that fascinates me most about professions. Take, for instance, the military profession. In the nineteenth century there were various academies; Prussian military academies that trained generations and generations of officers on the concepts of planning, of military strategy, on mobilization, and so forth, and when the test came—which was the First World War in 1914, after the Schlieffen plan collapsed—the whole grand theory of the military strategists was reduced to ashes. In the end they had to establish an alliance with the so-called industrial-military complex and to mobilize society, because all of a sudden the professionals recognized or failed to recognize that war is no longer between two professional armies, but war is total. War being total, the Schlieffen plan had only one function: to destroy the enemy forces, but not to destroy the society that they had to deal with. Four years of a campaign had succeeded in demonstrating that the military were not successful in under- standing the type of war they had not prepared themselves for.

The social sciences and sociologists have developed a grand theory that is called the *general theory* and the *unified theory* of social science. In the 1950s and 1960s, there was not a professor of sociology or political science or international politics who did not have an answer to every issue in American society. But they have not discovered anything really that was taking place in American society —the racial problem, the so-called energy crisis, and a few other things. Mostly they have opined and written grand theories that were called *conceptualizations;* some of which were middle-range theories that were also called *empirical studies.* But on the whole, the social-science profession collapsed because it did not meet the issues at hand. Needless to say, those professors talk about both the modernization of societies, which had no intention to modernize, and the different courses of modernization that have failed.

The diplomats have their own grand strategy and it is called *national interest*; in the name of national interest, everything can be interpreted. National interest is usually a self-designed cloth with which the diplomatic profession clothes itself. The most interesting intellectual way to understand American Middle East foreign policy in the last twenty-five years is to psychohistorically analyze the members and the practitioners of American diplomacy in the Middle East, because they were the ones who conceived what American national interest was in the area. They were touting the so-called national interest and some of them became the victims of some of the failures of the grand idealistic concept of the universe, which intellectually and psychologically was well rooted in the type of Calvinism that Mr. Wilson was born into, bred on, and subsequently enhanced.

The other thing, as I said, is the cultural aspect, and of course the last and most significant of the concepts that this particular diplomatic corps had in mind in their grand strategy was the emulation and enhancement of *progressive,* anticommunist, revolutionary officers and intellectuals from Nasser to Kassim, and final convergence of all these.

This was American national interest, or what was interpreted as American national interest. I know of no American ambassador to the Middle East who has not in the last twenty years interpreted American national interest in any other way than what I am trying to summarize. This was the conception of the universe that they had seen.

The trouble with this type of professional is very much like that of the military in World War I, and American professors of sociology and social science, including myself, a political scientist. All have prophesied in the last twenty years about modernization and change. They have been wrong on every aspect of their interpretation, for they have seen the Middle East via their social, psychological, and personal intellectual interests and that is how they have interpreted the public interest. I am saying with all sincerity, no one should doubt the sincerity of these people, but one should understand whence this concept stems. So the diplomats were also wrong.

All of a sudden, by 1967 or a little before that, everything was shuttered down. The so-called Baghdad Pact, this theory against communism, was proven a paper organization at best. Progressive Arab officers were neither progressive nor modernist; the best of them merely emulated progressivism. And our best intellectuals and modern political writers do remind me that Nasser was not the kind of progressive members of the diplomatic profession expected him to be; he did not act accordingly. It was very must like the way the Schlieffen plan did not succeed in 1914, with all the good intentions behind Field Marshal von Schlieffen.

Another concept that has been developed is that stable Arab governments will be established under the concept of united Arabism, and so forth. That did not take place either, despite the sincere desire of American diplomats for that to happen.

Another important issue that has been discussed here time and again is American oil interest in the Middle East. It does not seem that American oil interests were well defended and protected by twenty-five years of diplomacy. Of course, from time to time one could hear explanations of this. For example, if I understand Ambassador Nolte correctly, he wrote in 1950 that the burden upon American diplomacy in the Middle East was Israel; if not for Israel, American oil interests would have been defended, and, if not for Israel, Nasser might have been a progressive officer and a few other things. I should remind some of those writers that the Persian Gulf, today for instance, has very little to do with the Arab-Israeli conflict.

There are three types of conflict in the Persian Gulf. One is an inter-Arab, between Arab regimes in the area. Another is between Iraq and Iran; another is the Soviet-American conflict that has some links with the Arab-Israeli conflict.

Therefore, I now turn back to my role as a professor, which is a much easier one, because I would not want to set up concepts and positions of American national interests for the diplomatic profession. I hope that some members of the diplomatic profession here or else-where will be able to pronounce much better than I what is the new perception of the Middle East, or is there a new perception? They may challenge my view that all these concepts and theories that they have followed have failed, for reasons other than the ones offered. They may argue with me that they have not failed. However, I am really in no position for two reasons to opine what American national interest is, except as a professor of political science and international politics.

First, I really don't know today who is making American foreign policy in the Middle East. This is, in my view, because of the failure in the last twenty-five years. Those who dominate the State Department on Middle East policy, as much as those who dominated the State Department in the 1950s on China, are in no situation any longer to defend positions that they have taken for the last twenty-five years, except for tentative solutions, such as the Rogers Plan and interim agreement and half of an interim agreement, and so forth.

I am not cynical at all. I wish that some of this *could* take place. But then again, that has to do with the psychohistory of the Arab and the Jewish peoples and not of the psychohistory of those who come from the Andover Seminary or other colleges, or from the American University of Beirut. This is one reason why I can not tell you what American national interest is.

The second reason is that I think as yet there is no cognition —maybe with the exception of certain intellectuals or certain practitioners in the intellectual profession, or maybe some members of the Foreign Service, and some members of the National Security Council, who have been more influential in American foreign policy than before—that revolutionary changes have taken place in the Middle East since 1967, for good or for ill, and therefore American foreign policy and American strategic interests must certainly be dictated or at least oriented to cover the kind of changes that took place after 1967.

Therefore, my only duty and function here, after I have been so critical, is to argue and say what I think was the revolution in the Middle East after 1967, and therefore what I think as a professor of political science, not as a foreign-service officer, should be America's national interests in the Middle East.

To begin with, the 1967 war demonstrated clearly, at least in terms of its consequences and in terms of the consequences of the subsequent war of attrition, that neither the United States nor the Soviet Union is interested in a conflict in the Middle East. And, in my view, if the United States and the Soviet Union are oriented or interested that there should be no conflict in the Middle East, then the parties in the Middle East should be at the mercy of national interests, whatever the national interests are, and it is subject to supposition what the national interests of the particular actors of the Middle East are.

I think that the serious conflict has shifted from the eastern

Mediterranean into the Persian Gulf. I think that this is also part of what has happened after 1967. First and foremost, if one reads carefully the message of Professor Kissinger to NATO, and if one studies NATO very carefully, the importance of NATO in the eastern Mediterranean will certainly diminish if the Europeans are not going to be viable partners; it has already diminished by now.

Second, and most important, neither the Soviet Union, from my understanding—and I have been doing research in Washington for about a year and a half among American diplomats and Soviet diplomats—neither Washington nor Moscow is interested in being harnessed to any type of conflict that the local actors have in mind or desire, whether they be Arabs, Israelis, or others. Of course, that calls for a very delicate crisis management, and certainly crisis management has been part of the whole Nixon Doctrine of resolving international politics.* One waits for the issue to become serious and tries to extinguish the fire at a time when it is very close to what sometimes the President himself says it becomes: a powder keg. One no longer sends bulldozers to destroy fifteen revolutionaries in Guatemala, but one waits to see whether the Guatemalan or Chilean revolution is developing. I think that sooner or later—at least if the United States and the U.S.S.R. are serious about what they have in mind, (which is more important), their greatest concern is their *own* safety and sanity, which has to do with arms control, trade, and a few other things—the so-called powder-keg situation in the Middle East will go elsewhere.

That brings me to the Persian Gulf, and I think I have discovered nothing new, because it has been discussed all throughout this conference, and to project what I conceive or perceive it to be would not contribute. I am not saying that this is what the diplomatic service conceives or perceives to be the problem in the Persian Gulf and the type of American attitudes that have to be considered in terms of the Gulf.

First and foremost, I think the lessons of the last twenty-five years are that, if some professors of political science, some grand theorists, missionaries, and other zealots are not recruited to advise the government, the chances are that grand theories will not take place and disasters may not occur in the Persian Gulf.

The energy crisis must be discussed in two contexts: one, in the context of the energy crisis itself; the second, in the general global context of energy and financial problems of the United States. For

* And prophetically I was vindicated; this is exactly what Kissinger's role has been since 6 October 1973.

the energy crisis will not be restricted to the United States. It will be a European and a Japanese energy crisis. Furthermore, if the dollar has to be further devaluated because of Arab sheiks, and so forth, who will accumulate, according to Mr. Akins, close to 100 billion by the year 1985, then it becomes a universal problem. Therefore, I think we should take the energy crisis into a discussion of general international politics, into a discussion of the future of the relationship between industrial and nonindustrial countries, and among others we may also discuss the Middle East.

It is an Arabist orientation, I think, to link the oil crisis to crises in the Middle East. My opinion, as a student of international politics, is that the Persian Gulf has an autonomous life of its own. The concepts of what are the dynamics of the Persian Gulf vis-à-vis its relationship with the rest of the world will determine the future of the Persian Gulf and will determine the future of the relationships between the industrial, energy-hungry powers and the producing, nonenergy-consuming powers. This is the important issue.

Therefore, I think that the global American policy is the policy that should be dictated in terms of conflicts in any or every area with which the United States' economic, physical and domestic health, and future and development must be concerned. I dread the idea that the energy crisis will fall into the hands of some specialist of a particular area in the State Department. That could be the most disastrous of all things to the energy crisis; for example, if it falls either to experts on Japan—because Japan may undergo a crisis that will have its effect upon the United States—or experts on Europe, or those who are so-called experts on the Middle East. But for some reason or other, the original conception had to do with bureaucratic politics and with routine more than thinking; that is the reason why Professor Kissinger was trying to ignore, to avoid and to go around the various departments and geographic bureaus. That sort of conception must be established that should circumvent the geographic and specialized areas of concentration. And therefore American economic and strategic interests in the Middle East are connected with the *global* American concepts concerning its attitude toward the future of energy in the United States.

I shall give you only one example where area specialists may dwindle and may collapse if they have to carry the burden of the policy. Take the issue of the struggle between "revolutionary forces" —and I put it in quotation marks—Fedayeen forces versus "conservative," traditional Arab sheiks, and the struggle that is going to take place between Iran and Iraq on every square inch of the Persian

Gulf. These are two areas in which the United States can do very little, and if it ignores it benignly, the chances are that the global policy will have a better chance than otherwise.

The global policy has to do with the relationship between the government and the independent oil companies. The multinational corporations no longer can claim that they are public servants. I agree with Senator Jackson, whose statement I remember very clearly, that it is the function of the United States government to handle its relationship with oil-producing countries, rather than the multinational corporations, which at best represent their own interests and not always necessarily the American national interest. As the case of the I.T.T. in Chile demonstrates, they have not represented American national interests. I think that the United States and Chile are both very lucky that the I.T.T. and the C.I.A. did not succeed in completing the deal that they had in mind. Through the various testimonies, I detected that the United States government on the whole was oscillating, as to whether to intervene; at least Mr. Helms and Mr. Kissinger were not as convinced as people were convinced twenty years ago that there is a convergence of interests between I.T.T. interests on the one hand and American national interests on the other. They are not the same interest. So should be the case with oil multinationals. The true interest of a political community are not convergent with either the concepts of national interest defined by a multinational corporation nor with the concept defined by the high priests of the national interest.

If you want another example out of the Middle East, I would take a high priest of the national interest, Mr. George Kennan. He has been right and wrong on Russia so many times that I can not make up my mind at what times Mr. George Kennan's counsels were accepted or rejected. I was terribly upset to read Ambassador Bullitt's memoirs. And what do they tell us? He came with tremendous goodwill to Russia, and all of a sudden he discovered that there was something in Russia that is so contradictory to everything that he as a puritan, as a capitalist, as a Midwesterner believed. He became so bitter and people around him began to develop all sorts of theories that were not relevant any more to the situation in the Soviet Union, but that were relevant to the crisis and the tragedy of Ambassador Bullitt himself.

If you read Charles Bohlen, it is the same story. He was not the wisest of all men; he was a good interpreter. But he was a witness to history: I am witnessing that history again from time to time and I see that the professional has not succeeded very well in interpreting the Soviet Union, for he interpreted it in a similar way to the American missionaries who interpreted China in the 1950s, or to the way in which American missionaries interpreted the Middle East for a good century and a half.

I would also say parenthetically that it is quite interesting now that all those members of the American Foreign Service who were martyrs because of the viciousness of Joe McCarthy have now come back to life after being told twenty-five years ago that they were wrong about China—Professor Fairbank and others. And they are wrong about China again. Read Doak Barnett, who was one of the group who came back from China and had doubts. China is not that united, cohesive society that is going to become a great power tomorrow. It might be the power of the twenty-first century, but not the power of the twentieth century. These people who were wrong twenty-five years ago have a right to be right, because they have been exonerated; exonerated because Joe McCarthy has made them martyrs. But that does not make them any more right about China now. They have not been in China for twenty-five years, and they have been taken on a guided tour by Chou En-Lai. But if Chou En-Lai departed from China, the situation in China might not be the same. Professor Schwartz has written a very important book on China. You can not write a book, he said, only a collection of essays. It is called *China in Flux*. So is the Persian Gulf in flux, and the best thing is not to have doctrines, not to have theories, neither from professors nor intellectuals. Intellectuals have the right, of course, to have doctrines so long as they do not influence policy. So have professors of political science, so long as they want to remain professors of political science in their respective universities and not interfere with the operations of government, which I understand some of my colleagues believe they should do.

Therefore, I think that any dogmatic position that is governed by a wave of hysteria that is taking place, concerning the energy crisis, can not be resolved by grand doctrines. Moreover, the whole question of oil energy in the Middle East is a global question and not an area question and should not be relegated to the professors and foreign-service officers who are specializing in the Middle East. Maybe we need a special kind of National Security Council for the energy crisis—all of which frightens me, because there we have to compromise and have a committee and a doctrine that people will have to follow, and diplomats this time would not have a mind of their own but would have to follow it without a mind of their own, which is even worse.

It would have been, as you can see, a much easier course for me to make a list of what American strategic interests are. Furthermore, a point that I have not mentioned is that a revolution, maybe a cumulative revolution in the United States, is taking place, by which the consensus on foreign policy, if I may use that term, is no longer accepted by all opinionative segments of the United States. Who are the silent majority? They are those who are not members of the opinionative groups, for example, professors, ambasadors, intellectuals, *New York Times* correspondents. The latter are, of course, the ones who define the others who are not opinionative as the silent majority. But we have discovered that this majority is, in fact, very opinionative; they have demonstrated in one election after another that they are opinionative and, also, that they are very shrewd. All these silent majority members who were thought to have no opinion because some professors, ambassadors, intellectuals, and generals have never talked to their own wives to understand really what was going on. Therefore, I would think that the intellectual and social revolution that is taking place in the United States should make many of those who stayed at the helm of decision do some rethinking about what American national interest is. For it can no longer remain the domain of the professional diplomats, the domain of professional historians and political scientists, or of the professionals in violence, (namely, the military), or the domain of the professionals in secrecy and in deception, (the intelligence services). It should be the domain, among others, of whatever is called the American people. I know it is a very amorphous concept, but there are certain changes taking place and they certainly would be more serious if gas, electricity, and other day-to-day commodities were to pinch the average American—that silent member of the silent majority, who is not silent, who is opinionative, and who may have his own opinions. These opinions should also be taken into the consideration of the formulation of a global policy.

Therefore, in summary, I feel very strongly that so far the United States has been treading from the management of one crisis to another, whether it is grand crisis management, in Haiphong or Moscow, or is a petty crisis management, Jordan or maybe tomorrow Lebanon. Maybe for the time being crisis management is more efficient and more secure in view of new American-Soviet relations than any other type of policy. Maybe it is a time to pause. Maybe it is time to be hesitant. Let us be confused for a while; let us not have position papers that are so clear; let us be skeptics; let us question and not come to conclusions concerning policy before the basic questions have come to the fore, before they have been analyzed. From all that I have read on the energy crisis, I have not been convinced as to whether there is one and, if so, what type it is. I am not convinced who is motivating it, who is the power behind the scenes that moves it, whether the oil company, the consumer, or the producer. We have not decided yet on the elements of the conflict, so how dare we have a policy if we have not decided on the elements of the problem?

Unfortunately, I have to say in a note of sadness that we prefer to work by way of organizational momentum rather than by the organization of momentum. We prefer normal politics to innovative politics. And therefore what I feel is that there is still a frozen contingent of mind and of position in the American government, whether it is in the State Department or in the National Security Council or in the various offices; for example, the International Security Administration of the Defense Department or in any governmental agency that handles the Middle East. There are vestiges of wrong thinking, unthinking, no thinking, that may become policy. Policy has a momentum of its own, that has a rationalization of its own. Then a new generation of Americans will say again: you lied to us. And this generation will say: we did not lie to you. If you only had known how bad a man Stalin was, you would have talked differently. If you had only known how the crisis of energy was; if not for us, you would not be driving a car, a father will say to his son in fifteen years. Meanwhile, just as in 1960, we did not know there would be a Vietnam and in 1973 we are supposedly over it, I am not in a position to say what will be five years from now. So that I don't know how the particular father will explain to his son why he lied; he did not lie, because he did not really study the situation.

I think that what is necessary is to take stock, to begin thinking anew in terms of the dynamics of the Middle East and to relate to the Middle East in terms of a *Middle Eastern* problem, not in terms of an energy crisis problem—to relate to the Middle East maybe in terms of American global policy with the Soviet Union, but not of love with Arabs or Zionists. Either one of them will be a burden in the end on either one of the great powers, because it is natural for the small powers to be a burden on the great powers. It is in the nature of the most successful small powers to squeeze and to influence, to get as much as they can and give as little as they can in return to the great powers and to take from the great powers. It is in the nature of small states, who must survive by virtue of their influence on the great ones that they have to squeeze. Therefore, if you make a cost accounting, which I don't think is the best and most apt study for politics—look at the McNamara cost accounting system in Vietnam—but if you do take a cost-accounting analysis, I don't know if the effort is worth it, to make love to country X, to make an alliance with country Y, to restore relations with country Z, before a general concept of America's global policy toward specific and general issues is established. Let us rescue American foreign policy from the experts. Thank you.

MR. FINGER. Thank you, Professor Perlmutter. May I say that I feel twice cursed, having been for a long time a foreign-service officer and now a professor. It makes me almost afraid to speak this evening.

PROFESSOR PERLMUTTER. I am only half as guilty as you are.

MR. FINGER. It is now my great pleasure and honor to call on Mr. Eric Rouleau to discuss with us "Peace Without the Palestinians?"

Peace Without the Palestinians?

by Eric Rouleau

MR. ROULEAU. The Palestinians are today in the news. They are having serious trouble in Lebanon. There is heavy fighting that I think was going on only this morning, and casualties are said, according to the *Wall Street Journal* to number in the hundreds. Are we going to witness a new bloodbath like the one we witnessed two years ago in Jordan? Is this May 1973 going to be called *Black May* after Black September?

For a very long time most journalists or observers thought that this was not possible in Lebanon, because the situation in Lebanon, they pointed out, was quite different from the situation that used to prevail in Jordan. One of the first arguments was that the population in Lebanon was not political, that nearly half or more than half the population were Muslims, and that by and large the Muslim part of the population was pan-Arabist and for the Palestinians; therefore, it would be very difficult for the Lebanese government to take a stand that would become damned by at least half the population.

Another reason that was advanced is that the foreign policy of Lebanon would not allow it to take a hostile attitude toward the Fedayeen, because Lebanon needed all the other Arab states for its

155

trade, for its economy. It was necessary for Lebanon to have a so-called balanced attitude toward the Fedayeen.

Today, probably due to the fact that things are turning out differently, people might make a slightly different analysis. One thing one has to say is that there has been a growing disaffection of the Lebanese population toward the Fedayeen. I had the opportunity to see that with my own eyes last autumn. I was touring the Fedayeen bases in Lebanon not far from the Israeli frontier, and I was being accompanied by some Palestinian leaders, Fedayeen leaders. I discovered that they had to take circumventing roads to reach our destination, and I asked them why are you doing so? They told me there are some villages, several villages that would not let us go through because they do not want to have anything to do with us. Well, this can be explained partly by the fact that those villages were subject to very heavy Israeli retaliation and they did not want to have any trouble with the Israelis. They asked the Fedayeen or they told them, "Please do not come to our village or you are going to be in trouble."

But the Fedayeen leaders also admitted that there was political disaffection toward them and they did not want to have anything to do with it. So I suppose the Lebanese government is taking advantage of the fact that at least part of the Muslim population is not today so much in favor of the Palestinian Fedayeen.

Another reason is that the Arab states with whom Lebanon has to have good relations have themselves become much more lukewarm toward the Fedayeen. In 1970, in spite of the very strong support the Fedayeen got from most Arab states and from Nasser himself, it took fifteen days to stop the bloodbath. The Fedayeen were heavily beaten, yet Arab states friendly to them could not stop it. This time in reading the papers—I was in the United States when this thing started—I found the Arab reaction very, very weak, very mild. Sadat sent a representative to speak with President Franjieh and that sort of thing, but nothing really strong happened to stop what could have become a very serious debacle. That is another reason why the Lebanese government is not worrying so much about what it is doing to the Fedayeen.

The third reason, which is very important, is the fact that Lebanon can not afford to maintain the Fedayeen after the recent, very heavy retaliation raids of Israel and especially the last raid in Beirut. Lebanon is a peaceful country that is practically entirely concerned with commerce, trade, economics, and tourism. It has a kind of gendarmerie. It has not got an army, really, and I heard from a very important Lebanese member of the cabinet a few months ago that they even had to return some very sophisticated armaments to France. They said they bought it but "we don't want it because we might be tempted to use it against Israel and we don't want to do that." Why? Because retaliation might be so strong that Lebanon just could not stand the military power of the State of Israel.

So one can deduce from this kind of analysis that the Fedayeen movement is certainly going through one of its severest crises and maybe—one can not exclude it—we are witnessing perhaps the period of collapse of that movement. It has been liquidated in Jordan. It might be very easily liquidated in Lebanon; I am not sure, but it is a possibility. It is already under very strict control in Syria in spite of Syrian statements in favor of the Fedayeen, and also in very strict control in Egypt. Radical or so-called radical countries such as Algeria and Libya have practically abandoned the Fedayeen. From time to time there are statements in their favor, but I hear from people, who are reliable sources, that not only Libya and Algeria, but also Saudi Arabia are just not paying them the money they promised to pay them, or have asked to postpone the payments; therefore there are very strong pressures on them. And what is even more important, they have been practically liquidated on the West Bank, if not completely in Gaza, so they have not got much left as an armed movement to sustain their efforts in view of implementing their political objectives.

Why is everybody hostile to the Fedayeen? After that kind of analysis, one has the impression that everybody is hostile, and this is very largely true. There are various reasons. For Israel it is the most obvious: the Fedayeen are not challenging just Israel's expansion on Arab territory taken since 1967, they are challenging the state itself; it is no wonder that the Israeli would take such a strong stand against them. Arab conservative states don't like the Fedayeen, even if they say the contrary, for the simple reason that words like *armed struggle, revolution, socialism, antiimperialism, Marxism, Leninism,* are also very understandably not popular in conservative states such as Saudi Arabia or the oil emirates of the Persian Gulf. Even in Arab progressive states or so-called progressive states, the Fedayeen are in fact not very popular. That is also for other reasons, because they constitute or they constituted a challenge to the authority of the states, whatever the state is. They tended, even if they do not do so right now, to constitute a state within a state; something that a man like Nasser or President Hafez al-Assad in Syria would not tolerate.

Another reason is that they present a challenge—maybe not to the state, but to the policies of that state—to what are considered sometimes as national interest, rightly or wrongly. Nasser thought that the national interest of Egypt was to obtain a settlement in the Sinai as a primary objective, and the Fedayeen thought that would be a kind of betrayal and therefore there were at least the seeds of confrontation between a progressive Arab leader and Fedayeen leaders who might be as progressive or even more in their own domain.

Then, with respect to the foreign powers, why are the foreign powers against the Fedayeen? I am thinking of both the West and the East. They also constitute a challenge, to their interests, for one thing, and that might be the oil interests in case the Fedayeen should start blowing up pipelines. In that case I don't think the United States would have to consider a global situation only, but would also have to consider the Middle Eastern situation and see what is happening there, why pipelines are being blown up. And there is no doubt that the anti-American trend of the Fedayeen movement does not satisfy the American policymakers, and some of them are probably thinking of the future; therefore, I don't think that the Fedayeen can be popular with American policymakers.

As for the communist countries, it is another type of contradiction. The Fedayeen movement in its objectives is obviously going against the foreign policy of the U.S.S.R., to pick out the U.S.S.R. The U.S.S.R. is dedicated to *peaceful coexistence*. It wants to improve its relations and its special trade relations with the United States, and the Fedayeen are a challenge because they are speaking of armed struggle, talking of destroying the State of Israel—objectives that do not fit in with the foreign policy of the U.S.S.R., in spite of the fact that the Russians are giving arms to the Fedayeen, at least in an indirect manner.

But despite that, I think the international community should assume part of the responsibility for the Fedayeen's violence and uncompromising attitude. Recently while I was in Beirut preparing for a series of articles on the Palestinians, I had toured Jordan, Syria, Lebanon, and then Israel and the occupied territories. While in Beirut I was speaking with a Palestinian leader and asking him that very question: "Why are you so uncompromising? Why don't you try to see that there are forces in the world, there are possibilities?" And his answer was very direct. He said: "Have you ever heard of anybody, any state, any international body proposing anything to us? Then you could measure the response you have, whether it is negative or positive. We have been kept out of any kind of settlement." And I thought he was right even when thinking of the Resolution 242. Resolution 242 merely says that a just settlement of the refugee problem will have to be found. It is rather a curious phrase when one thinks that, after all, they could have included the Palestinian people; the United Nations could afford that. There was not even a word about a resolution, which had been voted every year by the General Assembly, giving the Palestinians their right to choose between repatriation, return to their homeland in Israel, or compensation. Even that did not figure in the Resolution 242. In fact, Resolution 242 was just a compromise at a certain moment. It reflected a kind of power balance between two groups of states—that is how I see it anyway—a group of states friendly to the State of Israel and a group of states friendly to the Arab states, and that compromise was found. The Palestinian movement was not a significant factor in international affairs. They did not have a strong body. They had not exercised enough pressure on any state so that a compromise would include them. They were just left out anyway, because I think at least that solving a refugee problem is solving a social problem and it is not solving a political problem, which is even more dangerous than a social problem sometimes. That is the second reason why the Palestinians feel that they have been completely excluded from any kind of international settlement.

A third reason is Israel's attitude toward the Palestinians. If Mrs. Golda Meir is prepared to recognize the southern Syrians, as she says, she does not feel there is a Palestinian people. In a recent statement she said it quite clearly that she does not think they need a state anyway. One would think that it is quite unnecessary for such statements, but unfortunately such statements get so much publicity among the Palestinians that I don't think they contribute very much to the cooling down of heads and to a peaceful settlement—so much so that the Palestinians, at least those I know and those I have met in the past fifteen or twenty years all over the Arab world and not only in the Arab world, feel very strongly Palestinian. Whether we consider them as people or not, in Kuwait, in Saudi Arabia, in Egypt, in south Arabia, those Palestinians I met felt very Palestinian. They just *felt* Palestinian, and I felt I could not discuss with them whether they existed or not as a nation. Many of you probably know that they are sometimes nicknamed by the Arabs, I mean the Arabs other than the Palestinians, as the *Jews of the Middle East*. They are either envied or despised and they are considered aliens anyway. They themselves feel alien. I remember speaking to what I thought at the beginning was a Kuwaiti high official, and during the conversation he came out and said, "I am Palestinian." He had the Kuwaiti nationality. He was completely assimilated. But he did not *feel* assimilated. He felt he was excluded from the state.

What is worse in a way, all those Arab states that are developing countries are generating their own labor force, their own elite, their own intellectuals, their own engineers, their own diplomats, and they don't like it very much when the Palestinian takes what they regard as the job of a local Arab. So in my view the problem is becoming more and more serious, because if one had the impression a few years ago, say ten or fifteen years ago, that at least some of the Palestinians were being integrated, I have the feeling today at least that there is a process of disintegration and of expulsion of the Palestinians.

Then there is the last point that I think also contributes to the uncompromising attitude of the Palestinians—a general trend in the West especially to consider them by-and-large as groups of bandits, criminals, terrorists, without any qualification. Sometimes those who severely condemn terrorism are the victims of terrorism, of another type of terrorism. I am thinking of a man like Kamal Nasser, who I would not be ashamed to say was my friend. I knew him for ten or fifteen years; I knew him as a poor refugee in Cairo; and I saw him when he left the occupied territories of Jordan in 1968. He told me then that he had tried very hard to convince Israeli officials—he had met Mr. Suzul, the Minister of Police, and many others—at the time trying to convince them that there might be a way for the Israelis and Palestinians to settle. He came out with despair and he joined the P.L.O.; I saw him as a P.L.O. functionary, and he told me: "I really thought there would be a possibility, but the Israelis are uncompromising." This man, I am sure—because I had known him well enough and I had had long conversations with him only a few weeks before he was killed in Beirut in that raid—was personally not in favor of terrorism; that is to say, that kind of thing, and I suppose people will say rightly that it is the sort of thing that does happen in wars. I would also say terrorism is a phenomenon that happens in conflicts. But to go as far as saying that all the Palestinians are bandits and criminals is not a positive way of helping them toward more compromising attitudes.

But they are responsible largely for their own failures and for the hostility others are demonstrating toward them. They demand recognition as a nation and yet they refuse to recognize the existence of an Israeli people and its own national rights. I think that is a big failure on their part, and they should not be surprised if on the Israeli side people take such a severe attitude toward them. They call for the creation of a secular state, which I think anybody with some political understanding would think is utopian, at least for the foreseeable future. This so-called strategic objective that they defend has contributed substantially to their complete isolation in the world. In Israel it is very clear that no Israeli would accept the idea that his community is going to be reduced to the status of a religious cultural minority in a state that although secular would be Arab and linked up to the Arab world. It is not reasonable to think that an Israeli, who would just look at the Arab world today and see what the fate is of the minorities, would accept the idea of being a minority in an Arab state within an Arab world. So I think that that very objective is something that is harming the Palestinian leadership and the Palestinian position in Israel itself very much.

It harms them also around the world, because the whole world, all the members of the United Nations, have recognized the State of Israel and the existence of the State of Israel. It is utopian to think that any state, whether hostile to Israel's policies or favorable to Israeli policies, will in any way accept or contribute to the destruction of the State of Israel. I think that they have lost all credibility on that point, at least among the Palestinian people itself. Palestinians who are not indulging in politics, who are just plain, common citizens, either of Jordan or living in the occupied territories, can very well see it for themselves—and I have heard many of them tell me so: first, the power of the Israeli state; second, the support that Israel has on a worldwide scale; and third, the weakness of the Arab world and the weakness of the Fedayeen movement. So, to tell them that they have to sacrifice their lives to attain such a strategic objective, which Mr. Arafat himself recognizes will not be attained until some future generations, is wrong and is in a way childish. So the Fedayeen movement has itself contributed to isolating itself by such unobtainable and utopian objectives.

But what is more serious is that this objective, in which most of them, I would say, do not believe, (which is what they would say in private or will let you know in private), has been turned into a kind of sacred cow that paralyzes them and their political and diplomatic action. In fact, they have deprived themselves of a strategy and tactics; I do not think they have a clear strategy. I do not think they have any tactics. The only tactics they have, which I think are very negative, is no. They say "no" to everything, and that is the worst thing that can happen to any political movement, whether revolutionary or not.

There is also another aspect of political infantilism, and that is the 1968 charter that speaks of armed struggle as "the only way to liberation." Again they deprive themselves of all kinds of means of action—political, economic, and other—that are usually used by political movements all over the world. And once their fighters are either arrested or killed, as is happening in Israel and has happened in the ocupied territories, they remain empty handed; they have nothing more to do in their struggle.

But in spite of that very dark picture that I have just given you, I think that there are signs of change within the Fedayeen movement. Last fall in the National Council they discussed this question of armed struggle being the only way to liberation, and they made some slight implication but an interesting one. One hears today of the National Council saying that armed struggle is the *main* instrument of liberation. This might also be a bit excessive, but still there is a sign that at least some of them are thinking of other means; that is, political and diplomatic.

You do meet Palestinian leaders in Beirut and elsewhere who in private—we can perhaps discuss why they are not saying it openly—are saying that diplomatic compromise is possible and that they are prepared to show more flexibility.

Another thing that has happened recently that is important is the open condemnation of terrorism in official statements issued by the Democratic Front. You do find in other organizations—but again they say it in private—people who themselves condemn terrorism and are not for it.

Another recent development is the conference that is being held in Bologna in a few day's time, where Israelis, Arabs, and Palestinians are going to attend; Mr. Arafat has agreed to send a delegation to a conference that is in favor of Resolution 242, by and large. Mr. Arafat is sending a delegation of the steering committee, although he did not agree to Resolution 242 and thought it was quite unfair to the Palestinians, but he was still sending a delegation to discuss the matter. These are very little signs, but I think that one in such a desperate and bleak picture has to register every sign of intelligent political attitude.

Another point: Kamal Nasser before his death asked me why France wasn't doing something to call for a Geneva-type conference; the one that put an end to the Indo-China war, when France was fighting and not the Americans. He said he felt sure the P.L.O. would be very happy to participate in a conference with Arab states, the Palestinians, some western European countries, Israel, and the eastern communist countries. Then he said that maybe we can do something with everybody there, with the Israelis, of course, but also with some Arab states and some communist states who are going to be sitting next to the Palestinians.

I think that Palestinian leaders also would admit in private that the implementation of Resolution 242 would be something quite dangerous for them and for their movement, that it would cut them off from the mainstream of the Palestinian people. They admit that, in the occupied territories in particular, many Palestinians are prepared to accept a Resolution 242-type settlement by which they would return to Arab rule even if Palestinian aspirations were not totally satisfied. I was very surprised to hear Palestinian leaders admit in my presence that they were going to have a very good time if the Resolution 242 is implemented, because many people are yearning much more for peace and for a settled life than for some ideal kind of solution.

This brings me to the last point. I think that the Fedayeen movement is much too weak today to be able to generate by itself positive attitudes. I think that we should all try to help them reach their positive attitudes, and when I say "we" I mean the international community and, of course, Israel. I think the starting point of any kind of positive action is that the international community should recognize that the Palestinian refugees are not just refugees, that they are a people since they consider themselves a people, and that they have national rights. I think it is very important that Israel do this herself. I don't think it will cost very much for Israel to recognize that. It would be very positive if the Israelis, who are after all the stronger of the two parties—a country that is strong militarily, economically, and technologically as well as psychologically—would take a first step, but of course also insisting that in exchange the Palestinians should do the same thing. That might be a starting point for something that could be worked out. Unfortunately for the time being the Israeli government—I don't say the people, I think many intellectuals in Israel are questioning that kind of policy—does not want to give the right even to those Palestinians in the occupied territories who wish to organize themselves into a movement in order to engage in negotiations with the State of Israel and to create a so-called mini-Palestine on the West Bank and Gaza. Even these people have no right to organize themselves into a movement. I think the Israeli government just wants to ignore the political aspects of the Palestine problem and is pursuing the policies of General Dayan, among others; the policy of faits accomplis or accomplished facts.

This, I think, is working today; there is no doubt about it. But I think it is a dangerous policy both on the part of Israel and on the part of the international comunity, because it is now serious. The Palestinian nationalism is authentic. This Fedayeen movement can be crushed, but new national movements will arise, as has been demonstrated in the past, and therefore I think the attitude is dangerous for Israel and the international community to ignore them.

I do not think that any lasting peace will be possible without the consent of at least the majority of the Palestinian people. The protagonists, for people who are wondering why there are no protagonists, protagonists for rapprochment, will rise and appear, and attitudes will be adopted by all those concerned for a permanent peace in the Middle East. Thank you very much.

MR. FINGER. We are now going to have a brief general discussion before the next series of statements. Several people have asked to participate. It is obvious from the number that if those who participate take too long, others will not have an opportunity. So as a general ground rule, we should have a limit of five minutes to any statement now made, except for those who have prepared statements, of course. If you can say it in less than five minutes, that is even better. Mr. Osman of Egypt has asked to speak from the rostrum. I now give him the floor.

MR. OSMAN. Mr. Chairman, I am encouraged to take the floor at this particular stage of our debate by what you had said yesterday that you would do your utmost to make this debate a free one. Well, I must admit that I am disappointed because so far the debate has gone in such a way that only one perspective of the Middle Eastern crisis has been exposed, whereas the other aspects have been completely neglected and not even mentioned. Had it not been for the interesting intervention made just now by my friend Mr. Rouleau, there would not have been one single mention of the Palestinian element in the Mideastern crisis. The debate so far, ladies and gentlemen, has dealt with the Middle Eastern crisis in terms of power politics, big powers, and world balance, and so on, and I am afraid these concepts, no matter how valid they are, and they are indeed valid, do not really come to grips with the matter. They don't contribute directly to the very ingredients of the tension now existing in this area.

Yesterday and today we have listened to some contributors who spoke about the annexed lands taken from Egypt, Syria, and Jordan, occupied by the Israeli forces since 1967 with a view that they are *new facts*. Well, they have been called *new facts* by Dayan, but I

submit it is not up to Dayan to determine the geographic, demographic, or physical situation in the area, to affect the very structure
and fabric of the Middle East. These aspects should be determined on
the basis of principles of international law, the U.N. Charter, the
right of self-determination, and by abiding with the United Nations'
resolutions.

Another contributor preached annexation of the territories
occupied by Israel and warned wholeheartedly and with touching
zeal against returning them back to their legitimate owners, namely
the Arabs.

Yet another speaker saw fit to label the United Nations' resolution
as one-sided. He conceded, however, that there is nothing wrong with
the U.N. except with its membership. One can only wonder what
to this particular contributor would appear to be an evenhanded
resolution. Would it have been an evenhanded resolution if the
Security Council condoned the state terror launched by Israeli forces
on the ninth of April last in the midtown of Beirut and its outskirts?

Mr. Chairman, I would like to allude to what has been said this
morning by Professor Gottlieb about what he termed the hardening
in the Egyptian diplomatic stand as far as the Middle East crisis is
concerned. Professor Gottlieb, I am sure you are aware of the fact
that what you yourself said about the flexibility existing in our
stand still exists. We have accepted Resolution 242. We adhere to it.
That resolution, as I said in answering Professor Kerr, was published
in the Egyptian press on many occasions, more than once, and as for
the hardening or the claimed hardening in our situation, I fail to
make a parallel between that and what has been said by no less an
influential leader than President Nixon himself when he said, and I
am quoting, "Egypt was really forthcoming more than we expected."

Ladies and gentlemen, there was not a single reference in this
debate to the U.N. Charter. Equally, there was no reference to the
principles stipulated in that Charter. There was no mention of the
principles of self-determination. Mr. Rouleau rightly said that unless
the Palestinians contribute in determining their own future, unless
their inalienable rights are acknowledged primarily by Israel, the
tension in the area will continue and will persist. It is not up to the
superpowers only to find a solution, a lasting one, to this problem.

I must also add that with due respect and esteem for the professors
and academic figures who took part in this debate, they seem to have
ignored the fact that because that area did not really take part from
within in shaping its own prospects and its own future, the problem
of the Middle East existed, does exist, and unfortunately will continue

to exist for the foreseeable future. So let us give a chance to the Palestinians, let us think not in terms of superpowers and world balance, but rather in terms of justice and abiding by the U.N. Charter in finding a solution to that problem.

Incidentally, I want to refer to the title of our debate, which is *The Search for Peace in the Middle East.** Search for peace does not come through coercion, does not come through intimidation, which are the two poles of Israeli policy in the area. Search for peace can be achieved and attained only and solely if the territory occupied as a result of the Israeli aggression in 1967 is restored, only if the inalienable rights of the Palestinians are acknowledged by the international community and by Israel itself.

MR. FINGER. I might say, Mr. Osman, that we have not by any means finished our agenda. I can assure you that my own statement will refer to the United Nations' Charter; that not only Mr. Rouleau, but also Professor Kerr took into consideration the Arab viewpoints; and a number of speakers including yourself did address it last night. We shall continue to strive for a free and balanced discussion. Professor Kerr has asked to make some additional remarks and I now call on him.

PROFESSOR KERR. Thank you, Mr. Ambassador. I would like to make a few brief remarks about a number of comments we have had today; I hope that my friend Mr. Perlmutter will not take it amiss and not take it as any personal reference at all if I say that I was a little surprised that the topic of American interests in the Middle East should have been defined by an Israeli participant. I would therefore like to take the liberty of making some comments that touch on Israeli interests, I being among other things an Arabist, an academic of quasi-missionary background, and so forth.

Mr. Lerner spoke this morning of the possibility of peace arising out of a stable situation in occupied territories, economic integration, rapid economic progress in these territories, and so forth; it seemed to me that perhaps there was something parochial about this concern. If we look at the prospects of peace in the region in terms only of internal events inside territory controlled by Israel—even if we were to accept all the things he said about that situation, which I would have some difficulties about—we remain with the problem of the major areas: Israel's relations with Arab states further afield, Israel's relations with the great powers, and in turn the great powers' relations with other Arab states, such as Egypt, Saudi Arabia, and others. We

* Original title was *The New World Balance and the Search for Peace in the Middle East.*

went on to hear about oil, and we were told by a series of speakers that whatever the ramifications of the oil crisis may be, we can not get away from the fact that the bulk of our dependence is going to be in coming years on Arab oil. I do not think that this can be waved aside by pleas for a more global approach. I did seem to detect in Mr. Perlmutter's remarks a kind of suggestion that we should not think of the oil crisis as involving particularly American-Arab relations. He also seemed to suggest that because the struggle in the Middle East was shifting to the Persian Gulf, perhaps the Arab-Israeli conflict could be downgraded in our concern.

I suggest that we really do have to come back to this bedrock problem of American dependence on Arab oil. It seems to me that the problems arising out of that dependence can take two courses. One of them is that if our policies do not change, if we continue, as many of us do in this room, to apparently regard American support for the existence of Israel as synonymous with support for whatever particular policies Israel chooses to follow, then it seems to me we are facing the same problem of lack of planning that Mr. Smith spoke about in talking about oil; that we will find ourselves one day in an increasingly explicit situation in which not only the Egyptians may be ready, as someone put it, to commit suicide by launching an attack on Israel that can not succeed, but we may also find that social, political, and psychological conditions will deteriorate in one Arab state after another—starting perhaps with Egypt, the most populous state with many serious internal problems in the best of times—and spread to other countries, such as Saudi Arabia, where the oil is produced. And if we reach some kind of Armageddon through this path, then we may face the time when we shall have to choose between adapting our policies in ways that do not seem desirable to many Americans or alternatively sending the marines and the paratroops to the oil fields—a possibility that has not been altogether discarded by even some members of Congress in recent statements.

The other tack is to do some planning now and to try to give some credence, some confidence, some political capital, some basis for hope to those elements in Arab society who would genuinely like to see some form of stability combined with progress restored to their society and who do not welcome the possibility of an Armageddon-like confrontation with the United States, but who may find themselves drifting toward it through lack of control.

It seems to me that perhaps Egypt as well as Saudi Arabia fall into this situation. I would just like to assure Mr. Osman briefly that my comments yesterday were intended to suggest that perhaps there is room for debate about what the long-range intentions and motivations of Egypt might be, but that my own judgment is very much in concurrence with his: that for a variety of reasons, that there have not been opportunities to discuss fully in this meeting, the Egyptian government as well as some more conservative governments have many reasons to fear the advent of chaos, nihilism, and despair in their own societies and therefore have very powerful reasons to hope that the oil crisis will not become their crisis or that of the United States either.

However, the only way to take this second tack is to look beyond the narrow concerns of Israel's position in the occupied territories and look more seriously at the prospects that she might find some basis for a long-term relationship with the Arab world as a whole, which will require some significant give on her part. Thank you.

MR. FINGER. Thank you, Professor Kerr. Mr. Bastuni has asked for the floor. Mr. Bastuni is a former member of the Israeli Knesset, an Arab member, as I understand.

MR. BASTUNI. Mr. Chairman, I would like to say a few sentences about what was discussed yesterday and today about Peace III of the conflict in the Middle East. I think that is of vital importance. It seems to me that the political thinking that is today governing most societies and peoples in the Middle East is outmoded, and these premises, values, and thinking are incapable of producing any dialogue between the Israeli society and the Arab countries. I don't believe that the Zionist form of thinking that came about at the beginning of the century is capable today of bridging the way toward the peoples around Israel. On the other hand, I don't think that the idea of Pan-Arabism, or let us say of Pan-Islamism in Islamic thinking, can really produce peace in the Middle East. I think these ideas have no place today in our own societies.

If one thinks in depth on the matter, I think the Middle East is not composed of one homogeneous people, of one geoeconomic unity, and one has to differentiate between all of the elements. There are Palestinians, Syrians, Iraquis, and Egyptians, and so on, but the word and the semantics of Arabism have been widely misused.

This brings me to the question that bothered us so much in the last decade: Who is an Arab? Who is a Jew? I think the idea of world Jewry is a myth, because in Israel today after twenty-five years and new generations, an Israeli society has been created that has some ties with Jews outside, but we have to draw a line of demarcation between the Israeli society, which is not necessarily a Jewish society—there are also non-Jews in Israel—and world Jewry, with all their affectionate ties. We must look at the Middle Eastern situation with new glasses and a new prism. We have to not be so simplistic as to say the war is between Arabs and Jews. Who are the Arabs and who are the Jews? I think that is of vital importance.

My second point concerns what was spoken about supremacy. I think Professor AlRoy advocated his thesis about the inevitable situation in the Middle East. I would remind him of two facts: one, China twenty-five years ago was primitive, was an agricultural society, and its civilization was seemingly decadent. Today China, through its own revolution and its own view, has become one of the super-powers in the world. So this does not prevent the peoples in the Middle East from renewing their society through social revolution, through social change that I think is inevitable. I don't know when it will come, but I think one day it will come.

I think, additionally, there are no myths in history and there are no miracles. Today one knows all the facts about the War of Independence in 1948. In 1948 the Jewish *yeshuv,* which means the 600,000 people who were living in Palestine, mobilized in quantity more armed forces than more than five of the Arab countries who intervened in Palestine, and that is the reason why the Jewish *yeshuv* won. Let us not be mystic about this fact. I don't think if one wins a war, one concludes peace.

Two more remarks, if I may, about Islam. One is how, in the Koran, when it says *Muhammad Razullah, Muhammad Razullah* means not Muhammed the representative of God, but Muhammed the messenger of God. This makes a difference.

The second thing that I will mention is that the schism in Islam started immediately after the death of Muhammed himself. I think the attitude of Ali Albitonim and his ambition to be Caliph created a schism that has spread through the history of Islam, and I think one can not only discuss Islam without discussing Ismail Khoja, Kharijites, Wahabis, Bahai, and so forth, which are four areas of sects that have dominated Islam.

Last, I would like to endorse Mr. Rouleau's recommendation. I think it is high time that most of the countries in the Middle East, including Israel, recognized the national entity of the Palestinians and their right to self-determination. I think that as an Israeli citizen I must say that most of the political atmosphere has to be changed, has to be changed because Israel has to recognize the Palestinians as an entity. I think Israel has to clarify its own policy vis-à-vis the occupied areas in the future.

Israel has to stop all kinds of settlements in the occupied areas. These occupied areas are not part of Israel; they are occupied and, as such, we have to change all of our attitudes and all of our policies toward the occupied areas.

One point to Professor Kerr: I think one has to distinguish between two entities that you mentioned, between Pinhas Sapir and Ari Eliav. I think the motivation of the attitude of Pinhas Sapir is different from Ari Eliav, because Sapir is worried about the Judaism of Israel and so he is against integration, whereas Eliav has arrived at that position from another point of view. He said this is a moral question for the Jews and, as such, I think that is quite right, because I am personally against any occupation, against even the occupation of Egypt in the Gaza Strip, the occupation of Jordan in the Western Bank and the occupation of the Israelis in both. I think that as such, this phase will pass.

I would like to remind you of public opinion in Israel, rather than the opinion of the establishment, of which the opinion of Pinhas Sapir is a part. Immediately after 1967 there were opinions of other people and one of them was a very distinguished person named Isa Smalanski, who wrote an article in 1967 in which she said quite frankly that the Jews have no right to dominate other people and the only way out is to clear the occupied areas, namely the Gaza Strip and the West Bank, and leave the Palestinians to the determination of their own fate by themselves. I think it is high time for Israel to reorganize its own policies toward the Palestinians. Thank you.

DR. RONALL. In endorsing some of the approaches of Professor Kerr, I feel myself compelled to express some puzzlement about statements of Professor Perlmutter and his warning to keep Middle Eastern affairs out of the hands of experts. I have seen very little indication that matters concerning the Middle East are really kept within the ivory tower of Middle Eastern experts. One speaker this morning—Mr. Smith of the *New York Times*—takes the liberty of reminding our audience here on the contrary; he, in a somewhat complaining voice, stated that energy problems in the United States are being dealt with by forty-four different agencies. So I can not endorse a statement that it is kept in the hands of the experts.

The same applies, I would say, to the enterprise that has been instituted by the Ford Foundation that is just now in the process of compiling a worldwide energy report.

If you look around on more general questions concerning the Middle East, let us say readers' letters to the *New York Times*, *Time* magazine, and other public media or on television, I can not see any trace, I am afraid, that Middle Eastern questions are being kept within this allegedly closed circle of Middle Eastern experts.

In addition, our institution of Congressional hearings before passing legislative acts in general does not limit itself to one kind of expert, but as far as I can see from recent hearings on energy and other problems, tries to take as wide a range of sources and members and participants as possible. Thank you.

MR. FINGER. Thank you, Dr. Ronall. I now call on Dr. Heskal Haddad, who grew up in the area we are discussing.

DR. HADDAD. Thank you, Ambassador Finger. I appreciate the opportunity to speak to this audience. I would like to discuss the Palestinians, with particular reference to the refugee problem.

To the average American, any mention of refugees in the Middle East means only Arab refugees from what was once Palestine. The tragedy of the Jewish refugees from Arab countries is rarely remembered.

In 1948, close to a million Jews—974,000 to be exact—lived in Morocco, north Africa, Egypt, Iraq, Syria, Lebanon, Yemen, and the Arabian Peninsula. What's more, their antecedents had lived in these lands for hundreds of years.

In sharp contrast, fewer than 150,000 Arabs resided in Palestine in 1917, when the Jewish immigration began. By 1948, their numbers had grown to about a million. Therefore, at the time of partition, the number of Jews in Arab countries almost exactly equaled the number of Arabs in Palestine. There, however, the similarity ends.

In 1948, having been defeated on the battlefield, the Arab League sought to destroy Israel economically. Boycott was one weapon; the other, which surprised the world, was the expulsion of Jews from the Arab states. To conceal their true motivation, the Arab League explained this policy as part of a population exchange. A *quid pro quo* . . . their refugees for ours. In reality, the flood of indigent Jews was designed to bankrupt the already war-drained state of Israel. Needless to say, the Jews who left Arab lands left with little but the clothes on their backs. Virtually all they owned was expropriated, and no accounting has ever been demanded by the world court that is so quick to condemn Israel in all such areas.

In this matter, I speak from experience, having been expelled, not just from Baghdad, where I was born, but from the country where my ancestors had lived for 600 years. Although I had completed medical school—in spite, of course, of a strict Jewish quota—I was even denied the credits I had earned. My individual case is unimportant. I state it only to show that the problems of approximately a million Jews were at least as tragic as those of the Palestinians.

However, there were two major differences in these parallel dramas. First, the Palestinians left of their own accord, while the Jews were forced from their homes. Of even more importance, the Arabs who fled were not welcome in the many underpopulated, oil-rich Arab states, while the expelled Jews were quickly assimilated and now constitute sixty percent of the population of the small State of Israel.

Leaving the refugee problem, we reach the second point always put forward by the self-appointed Palestinian leaders. "We, the Palestinians," they say, "are a nation unto ourselves."

If they do, indeed, consider themselves a separate national group, unallied with other Arabs, why did they not say so in 1947? Instead of declaring then that they were an independent people, living in Palestine, and desiring independent statehood, they took their orders from other Arab states.

We may also ask why they didn't make their claim to nation-hood when the late King Abdullah annexed the West Bank. Why didn't they insist on their "rights" during the twenty years in which Egypt exercized control over the Gaza Strip? The Fedayeen existed then, and they could have fought for their "rights" then as they are doing now. Obviously, these "rights" are of recent origin, and were encouraged, if not created, as a political weapon. Since conventional and economic warfare had failed to annihilate Israel, perhaps politics could be used to erode it, bit by bit.

Incidentally, it should be understood that Israel is not intent on destroying the Fedayeen as such, but is simply trying to protect the rights of *its* citizens. What many don't realize is that the Fedayeen are as much a threat to the Arab countries as they are to the Jewish state. More of these terrorists have been killed by Jordan and Syria and Lebanon and Iraq than by Israel. Hopefully, one day it will become clear to all that murderers are a menace to *all* civilized states.

Thank you.

MR. FINGER. Thank you, Dr. Haddad. The next speaker on my list is General Burns.

GENERAL BURNS. Mr. Chairman, I was rather surprised that neither in the speech by Mr. Middleton yesterday, which was on economic interests in the Mediterranean and the Indian Ocean, nor in the speech by Dr. Perlmutter today on the American strategic and economic interests in the area, nor in the speech by Professor Lerner, which was supposed to deal with economics, has any mention been made of the effect of the closing of the Suez Canal. This is one of the things that is hoped will be achieved in any settlement in the Middle East, the opening of the canal. Besides the effect on the distribution of oil, which is one of the problems we have discussed today, it has a great effect on the cost of trade between Europe and the countries surrounding the Indian Ocean. It is possible that Ambassador Finger will be touching on that point himself, because that could come up in the purview of what he has mentioned. This seems to me to be an important part of the problem of the Middle East and any solution that might be found to it, and it is rather surprising to me that no one has raised this point so far.

MR. FINGER. Thank you, General Burns. It is a very good point. I hope Mr. Roy Atherton will deal with it. The next speaker I have is Professor Lerner.

MR. LERNER. I first want to correct a misunderstanding. I have heard that I was interpreted as saying that Mr. AlRoy had said that the Arab people are not capable or willing to fight. This is not my intention. I agree with what he actually said, which was not that, but that the objective conditions of development have made them incapable for some time of destroying Israel.

I want to say a few words in response to Mr. Rouleau, whose remarks I found extremely interesting and I find myself very much in agreement with them. There are two points, though, that I would like to ask him about. I make a sharp distinction between the fait accompli argument of Dayan and the denial by the Prime Minister of Israel that there is a Palestinian nation. I think it is very difficult for anybody who is not a very tied-down diplomat to deny that there is a strong Palestinian national feeling, and if there is a feeling, there is a nation just as much for Palestinians as for Jews. This is not the issue. But I do think that I find myself in sympathy with the kind of things that Dayan is doing, although I disagree with what Golda Meir said. I do not believe that these faits accomplis, the settlement of Jews in some of the occupied territories, are inimical to the ultimate settlement together with the Palestinian nation. There are Arabs, Palestinian Arabs in Israel; there will be and there should be Israeli Jews in the Palestinian nation; and there should be and there has to be freedom of movement and freedom of trade. Otherwise, there is no viability. So I would think there is no contradiction.

I believe that Sapir's and Golda Meir's objections to the territorial annexation spring from an undue concern for Peace II—from an overconcentration on getting a settlement with the other Arab nations rather than with the Palestinian people. For a settlement with the

Palestinian people, there is no necessity for refraining from having Jews living in the Palestinian part any more than for Arabs living in the Israeli part.

I must admit that I have been taking a rather narrow view. I am sure that even if there is a solution to the Israel-Palestine problem with Peace I or Peace II, this will not solve any number of other problems in the Middle East, such as the Suez Canal, which seems to me to be not a matter of very great concern to Israel at all or to the Palestinians. It may be important to Russia, to India, to Britain maybe, to America, to Egypt, but not to Israel and this part of the Middle East that I was concentrating on.

I would like to make a sharp separation between two problems in oil. I am worried about the world running out of oil. The way oil is being used now is going to cause very serious troubles everywhere no matter who gets the money. I am not worried about one hundred billion dollars or three hundred billion dollars being accumulated by the people who are sitting on the oil, because the alternative is that they be accumulated by the oil companies or they be given as subsidies to the people with heavy motor cars. This is not important for me even if the Arabs should invest the money in buying up factories in the United States or elsewhere. It is no worse than other international corporations doing the same thing.

The important thing about the oil problem is the fuel, and not the worry about the money going from the oil-using countries to the oil-producing countries. It is, of course, another worry altogether if great sums of this money are diverted toward military attacks on Israel.

MR. FINGER. I call on Dr. George Gruen.

PROFESSOR GRUEN. Just a few questions; one on the energy situation. I don't know if Mr. Smith is still here, but this is directed both to him and to Dr. Ronall. I am surprised that no one mentioned coal liquification or gasification among possible alternatives. I am not an expert on the subject, but I understand that this is an example where the technology is already at a stage where it could be utilized rather soon. Certainly we have more than enough coal to last for several centuries. Similarly, geothermal energy is on a level where apparently it can be utilized with just some refinement of petroleum technology. According to a study recently completed by a National Science Foundation-sponsored commission, headed by former Secretary of the Interior Walter J. Hickel, they estimated that by 1985 geothermal energy could generate something like a third of the present electric energy requirements of the United States. And do so without any foreign currency cost. I understand that something like nuclear fusion and solar energy are way off at the end of the century or the beginning of the next century, but these seem to be alternatives that are possible within the foreseeable future. I would like some comment by the experts on that.

I was very much struck by Professor Lichtenstadter's comment about the pluralistic society under Islam. Having studied the period, that certainly *was* so in the Ottoman Empire where the *millet* concept was defined to give a fair measure of autonomy to different religious groups as cultural groups. What seems to me has happened, unfortunately, is that in the Middle East they have learned our lesson of modern Western nationalism too well. Maybe they pay too much attention to Western political scientists, and conclude that the ideal state has to be a clear, simple, homogeneous national ethnic state, like the Frenchmen in France. When an attempt is made to carry out this monolithic concept in a country like Egypt, minorities suffer. The position of the Copts illustrates this. The Christian Copts, who after all are descended from the Pharaonic Egyptians, are not fully comfortable in their own country because they do not happen to be Sunni Muslim Arabs. The problem of the Kurds in Iraq is another similar analogy to this. And Zionism is in a sense a reflection of the same kind of modern political nationalism that is not as pluralistic as the Ottoman *millet* system was. I would like some comment by Professor Lichtenstadter or by someone else as to the present-day salience of the religious factor in political controversy.

A majority of Israelis are not Orthodox Jews. We do get occasional statements by the former Sephardic chief rabbi and other religious spokesmen that no government has the right to give a single inch of the Promised Land away. Again the question is, how is the Promised Land defined?? Which chapter of the Bible do you use?

I was even more disturbed, though, by the speech—and I checked rather carefully because I did not believe the translation when I first got it, and I checked it from three different monitoring services—a sermon that was given by President Sadat slightly over a year ago on 25 April 1972, on the birthday of the Prophet Muhammed, when Sadat said in a mosque in Cairo that "the most splendid thing that the Prophet Muhammed did, blessed be his memory, was to drive them [the Jews] out of the whole Arabian Peninsula," because they were "men of deceit and treachery." Muhammed was angry because some Jewish tribes had concluded a treaty with his enemies in Medinah. But the point is not the history lesson Sadat was giving his congregants, which does not bother me, but his conclusion that "we shall never conduct direct negotiations with them [for example, the Israelis] because we know our history and their history with the Prophet in the past. They are a nation of liars and traitors, contrivers of plots, a people born for deeds of treachery. . . ." In other words, Sadat is attributing the vices of whatever Jewish tribes were in Arabia at the time of Muhammed to the present-day Israelis. Sadat concluded by promising his listeners that at next year's anniversary of the Prophet's birth "we shall celebrate in this place not only the liberation of our country, but also the defeat of Israeli arrogance . . . so that they shall return and be as the Qur'an said of them: 'condemned to humiliation and misery.' "

I wonder whether this was said as empty rhetoric out of frustration. Certainly an Israeli who hears this monitored broadcast—and people in the Israel Foreign Ministry listen to it in the original, they tell me, from Radio Cairo, since they know Arabic—must begin to question what are the prospects for peace and what are the true intentions of the leadership in Egypt. I would like the Egyptian representative to say how this kind of rhetoric can improve the prospects for peace. Certainly some individual Israel statements have also not been helpful, but this is a formal speech by the President of Egypt.

A final point and question that relates to the United Nations' resolutions. There are two that come to mind. Mention was made by General Burns of the Security Council resolution about the Suez Canal. I recall there was a 1 September 1951-Security Council resolution adopted without a single negative vote and therefore it was the will of the United Nations—according to Dr. Stoessinger's conception—in which the Council held that the Armistice Agreement between Israel and Egypt had taken on a permanent character in that it barred any military solution. Although it left open peaceful political changes, since violence had been ruled out as a method of solving the original conflict, the Egyptians were therefore not entitled to exercise the rights of search and seizure and blockade, and therefore the international community as well as Israel had the right to ship goods back and forth through the Suez Canal. That resolution was ignored, and in 1954 when there was an attempt by the Western powers to politely remind the government of Egypt of this resolution, the Soviet Union vetoed the resolution to which it had previously acquiesced. The Soviet gentleman can explain why there was a change in Soviet policy.

The last resolution I would like clarified is the famous Resolution 242, which is really the basic compromise that we are dealing with at the moment as a possible diplomatic solution. It is very interesting to look at the history, as I did in a brief article on it a short time afterward. The original concept came out of a speech by President Johnson a few days after the war. It was incorporated in an American resolution introduced by Ambassador Goldberg that had five key operative paragraphs in it. If you look at the compromise resolution that was adopted, which has Lord Caradon's imprimatur on it, there are four operative paragraphs. The fifth one that got lost in the shuffle would have had the Council affirm the necessity "for achieving a limitation on the wasteful and destructive arms race in the area." The reason for the deletion of that paragraph, I was told, is that the Soviet Union at that point was busy rearming Egypt and did not want to freeze the arms race at that time until it had rearmed Egypt.

We have heard very interestingly from Professor AlRoy last night that the military balance is so obviously in favor of Israel that there is nothing that the Russians nor anyone else could do short of military intervention, which they supposedly will not do because of the summit conference and the détente; there is no point then in further escalating the arms race. I wonder whether now might be a good time for the United States and the Soviet Union, maybe with the French or all the permanent members of the Security Council to get together and at least on that level reach an agreement not to escalate the Middle East conflict to a new stage of armaments. In other words, to reintroduce that fifth operative paragraph.

MR. FINGER. In order to elicit some answers to your question, I call first on Professor Lichtenstadter and then Dr. Ovinnikov, who has also asked to speak.

PROFESSOR LICHTENSTADTER. I would like to answer the point that Mr. Gruen made with regard to the Israeli tribes that were expelled from Medinah. I mentioned it before briefly in my own speech, and in an article published some years ago I said that this was the only cruel act that the Messenger of Allah ever committed. (By the way, I used the term *representative* instead of *messenger* only to clarify his task for a non-Islamic audience.) The Prophet did expel the Jews of Medinah because he realized that they were absolutely not integratable into his *ummat al-Islâm*. You will remember that he included the Jews of Medinah in his *ummah* and gave them religious freedom, which I characterized as a great and unusual attitude, probably the first instance of religious freedom in history. When Muhammed experienced the constant objections of the Jewish community in Medinah, not to his mission, not to Islam as such, nor to his monotheism, but to his misrepresentations of the biblical stories and their own concepts of revelation, only then did he realize that they would disturb the unification of his Arab-Muslim community.

By the way, I have my own views on the origin of the so-called biblical stories in the Koran. The Jews of those times misunderstood the Prophet's representation of the biblical stories just as the Muslim commentators and the Western, modern Orientalists misunderstood them. He did not quote *biblical* stories, not the Torah, the text of which the Jews could show him and prove him wrong; he was talking in terms of very ancient Near Eastern myths that came to him in an oral tradition different from the way in which the same myth came through the Bible to the Medinian Jews. I have been attacked for my protection and my apologetic explanations of the Prophet's actions against the Jews of Medinah; I have even been accused of protecting him from the accusation that he acted almost as Hitler did against the German Jews, on the same grounds. But one has to keep in mind that what Mohammed did happened in the seventh century A.D., and the comparison with Hitlerite style of extermination is, to say the least, unfair and unjustified.

MR. FINGER. I now give the floor to Dr. Ovinnikov.

DR. OVINNIKOV. Professor Perlmutter's talk put me in a very delicate situation, because he reproached both professors and professional diplomats. Wearing both hats, being a doctor of history and a minister in the Soviet Mission of the United Nations, I should somehow take sides with one half of myself. I will say that I tend to agree with myself as a diplomat, because what we are looking for is very often pie in the sky, but diplomats stand with both their feet on the poor sinful earth where we all are. I still submit that the main thrust of our discussion is a wrong one. We should not have discussed whether outside powers could afford a settlement at all in the Middle East, because what is the crux of the situation there, in my view, is that the very situation is an abnormal one. It is abnormal first because it contradicts the well-established norms of international law, because it contradicts the principles of the United Nations' Charter, because it contradicts a number of resolutions of the United Nations; second, because there is a hotbed in the Middle East of tension, conflict, war. This is the real situation there.

Of course, all the aspects that have been discussed here—for example, the energy crisis—involve the interplay of power politics in the Middle East. They are perhaps important, but only to a certain extent. The crux of the problem is that for almost six years there has existed in the Middle East a situation under which the territories of three Arab states are being occupied. Is there a solution to this abnormal situation? The solution is the establishment in the Middle East of a just and lasting peace. Because if an imposed peace is not just, it can not be lasting. The only difficulty now is that someone, the Israelis in my view, do not want peace, whether just or stable, because at a certain period in time they were in favor of secure and recognized boundaries, but this is not how they understand their security. They are now in favor of defensible borders, which means that these borders will bear the weight of their conquest, and this is what makes the situation so abnormal.

I submit that until a just and lasting peace is established there, no other solution is possible. Or if it is possible in theory and in life, it can not be stable.

What are the means for a possible solution? They are numerous, but practically only one thing is necessary: the willingness, the will. The basis for any solution, in my view, is total withdrawal of the Israeli forces from all the territories of their conquests that are occupied, and second, respect for lawful rights of the Arab people of Palestine. Only a peace that is based on those two premises can be a stable one.

The ways and means are numerous, as I have said. Bilateral negotiations between the Soviet Union and the United States could contribute; the five permanent members of the Security Council could negotiate; or the discussion in the Security Council itself could contribute, because in the Security Council not only are the permanent members represented, but also the non-permanent members representing all geographical regions have an important role. So only one thing is missing: the political will or political willingness. The ways and means can always be found. Thank you.

MR. FINGER. Thank you, Dr. Ovinnikov. I have been asked to make just one exception on the understanding that we have a two-minute rule. Professor Perlmutter has asked to speak and I understand it will be two minutes. I now call on him.

PROFESSOR PERLMUTTER. It is only a point of information. I do consider, if you will remember, professors and diplomats in one coalition. Now, some are intelligent and some are unintelligent, and the unintelligent ones should not participate in the same way as others do, but it is very difficult to distinguish between the two.

The other point is, since you know I am a globalist, I do consider again that one of the major international conflicts in the world is the Soviet aggression toward China, and the Soviet occupation of Chinese territory. I am certainly convinced that if the Soviet Union would abide by the Charter of the United Nations and return some

Chinese territories to the Chinese, the chances for international peace and security are certainly much more prospective than the ones in the Middle East, for at least the Soviet Union is a great power that can afford its generosity and magnanimity toward the Chinese. Thank you.

MR. FINGER. I now have great pleasure in introducing Ambassador Richard Nolte, one of those who is both professor and diplomat, as former United States Ambassador to Egypt.

American Relations
with the Arab States and Israel

by Richard Nolte

MR. NOLTE. Thank you, Mr. Chairman; perhaps I should say twice blessed and twice cursed. In any case, I lay claim to being the shortest tenured ambassador in the annals of the American Foreign Service. I was appointed American Ambassador to Egypt in 1967 and actually arrived on the scene in Cairo on the 21st of May—how could I forget?—1967. Three weeks later I departed Egypt on a boat with four or five hundred other Americans, thus ending my twenty-one-day economy tour.

In speaking this afternoon I would like to emphasize that I do not speak as a representative of the United States government. My official connection with that institution was very brief. It did not precede by much the singular events of 1967, nor has there been any connection since. I speak as a private citizen but not entirely without a prior awareness of the Middle East.

My first visit there was in 1948 just before the establishment of the State of Israel, and so in a sense my interest in the Middle East and for some years my intimate connection with it—I lived there— extends during the whole life of that new state.

I first became aware of the Middle East after the Second World War when I came back from being a pilot and decided to go to Oxford and take up the wildly improbable subject of Oriental studies on the basis of fellowships that I had won both there at Oxford and here at the Institute of Current World Affairs, which institution I now direct.

I remember coming back from the war aware that the Middle Eastern area would be of considerable and growing importance to the world and to the United States by reason of strategy, geography, oil, all the lessons of the war. But my first introduction to the heat and feeling and emotion involved was a full-page ad in the *New York Times* sometime early in 1947, late in 1946—I have forgotten exactly when—that featured a quotation signed by Ben Hecht : Every time a British soldier is killed in Palestine, we make a little holiday in our hearts.

Now, that was a rather ungentlemanly thing to say, even about British soldiers, even in Palestine, and I reacted negatively to that vehemence. But it was an accurate introduction to the kind of feeling that existed then and does still, even more so, in and about that region.

My own aproach to the Middle East was conditioned more by my studies just after the war at Yale University Graduate School with Arnold Wolfers and a distinguished group of graduate students. We gained a perception of the iron reality that has dominated foreign policy of nations, certainly of the great nations, since the end of the Second World War. The Cold War has been that dominant, distorting, polarizing fact that has governed relations between the United States and the Soviet Union in particular ever since that time. That global competition, carried on all over the world at a level of intensity varying with time and place and by a variety of means from propaganda and aid programs, right up to other people's wars or proxy wars, has left its record of high points or crisis points, waymarks of the struggle. One can recall the Czechoslovakian takeover in 1948, and China in 1949, the Berlin Airlift in 1948–50, the Korean War 1950–52. Then the Russians invented the hydrogen bomb, and then we had Berlin again, and Cuba, the missile crisis of 1962. And then the Congo in 1960–64. All during this period the Middle East was by no means unaffected by the Cold War's influence, and in fact, one can say that the Cold War really began in the Middle East when the Russians in 1946 refused to withdraw their troops from Iran according to treaty along with the United States and Great Britain. This led to the first confrontation between the United States and its partners in the Security Council and the Soviet Union.

Reacting to what amounted to an ultimatum by the United States, the Russians agreed to withdraw their troops, and the first, shall we say, *encounter* in the Middle East ended in something of a victory for us and a setback, at least as we saw it then, for the Soviet Union.

But this went on. In the winter of 1946–47, one of the harshest in the history of Great Britain, compounded by a massive coal shortage and the exhaustions of war, the British government was forced to announce that it could no longer carry the Cold War burden in the Middle East. Specifically, it could no longer support Turkey in its struggle to resist Russian pressure to cede the easternmost provinces and to share control of the Dardanelles. Or Greece, where the communists had achieved control of more than three-quarters of the country and were in visible distance of winning that contest.

The American response to the threat confronting Turkey, Greece, and Iran was prompt and the new policy soon acquired a nickname : the *Truman Doctrine*. The Truman Doctrine meant cash backing and military assistance in very short order, and this first American response to the Cold War threat in the Middle East was a successful one if we judge it from the standpoint of the present; we are still in reasonably good relations with all three countries, and they are all still independent.

The success of the Truman Doctrine might have been and indeed was thought to be a successful pattern for United States action when the Arab states, the so-called soft underbelly, became an area of competition between the United States and the Soviet Union. The security interests of the United States had led us to the Truman Doctrine, but at the same time we were making an intervention in the Arab world for quite different reasons, with a humanitarian motivation of major dimensions. It was major in the sense that the United States as a whole was committed to it, and major, too, in that it led to a very large support for the establishment of this new entity, the State of Israel, a support that has continued from that time to this and has been a really remarkable demonstration of generosity, official and private, by the citizens of the United States.

But in this double intervention in the Middle East, at the same time in different places for different reasons, we created for ourselves a dilemma that has plagued us right down to the present time : the conflict between the interests of American security and the humanitarian interests of the American people toward the State of Israel. This was a contradiction that had within it the seeds of potential violence, of very great violence indeed. The magnitude of the threat did not go unperceived, of course, by people on both sides of the Iron Curtain. The United States, having had one nuclear confrontation with the Soviet Union, has been concerned about the danger of similar confrontations elsewhere, not the least of which could occur in the Middle East; and as for the Soviet Union, its reluctance in 1962 to stand firm in the confrontation over Cuba seemed to continue in the Middle East, as elsewhere.

Nevertheless, the suspicion was that a confrontation might well occur anyway because both the U.S. and the U.S.S.R. were linked on opposite sides with Middle Eastern nations whose quarrel with each other transcended and outweighed for them any Cold War consequences.

United States' backing for Israel and Soviet involvement with Egypt meant that the quarrels of the Middle Eastern antagonists could ignite military conflict between their two great power sponsors. As for the Russians in their relationship with Egypt, it has been apparent that they have exercised a considerable measure of restraint both by their damping presence in Egypt, especially after 1967, and by their consistent refusal to supply long-range means of attack. The Russian aircraft supplied to Egypt could not make the round trip between the Egyptian airfield and, say, Tel Aviv, and Russian anti-aircraft rockets, however sophisticated, were not exactly offensive weapons. So there has been a degree of restraint there that was far more real than the martial rhetoric one heard from Cairo.

As for United States' control over Israel, this may or may not have been possible, but none has ever been exercised, except on one occasion in 1956 when the United States required, over a period of months, that Israel withdraw from Sinai after that previous war. Israel eventually complied and there ensued a decade of peace; but when that peace was ruptured by another war, it became difficult to argue that U.S. pressure, Israeli withdrawal, and the U.N. Emergency Force in Sinai had been a useful formula. That is the only occasion I can recall that Israel has been required to do anything that it did not want to do by anybody, and there was no reason to suppose after 1967 that the Israelis would listen very carefully to cautions of restraint by the United States. In fact, far more typical of the Israelis' attitude has been a shoot-from-the-hip readiness to attack, a sort of Wild West daring rather congenial to our American tradition of frontier readiness. This readiness to shoot first, which was learned in a hard school by the Israelis, nevertheless carried with it very real dangers for the United States.

Typical of this rough-and-ready approach was the bombing,

strafing, and torpedoing of the American ship U.S.S. *Liberty*, an electronic-surveillance vessel, in the eastern Mediterranean during the Six-Day War. The Israelis did a very effective job, killing about thirty-seven Americans and wounding an equal number, and there has always been the question : did the Israelis know that it was an American ship? It was just off the Sinai coast. Was it American? The Americans say yes, there was a big American flag painted on the side. But the Israelis have maintained that they did not know it was an American ship, and when they found out, the reaction was, "Thank God it was American!" But that is the point. They attacked, never mind whose ship it was. It was this kind of willingness to strike first and count the cost later that had within it the seeds of danger for the United States.

This realization led to Secretary Rogers's peace initiatives in 1969 and 1970, but in looking at the equation, the obvious question is : what is the Arab-Israel quarrel all about and why isn't peace somehow negotiable? Both sides profess they want peace. The Israelis certainly have never failed to stress the importance to them and their future of a peaceful relationship with their neighbors, and this is so obviously true for economic, military security, and other reasons that it needs no arguing. The Israelis want peace by all means, but prior requirement is security. Security comes first, security above all, security even if peace has to be sacrificed to achieve it.

Where does security lie in the sea of hostility, as Israelis perceive it, that surrounds them? The Israeli answer has been : security lies in military strength; and right up to the present time Israeli security has been defined ever more completely in terms of military power. This is in the Israeli view, the lesson of their whole experience. After all, Israel owes its establishment to the military success of a small handful of Davids against the "Arab hordes." And when it came to border marauding across the Jordanian frontier, military success again in the form of hammer blows at suspected Arab villages were successful in forcing the Jordanian government to stop the border crossings.

Again in 1956 a preemptive war was brilliantly successful and even more so in 1967. Success has a way of confirming itself. Military security was the only security, and it certainly had worked for all that period of time.

Again one feels that the military definition of security is, in part, in some measure a product of the assumption by the Israelis of the "civilized" values of the modern West, which puts a great deal of emphasis on strength, military strength, efficiency, technological sophistication, the ability to act quickly, to strike, and, to display the organization, power, and control of an up-to-date nation-state. Other nations were certainly putting emphasis on military might as the means to security and the United States itself was not laggard in this regard. At any rate, military security for Israelis is the only security. Even if it has to be achieved at the expense of that real long-range security that can only be gained through the peaceful acceptance of Israel by its neighbors. Israelis argue that this, nevertheless, is a necessary choice.

In my own view, the military definition of security is ultimately a trap for Israel, a trap that could be as lethal as Masada was in the past, and it is a trap that the Israelis must avoid by somehow converting their present military security into real security. How that necessity is to be recognized, first of all, by the Israelis, and second achieved, is a question that might baffle a Solomon.

As for the Arabs, they too want peace. They need peace, particularly the Egyptians, at least as desperately as the Israelis. A more pacific and docile population you are not likely to find on the planet than the Egyptians, and their need for peace and respite is certainly tangible. And yet for the Arabs, too, there is a prior necessity in their minds, and that necessity is what they call justice. For the Egyptians, justice has come to mean, since 1967, the return of the occupied territories of Sinai, or at least the promise that it can in time be achieved. To them, this is the very definition of justice and it goes to the heart of the United Nations' Charter and the unacceptability of territorial acquisition by force. Israeli withdrawal from Sinai has become the overriding component of the Egyptian notion of justice.

But an underlying, older, and more pervasive conception of justice is the notion that the Palestinians and particularly the Palestinian refugees were wronged, grievously wronged by the world, chiefly the West, and by the Israelis in particular; a wrong maintained ever since 1947–48 and continuing still. This wrong was the forcible displacement of nearly a million Palestinians from their homes in 1948 and since, and the refusal by Israel to let them return despite repeated U.N. resolutions, universal human rights, and all the rest. To Egyptians, as to all Arabs, righting the wrongs of Palestine underlies everything else as the basic requirement of justice. Palestinians, and by extension all Arabs, have not been regarded by the world, by us in particular, by the Israelis in particular, as being entitled to that same full humane treatment due to fully civilized people like ourselves or like the Israelis; and this Western scorn rankles and will continue to rankle until the Arabs in general and the Palestinians in particular perceive that the world has changed its views on this score. Inevitably, meanwhile, they are learning at the rough hands of the West and of Israel that the only way you can bring about such a change of view is to acquire military ability and to use it. Power creates respect.

So we have these two seemingly incompatible demands. Justice on the one hand versus security on the other hand, all focused on a very narrow piece of ground, with each protagonist able to draw on enormous outside power.

You would think, looking at it from outside, that one ought to be able to find an area of compatibility between the necessary needs of security and the necessary needs of justice; an overlapping ground in which enough of each could be given to both sides so that real peace could be the product. Indeed, the United Nations came up with such a formula in November of 1967—Resolution 242, which was a sort of package deal that still stands in the minds of most of us as the basic outline of an arrangement that would give to the Israelis a treaty of peace, recognized frontiers, a cessation of marauding attacks by guerrillas, unimpeded passage through the Suez Canal and the Straits of Tiran; all, in short, that the Israelis had been claiming up until the June war of 1967. At the same time, their opponents would achieve a return of the occupied territories, and some formula securing justice for the Palestinian people and the refugees in particular. Resolution 242 seemed to offer sufficient security, sufficient justice, and the hope of peace.

Because of the escalating conflict between Egypt and Israel in 1968–69, the United States became alarmed at possible Cold War consequences. The new administration began an effort to ameliorate the situation: Secretary of State Rogers's efforts, which turned out to be successful on the one side in that Nasser and subsequently President Sadat were able to say to the U.N. negotiator, Ambassador Jarring, that if issues between the other Arab states and Israel could be resolved, and if Israel would withdraw or promise in due time to withdraw from Sinai, Egypt would formally and publicly grant Israel the peace and recognition, free passage, and cessation of harassment that it had sought for twenty-five years.

A parallel question was addressed to the Israelis, saying if you achieve this twenty-five-year objective and get a peaceful arrangement with the Egyptians, and if the dispute with the other Arab states can be arranged, and if a formula can be arranged to deal with the Palestinians, would you then agree to withdraw from Sinai? The Israeli answer to that question was and is: No!

The impasse continues to the present time. It is an impasse that Israel alone can break, because no Arab government is powerful enough at home in the wake of defeat to accept the loss of territories under Israeli occupation. No government could survive in an Arab state that accepted that further surrender to injustice.

In the past year things have changed very considerably. There has been a weakening of the danger posed by the Cold War. The Soviet Union has made it clear that in any Middle Eastern competition it is not interested in being brought eyeball to eyeball with the United States. It has preferred in the SALT talks and in other ways, imports of grain and technology, to deal with the United States no matter what the United States' relationship was with Israel or with Egypt. This is bitter medicine in Cairo and was a major factor underlying the expulsion of the Russians from Egypt last summer by President Sadat—which the Russians accepted with apparent equanimity. The Russian preference for détente has taken much of the danger out of the Middle Eastern situation, making the Middle East for the present at least an area of far less concern to the United States.

What does that leave in the Middle East? It leaves the Israelis supreme in power. They have many times the military strength necessary to deal with all of the Arab states put together at any time. It leaves them in a position to make peace if they could bring themselves to decide on what kind of peace they want to make, and that apparently is an impossible task in Israel, given the coalition government. But they can continue to ride on the status quo indefinitely, the more so since the American position has been to endorse the Israeli position not only tacitly by not opposing it, but also quite materially in continuing to supply weapon, financial, and diplomatic support on a handsome scale. As for the Egyptian side of that equation, demoralization could not be more complete. They see themselves unable to achieve the mandatory objective, recovery of Sinai, by negotiation against a powerful Israel content with the status quo, nor despite bluster, can they do it by force, all the less so after dismissing the Russians.

One feels that this can not continue and that the Egyptian situation will break down inside with riots, violence, and who knows what destruction—and one can be pretty sure that among the initial and major targets would be anything American in that country.

That brings us to the problem of what the United States could or should do about the situation. Basically, in my view, it should begin to apply equal treatment to the nations of the Middle East, and to be consistent about it. The U.S. should recognize that the Arab-Israel quarrel is not self-liquidating, quite the reverse, and that the United States must act to help resolve it, or at least to insulate it from Cold War politics. This will require adequate security arrangements for Israel coupled with sufficient inducements and pressure to produce justice for the Arabs: withdrawal from the occupied territories as specified in Resolution 242, and recognition of the necessity to deal constructively with the Palestinian problem.

Particularly since 1967, the United States has given unequivocal support to Israel no matter what. This consistent behavior has raised a tide of Arab hostility and made it impossible for Arab governments, particularly in times of crisis, to deal with the United States. The Soviet Union has been the willing alternative. In the interest of peace, for the sake of Israel's ultimate survival, it is necessary for the United States to reestablish normal relations with the Arab states. In the present period of Cold War relaxation and the quasi-withdrawal of the Russians from Egypt, it may be possible at long last for the United States to act wisely, responsibly, and fairly in the Middle East. The Arab response could not fail to be positive.

There is another factor to be considered in all this. It may be that the winds of economic necessity will force the American people to ask why the Arabs with all their oil have become so bitterly hostile to the United States? In asking such questions we shall also find answers, and as a result I suspect American policy will move more swiftly than otherwise toward an evenhanded posture in the Middle East. I am referring of course to what is called the *energy crisis*. This is no doubt overstated in some quarters, but I believe it is real enough. One can anticipate that by 1985 or so, half of our oil will have to be imported and the great bulk of that will have to come from the Middle East. It is an irony, I suppose, not a very comfortable feeling, to realize that the proper behavior of nations is sometimes the result of pressure or force. It does not always spring automatically from morality, wisdom, or purity of heart.

MR. FINGER. Thank you, Professor Nolte. I now call on Professor Don Peretz of the State University of New York in Binghamton, who will talk about the Kennedy and Johnson administrations and the Six-Day War.

The Kennedy and Johnson Administrations and the Six-Day War

by Don Peretz

PROFESSOR PERETZ. Very often the current situation in the Middle East reminds me of an incident I heard about a man who fell off the fiftieth story of a skyscraper. As he was falling, he happened to pass the twentieth story where his friend was looking out the window and just happened to catch a glimpse of him passing by. The friend yelled out the window to him, "How's it going?" The falling man yelled back, "So far so good." After listening to Dick Nolte, I am not quite sure what floor we are on, maybe we are down to about the tenth or even the second floor.

I promised Mr. Merlin that I would talk about both the Johnson and the Kennedy administrations and their Middle East policies.

I think the Kennedy administration made a high-water mark in the change of American policy. Certainly under Kennedy there was a more sophisticated approach to international problems, especially those of the Middle East. It was quite different from the pre-Israel era when United States Ambassador Warren Austin in the Security Council debates on the Palestine problem called upon both

190

the representatives of the Jewish Agency and of the Arab states to resolve their dispute in a Christian-like manner. While Kennedy set a somewhat novel tone compared with that of the rather hectoring anticommunism of Dulles, I often ask myself: "Was there really any change in substance, or was this primarily a change in style?" It is certainly true that the Kennedy administration raised many hopes in the Middle East, as it did elsewhere in the world. The basis of these expectations was that this new younger generation of politicians and diplomats would have much more understanding of Third World problems than the Eisenhower-Dulles administration displayed. Kennedy seemed much more open to discussion than the rather doctrine-bound Dulles. Kennedy was furthermore much more tolerant and understanding of the Third World. Neutralism was no longer considered a mortal sin. Furthermore, he had been one of the very few United States politicians who seemed to give some overt expression of sympathy to the Arab cause, going back to the famous speech that he made on Algeria when he was still a senator. Even as a presidential candidate he took the very high political risk of daring to talk with Arab politicians. This he did in secret, but he *did it,* whereas other politicians who were running for office were reluctant to expose themselves to such risk, perhaps fearing that some Watergate-bugging incident might reveal their secret diplomacy.

After assuming office, the new Kennedy administration gave the appearance of a fresh approach to Middle East problems. Chester Bowles received a very high appointment in the State Department, and he too, was supposedly much more open-minded on questions of neutralism, a group of new ambassadors was appointed in the Middle East, many with language skills and with understanding for the countries where they were stationed, perhaps best exemplified by the very popular John Badeau, the administration's ambassador to Egypt.

But the cornerstone of United States policy still seemed to be based on the code word *evenhandedness.* This term *evenhanded* often causes a great deal of confusion. It seems sufficiently ambiguous to disguise any kind of action that the federal government wants to take. On the other hand, it offers promise of a balance of some sort.

Continued emphasis on the refugee problem was also a main element in the Kennedy approach. The rationale was that, if the United States could succeed in convincing Israel to make concessions on the refugees, there might possibly be some quid pro quo from the Arab states toward a peaceful settlement. This was underscored by the appointment of another Johnson mission.

Every president of the United States since Eisenhower has had some sort of Johnson input into the problems of the Middle East. President Eisenhower had his Eric Johnson, President Kennedy his Joe Johnson, and Lyndon Johnson had himself. Now I am waiting to se which Johnson Nixon is going to send to the area. The name Johnson has aroused a lot of suspicion in the Middle East, because of the extent to which the Johnson input has been used as a way of resolving American policy.

Actually Joe Johnson was appointed as a representative of the U.N. Conciliation Commission. There were unconfirmed reports that a Swiss diplomat had refused to undertake this mission because he saw no prospects for peace in the area, but the Kennedy administration prevailed upon Joe Johnson, who was then president of the Carnegie Endowment for International Peace, to undertake the task. After several visits to the area and after months of study, he reported that both sides had expressed willingness, but with reservations, to consider what he called *step-by-step process* that might lead to peace. However, he concluded there could be little progress apart from an overall settlement of the Arab-Israeli dispute, warning that the refugees would require U.N. assistance for at least another decade. He urged accelerated economic growth for the whole region, in which the refugees would be a part. Perhaps the most controversial part of his proposal was that the refugees be given an opportunity to choose between repatriation to Israel with safeguards for the country's security or settlement elsewhere. Both repatriation and resettlement would be undertaken simultaneously under U.N. supervision, on a step-by-step basis financed through a special U.N. fund.

Neither Israel nor the Arab governments seemed to find Dr. Johnson's proposal acceptable. Prime Minister Ben Gurion succeeded in convincing the Knesset to pass a resolution that categorically rejected it, for Israel was convinced that the proposal was designed and calculated only to destroy the Jewish state. By an overwhelming majority of sixty-five to seven, the Knesset endorsed Ben Gurion's stand, further resolving that the solution to the problem was resettlement of the refugees in the Arab countries.

On the other hand, most Arab officials were unprepared to accept a partial solution outside the context of an overall Palestine settlement, and refugee leaders furthermore charged that Dr. Johnson's proposals favored Israel. They called on the United Nations to enforce existing resolutions that supposedly would enable all the refugees to return.

Despite the lack of any concrete or substantive change in policy under Kennedy's administration, the emphasis on appearance and sensitivity to the problems seemed to raise him on a pedestal in both Israel and the Arab world, so much so that throughout the Middle East today you can find monuments, such as the John F. Kennedy Memorial built by the Israelis in Jerusalem, and the John F. Kennedy Information Service in Cairo, and John F. Kennedy Boulevard in Beirut. Kennedy lost responsibility for this problem at a time that was opportune, and therefore until today is regarded by people on both sides of the dispute as very sympathetic to their respective views.

I remember talking to a Jordanian military governor of Jerusalem before 1967. He told me how nefarious the Israelis were and what a great man Kennedy was. If only Kennedy had lived, this problem could have been solved. "But you know," I argued, "there is a John F. Kennedy Memorial that the Israelis have put up over there."

"Well," he said, "that is just part of a plot, only a trick."

There is little evidence and only the vaguest speculation to support the thesis that things would have been different had Kennedy lived. Reports or rather rumors in the more unreliable Arab press that the President's assassination was linked to an insidious Zionist plot to remove him because of his *evenhandedness* continued to feed illusions that Kennedy's policies would have been different than those of his successors. But in reality it was events in Johnson's administration rather than the man himself that conspired to undermine his credibility and his own evenhandedness.

There are a variety of reasons why things changed. First of all, the pressure of domestic politics became much heavier after the death of Kennedy. Vietnam absorbed American energies and American interests. The Middle East problem had become even more intractable, facing the United States with many dilemmas even before 1967. For example, in the U.N. efforts to seek evenhandedness through Security Council resolutions censuring Arab guerrilla raids and Israeli retaliatory attacks were usually frustrated by the Soviet Union, who joined the United States in condemning Israel; but, on the other hand, Russia vetoed all resolutions condemning the Arab attacks. Nor did repeated United States' warnings that it would not approve the use of force seem to deter either side.

Israel became increasingly disenchanted with the United Nations, while radical Arab regimes became even more friendly with the Soviet Union, thus vitiating the whole effect of any action through the United Nations. Thus, the goodwill, the sympathetic attitudes of President Kennedy lost their effectiveness as both Arabs and Israelis became increasingly bitter at America's inability to intervene with the antagonists. The Arabs resented continuing promises of American support for Israel's security, and Israel, fearing the growing influence of radical regimes and their closer ties with the Soviet Union, felt that the growing promises of American aid were far from adequate.

For example, in 1963 the United States initiated the first sale of the Hawk missiles to Israel. This tremendously infuriated all of the Arab states. However, Israel felt that these sales were hardly more than tokenism when compared to the large arms supplies that the Arab states were receiving from Russia. And so the situation went on until the outbreak of the 1967 war.

The 1967 war became a crucial test of big power willingness to avoid a head-on confrontation in the Middle East. You recall that in 1963 a hotline was installed between the Kremlin and the White House. But it took four years before that hotline was first used when Prime Minister Aleksei Kosygin called up the President immediately after the Six-Day War. This first use of the hotline indicated that there was a willingness to avoid a head-on confrontation.

Immediately after the war, having avoided the confrontation through hotline consultations and direct diplomacy, another crucial test set a new pace for diplomacy at the Glassboro meetings between Kosygin and President Johnson. The Glassboro meetings were the beginning of detente, the détente that reached its final peak with the visit by Nixon to the Soviet Union and the Middle East last year. Although there was not an overall agreement reached on Soviet-American policy in the Middle East, Johnson observed that there was American-Soviet agreement on many problems. "We have not yet solved all of our problems, but on some we have made progress, great progress," he said, "in reducing misunderstanding with Russia despite our deeply differing positions." Johnson said, "We have agreed that the leaders of our two countries will keep in touch in the future." This was a major breakthrough in Soviet-American diplomacy provided by the occasion of the 1967 war.

However, since 1967 there has been a gradual drift away from a policy of evenhandedness. This phrase was used less and less in the Johnson administration. Nixon attempted to revive it, but we heard little of the term *evenhandedness* in recent months or recent years.

After 1967 the United States was at a great disadvantage in the Middle East as a result of the Arab defeat. The all-out political commitment by the Soviet Union to rearm the Arab states led to renewal of the arms race in the Middle East.

In discussions with Soviet diplomats, their perception of the problem is quite different from that of most Americans, and certainly of the State Department. The U.S. government usually views this problem in terms of balance, a mathematical formula. For x amount of arms that the Arab states receive, Israel must receive a competitive amount based on the formula. The Soviet sees the major obstacle as one of Israel's military potential, not only in terms of arms and equipment, but also in terms of the whole military infrastructure of the state, including manpower, capacity to organize, and the ability to maneuver troops into the field within a matter of hours.

What might be learned from the Johnson and Kennedy administrations is that American efforts to find a peaceful solution to the Arab-Israeli dispute illustrate the difficulties of intervention by an honest broker when large numbers of American citizens have great sympathy for one party and either indifference or hostility for the other; when the second party has the full and uncritical support of a power that is in strategic, diplomatic, and political competition with the United States in the area where peace is sought; and where, because of great political and social unrest, radical regimes in the area suspect any overall American policy objectives. The wonder is that the United States was able to continue its role as an intermediary at all. Perhaps the explanation is that, although mistrusted by all parties, the United States was the only nation that the antagonists believed had sufficient power to influence the policies and actions of the other side in a way that would result in a settlement giving both even the minimum of satisfaction.

MR. FINGER. It is now my great pleasure to call on Mr. Roy Atherton, Deputy Assistant Secretary of State for Near Eastern and South Asian Affairs.

The Nixon Administration
and the Arab-Israeli Conflict
by Alfred LeRoy Atherton, Jr.

MR. ATHERTON. If there is anything that can be said about audiences on the Middle East, they have endurance. I suppose it is a truism to say that everyone approaches a problem or addresses a problem of this kind from the point of view of his own perspective, and I know of no subject on which this is more true than the Arab-Israeli problem. It is a problem that has many advocates of one side or the other, and sometimes too few truly detached observers.

My perspective that I am going to set forth today is to try to describe the policy of the Nixon administration toward the Arab-Israeli problem as it is seen by those people involved in making the policy and in recommending making and trying to carry out the policy. Others will view the policy of this administration from their perspective in perhaps very different ways. I am not going to try to judge it; I am going to present it as best and as honestly as I can and leave it to others to judge.

I think before I start this process, it might be useful to simply state very briefly the premises that underlie the policy approach of this government. Too often, our premises are left unstated and we assume that the other people know what they are when many times their premises are different, and misunderstandings arise that way.

Simply stated, the premises are these. First of all, it is in the interests of the United States to have good relations with all of the states or at least as many as possible of the states of the Arab world, and it is not in our interest to have bad relations there. Second, it is certainly in our interests to assure the security, the sovereignty of Israel, and to assure it in particular ways that Israel can itself defend its security and its sovereignty so that the United States is not called upon to intervene in any way to try to accomplish that end. Third, it is in our interest to avoid situations arising in the Middle East that would lead to confrontations between ourselves and the Soviet Union. Therefore, and finally, it seems to me self-evident that it is in our interest to work for a settlement of the Arab-Israeli dispute. Certainly a continuation of that dispute is not in the interests or to the advantage of the United States.

I am going to sound more like a professor than a diplomat, perhaps, for a few minutes, because I would like to try to analyze the policy in rather specific phases as I have seen it evolve. To begin, I have to step back just a bit before the inauguration of the Nixon administration because the phases really are those that are subsequent to the Six-Day War up to the present time.

Let me also make the preliminary comment that, while there may be differences or appear to be differences in the policy toward the Middle East between the Johnson and the Nixon administrations, they are not differences in substance. There has been a continuity in the substance of United States' policy. There has been a difference in the perception of the role of the United States in its relationship to the problem, and that is where the differences emerge.

I am going to run through four phases before I am finished, but the first phase is the period of roughly the first year after the passage of Security Council Resolution 242; roughly the calendar year 1968, the last year of the Johnson administration. This, it seems to me, was a period when basically we had adopted a passive posture toward the problem. We had been active at the time of the negotiation and development of Resolution 242, which, as has been correctly pointed out, embodied certain principles that were set forth by President Johnson in his speech of 19 June 1967, right after the war. With one exception, these principles appear in only slightly different form in Resolution 242, and they have become the basis of policy, so far as the substance of a settlement goes, of this administration. So there is continuity there.

But in 1968 the United States adopted a relatively passive posture, basically. Having actively set up this framework for a settlement, the decision was taken quite consciously that we would then stand back, urge others to stand back, and let the two sides of the conflict seek to come together and work out the details of a settlement based upon the principles of that resolution, using the instrument of the Jarring mission that was established by Resolution242.

By the beginning of 1969, the first year of the Nixon administration, the situation in the area had deteriorated. There was an increasing breakdown of the cease-fire along the Suez Canal, an increase in the militancy of the Fedayeen movement, and all in all it was apparent that the stand-aside posture had not produced what had been hoped that it would produce—namely, an interaction between Arabs and Israelis that would produce negotiations and an agreement.

The second major foreign-policy decision of President Nixon was to take a more active part in trying to promote a settlement. This was done in the context of responding to a proposal that had been made by President DeGaulle prior to the end of the Johnson administration that the then four active, permanent members of the Security Council engage in Four-Power talks to try to see if they, among them, could begin to stimulate some progress toward a settlement. The decision was that we would, in fact, engage in these Four-Power talks. This was taken roughly in February of 1969. Now, one has to remember that this was in the context of an administration that had launched itself with the goal of replacing an era of confrontation with an era of negotiations. The Middle East was just one area where it appeared at that time in the perspective of 1969 that perhaps the theory of negotiations could be tested. So this was part of a larger global view of the foreign-policy role of the United States as the Nixon administration began.

The Four-Power talks began, and parallel with these we entered into bilateral discussions all through the year 1969 with the Soviet Union. Both sets of talks, at least as we saw them and certainly our purpose in them, were basically to try to see if it would be possible to reach agreement among the major powers on a framework for the negotiations that we all felt had to then go forward in the context of the Jarring mission. In other words, not to impose a settlement, not to write up a settlement and simply put a blueprint on the table, but to try to get some more precision in an agreed interpretation of the ambiguity of certain paragraphs of Resolution 242. All of this was designed, of course, to move a situation toward a total overall settlement of the problem as rapidly as possible.

From the point of view of the United States, the principal outcome of this year of what might be called *active multilateral diplomacy* was the development of a set of positions that came to be known as *the Rogers Plan*. This did not appear full-blown from nowhere. In effect, it was the result of positions that we developed and put forward over time during the bilateral talks with the Soviet Union and also in the Four-Power talks in New York. The totality of these positions became the *"Rogers Plan" of 1969*. We viewed it at that time not as a blueprint for a settlement to be imposed, but as a framework that, if others would accept it, both major powers and the parties themselves, it would provide a fair and equitable basis for negotiating the details of a settlement. What one sometimes forgets is that the Rogers Plan of that period was not accepted by anybody. The Israeli reaction to it was very sharply adverse, and I think this is widely remembered because it was also very public. What one tends to forget these days is that it was also not found acceptable by some Arab governments concerned, in this case Egypt, and it was not accepted in its totality as a common position between the United States and the Soviet Union.

I would say that the bilateral talks that year with the Soviets were useful. I think they produced a certain common ground between us on what we were trying to achieve, but they did not produce complete agreement either between us or between the parties concerned.

We went into 1970 with the Four-Power talks pretty well stalled, although still meeting from time to time, with the bilateral talks between ourselves and the Soviets in abeyance, with no negotiating process going on, and with a continually deteriorating military situation on the ground. This was the time of the war of attrition along the Suez Canal; it was the period, lest we forget, that there was a large increase in the number of Soviet military personnel in Egypt, called upon by President Nasser to bolster his air-defense system against the increasingly deep Israeli air raids that were Israel's answer to the artillery war of attrition along the canal. It was a time when the Fedayeen were increasingly becoming a state within a state in Jordan and threatening to cross the cease-fire lines into the occupied areas and into Israel. So, all in all, the situation was one that, as it so often is in the area, seemed to be increasingly explosive, and of course with greater risk than there had been in other periods of the history of this problem of major power involvement and confrontation over the local conflict.

It was against this background that we moved really to the next phase that I would call, for short-hand purposes, *a phase of unilateral* rather than *multilateral American diplomacy*. We put forward in the summer of 1970 what some people have called *Rogers Plan no. 2.* What the Secretary announced in his public statement at the time was an initiative to stop shooting and start talking. Basically, it was a two-pronged proposal, at our initiative, designed to accomplish two things: to restore the cease-fire along the Suez Canal, and to get the two sides themselves committed to a specific and common negotiating formula that would require at least certain *verbal* concessions by both sides to get within what we hoped would be negotiating distance of each other. The cease-fire part of this initiative took hold; it is sometimes forgotten today that the cease-fire originally was only agreed to for ninety days. There were two further extensions. It has long since run out, so far as any agreement of the two sides to keep it is concerned, but it has continued into its thirty-third month on a de facto basis. The negotiating formula that was devised and was accepted after considerable difficulty by President Nasser, by King Hussein, and by the government of Israel did not lead to the negotiations that we had all hoped for.

Let me point out in passing that that negotiating formula, simple as it seemed, caused a major crisis in both Israel and the Arab world. In Israel there was strong resistance to the language in the formula under which Israel accepted specifically the principle of withdrawal from occupied territories, and the wartime coalition cabinet was divided. It broke up as a result of this, (certain of the rightwing elements left the Israeli government), so it caused a major political crisis internally in Israel.

In the Arab world it was bitterly opposed by those elements who were also opposed to Resolution 242, who were opposed to a peaceful settlement: the militant Palestinian leadership, the Fedayeen, as well as a number of Arab governments, further removed from the fray.

Despite this, the governments concerned did accept the formula and there was hope that we were at long last going to make that negotiating breakthrough.

The next thing that happened—and this is part of the history of the problem that again sometimes tends to be forgotten in its sequence and its consequences—was that one part of the cease-fire, that part which called for, and under which both Israel and Egypt agreed to, a military standstill within a zone on both sides of the Suez Canal, was in effect violated on the Egyptian side of the canal almost as soon as the cease-fire went into effect, and there were changes in the military dispositions. Now, granted, as Dick Nolte has pointed out, these were air-defense systems, these were not offensive weaponry; nevertheless, the Israelis felt that the fact that the defensive system was improved on the West Bank of the canal would inhibit their ability to use their air power if the cease-fire were to break down. So it was clearly a violation of the standstill part of the cease-fire agreement; so massive, as it turned out, that the Israelis broke off the negotiations under Jarring almost before they had begun.

That brings us into 1971 and the third phase of American efforts. The first phase in 1969, while it had had some useful by-products, had not produced any breakthrough as far as a settlement was concerned. And so we had to look for other possibilities rather than simply throw up our hands and give up, given the premises from which we were then and are still operating.

Still in the realm of unilateral rather than multilateral diplomacy, a new idea came along about that time, just at the time that the Jarring mission had become completely paralyzed by the effort that Jarring made to get simultaneous commitments from Egypt and Israel to a formula of his own. This was a formula to which the Egyptians replied, as we characterized it at the time, in a more positive way than the Israelis, in the sense that the Egyptian reply did say that they were, under certain conditions, ready to enter a peace agreement with Israel—the first time that an Arab government had formally on the record stated this for all the world to see and hear. And it had always been one of the things that we had been told, and I think quite rightly so, Israel felt was necessary before there would be any evidence of a psychological change in the Arab frame of mind.

The Israeli reply, while positive in many ways, did conclude with this final sentence : Israel will not return to the lines of 4 June 1967. We said at the time that we felt this was unnecessarily negative, that our interpretation of Resolution 242—while it does not endorse those lines of June 4th, the old armistice lines, as the only secure and final and recognized borders—certainly does not preclude those lines either. The Israeli formulation in reply seemed to preclude those lines and therefore go beyond what we had felt was an equitable interpretation of Resolution 242.

In any event, the diametrically opposed replies to Jarring tended very quickly to freeze his mission in early 1971, and it has remained fairly well frozen ever since then. But at that very point, a new idea was put forth and it was put forth interestingly enough—and this is why it was such a hopeful idea—not by an outside power, not from Moscow or Washington or Paris or London, but from Cairo; a speech by President Sadat in which he threw out the germ of an idea. It was not made precise and specific, but in essence what he was talking about was a settlement in stages, under which the first stage could be the partial withdrawal of Israel from the canal in return for which President Sadat said he would undertake to clear the Suez Canal to put it back into operation for international commerce. Mrs. Meir very soon after that stood up in a public speech and said that Israel was prepared to consider this kind of an idea. Then in private channels both governments let it be known that they would like the United States to try to be the middleman between the two parties in seeing whether or not this idea could be translated into something more concrete and into specific actions on the ground. Most of the summer of 1971 was devoted to exploring this idea of what we came to call an *interim-Suez Canal agreement*. It was one of the main focuses of Secretary Rogers' meetings when he went to the Middle East and particularly to Israel and to Egypt in the spring of 1971. It was the same subject that took Assistant Secretary Sisco and me back to the Middle East, in that case to Israel, in July and August of 1971, trying in quiet diplomatic channels to see if this idea could in some way be used as the basis for the beginning of a process of negotiations that would ultimately lead to the final settlement of this dispute.

When we felt that we had gone about as far as we could in long-distance diplomacy, travelling from capital to capital and communicating through embassies, we made a suggestion that perhaps what was needed was a more intense negotiating process. This is what, for want of a better phrase, we call *proximity talks*; the idea being that the two parties would send delegations to the same city and hopefully even to the same hotel, if not into the same room, and that the American middleman would then try to get a process of round-the-clock negotiating going to see if the differences on this issue couldn't be hammered out. The proximity-talk idea attracted a certain attention and, ironically, as so often happens when one side is ready, the other side is not. There were clear indications in October of 1971 that President Sadat was interested in the idea of proximity talks. At that point there were problems from the Israeli point of view. By the time those problems were sorted out between us and Israel in early 1972, Cairo had begun to lose interest, had begun to feel that perhaps this was not quite as attractive an idea as it may have looked in its earlier conception. I believe one of the problems was that it looked increasingly to President Sadat like a trap, like an end in itself; not a first step in an ultimate final settlement, but a new de facto situation that, once achieved, might freeze the situation on the ground indefinitely. We had been at pains to try to convey to the Egyptian government that this was not our concept, that we viewed this as only a pragmatic way to get a process started, and that we would see it as leading to an additional process. Nevertheless, the idea did not germinate and the rest of that particular year, 1971, really was spent in keeping this idea alive without any very active progress being made.

In a way 1972 was a year of pause in American policy, for a lot of reasons that I won't try to go into here. But we did come out of 1972 with the situation not any further advanced, although in many ways not set back from what it was at the beginning of the year.

Just one other observation about this fourth phase, this phase that we are really still in, in our post-1967 diplomatic efforts. While 1972 saw no progress on the negotiating front, it was a year when two developments occurred that have changed in very important ways the negotiating context, or the global context, within which the problem has to be dealt with. It was the year of the Summit meeting in Moscow, and while the Middle East was not negotiated at the Summit, there was certainly an exchange of views. There was no resolution of the differing perspectives and aproaches that we and the Soviets have of the problem, but what did come out of Moscow in the statement of principles was an agreement that the United States and the Soviet Union undertook to prevent or to seek to prevent local conflicts around the world from becoming the source of confrontation between them. This did not refer explicitly to the Middle East, but quite clearly it had relevance to the Middle East. This took the Middle East out of the major power arena to some extent. I can not be so naive as to say it is entirely out of the major power arena or ever will be, but I think it did take it out to some extent.

The next step that in some ways followed from this, although from a lot of other causes, too, was the decision by President Sadat in July of 1972 to ask the Soviet Union to withdraw its operational military personnel from Egypt. The major power factor in the equation certainly has been greatly reduced as a result of the events of 1972.

Very briefly, where are we today in the first half of 1973? We are in what I would call a *phase of review and exploration* of the problem. I don't know whether there is going to be a fifth phase and I would not attempt to characterize what that fifth phase will be, because we have not got there. The policy decisions have not been made, other than the basic decision that the problem has to be looked at, has to be dealt with actively, and can not simply be ignored.

In summary, I think it might be useful if I could give what seems to me a kind of balance sheet of the pluses and the minuses in the area as we see them through the perspective of those dealing in Middle East policy in Washington. Unlike most balance sheets, when I get through you are not going to be able to tell whether we are in the red or the black, and I am not sure myself. But at least I can cite some of the factors that are important to keep in mind, because so often if we just read the daily headlines, we hear about and read about the minuses and forget some of the pluses, and there *are* pluses. First of all, there is the continued adherence of the principal parties to Resolution 242, that framework for a peaceful settlement. Second, there is still a cease-fire, and I would like to make it very clear that we do not see the cease-fire as an end in itself. Obviously, it is a blessing in terms of a saving of lives and resources, but certainly it is not an end in itself. We recognize that the cease-fire on its own can not survive indefinitely without some political progress. Third, there is greater stability in some countries in the area than was the case as recently as two years ago. Jordan is a prime example, and it is very important. Jordan has a key role in any settlement; obviously that is where the heart of the problem still is, and it is one of the states on the borders of Israel and the occupied territories. Finally, the risk of major power confrontation has been greatly reduced. And one more plus, which flows in a way from the continued acceptance of Resolution 242, diplomatic options have not been closed by any party to the conflict. There has been tough talk, there has been belligerent talk, but I would note that even in President Sadat's last speech where he said that he has about lost hope and must get Egypt ready for battle, he nevertheless said that Egypt will continue to pursue the diplomatic avenues.

Those are not inconsiderable pluses, given the intractability of this problem over the years, and it is well to keep them in mind to balance the gloom and the depression that comes from reading the daily headlines.

On the minus side, very briefly, the principal negative is that there is no negotiating process. There has been no negotiating process on this problem in any meaningful, genuine sense of the word, not only since 1967, but not really since the armistice agreements were negotiated way back in 1949. The absence of any negotiations, of any progress toward a settlement, does lead to a radicalization of militant forces in the area; it increases and strengthens the hardliners and militants, and undermines the moderates who would like to see conciliation and accommodation. We have seen this increasingly in the growth of terrorism as a tactic of the Palestinian national movement, of the Fedayeen, who has moved increasingly from the political field to classical guerrilla warfare to terrorism in third countries, a process that I think is not going to be entirely eradicated until one begins to get at the roots of the problem.

Let me just say as a final word, to try to put all this in perspective: the United States does make certain judgments about this. One, we do not think that this status quo is a stable status quo, or that it is durable for any protracted period of time. Another observation that is very interesting is that, despite the fact that at one time or another our policy approach has been under attack by one side or the other, and in recent months in particular from Cairo, nevertheless, there does seem to be a general recognition in the area and in the world that the United States does have a role to play, not as a negotiator or a participant but as a catalyst, as someone supportive of a settlement. Probably there can not be a settlement without the United States being involved in helping to get that process going.

I don't know whether progress is going to be possible or not. Given the history of the problem, it would be foolish in the extreme to make predictions of progress. But within these basic principles that we have established—security for Israel, a settlement that will meet the legitimate concerns of all of the parties including the Palestinians, and the concept that an agreement must be a negotiated agreement arrived at between the parties concerned and not worked out by outside powers—within these principles, we are going to continue to work for a settlement. It is in the interest of the American government, of the American people to do this. Whether it achieves all that it sets out to achieve or not, the very process is important and therefore is one that we do intend to keep going. Thank you very much.

MR. FINGER. Thank you, Roy. I sleep much better knowing that you are in the State Department.

We are to adjourn at six. I can therefore call on just one speaker. The others we shall hear after dinner. Ambassador Jacob Doron has asked to speak. I now call on him.

AMBASSADOR DORON. I was glad today to hear mention made of the Charter of the United Nations, but it is not enough to pay lip service to the Charter, and I should like to remind the audience that in 1948, even before the 14th of May when Israel came into being as an independent state and was not yet a member of the United Nations, the Arab countries that attacked Israel were already members of the United Nations, bound by the Charter, and yet they openly, without any shame, without even trying to hide the fact of their aggression, attacked Israel in violation of their obligations under the Charter, their attack in those days was sharply denounced by many countries, including the representatives of the Soviet Union at the United Nations.

I was also glad to hear Mr. Osman mention yesterday that Egypt wanted peace, and today he reminded the audience of the fact that our colloqium title is "search for peace."* This is very good. But the trouble is this enormous discrepancy with which we are always faced between statements sometimes made abroad—always only for foreigners—and statements made for what is known as *internal* consumption, in other words for Egyptians or Arabs. And sometimes the very same statements, the same interviews reported in *Newsweek* or other American or European media are censored and doctored out of recognition in the Arabic version. Every slightest mention of anything that could look like a positive approach or, God forbid, mention of peace is scissored out and censored out of the version published in Arabic.

If Arabs want peace, as Mr. Osman said yesterday, we should be only too happy to oblige. But peace can not be presented to them on a platter ready-made without any contact whatsoever with Israel preceding it, and with all that has been lost in 1967 also arranged neatly on the same platter and handed back. This is a situation that has never existed in history, and it is very difficult to bring it about even now.

Quite often we hear from people—and by "we" I mean we Israelis, who are in contact with Arabs—that some Arab statesmen in private conversations say that they would have loved to come to an arrangement with Israel, to make peace with Israel, but that in this case they would be torn to bits by their own people at home. Personally, I don't believe this. I believe that there are very many people in Arab countries who really want peace, but their leadership

* Original title was *The New World Balance and the Search for Peace in The Middle East.*

does absolutely nothing—indeed it does it all to the contrary—to make it easier for those people to consider peace and eventually to agree to peace and not to tear those leaders to little bits.

All the internal propaganda media, the mass media, of the Arab countries are directed in a completely different direction and they do not make it easier for their people eventually to agree to peace.

I am not going to occupy too much time with Mr. Osman, but it does occur to me that when he said today that it was only Mr. Rouleau, and nobody before Mr. Rouleau, who mentioned Palestinians, he must have forgotten that a gentleman introduced himself as a Palestinian yesterday and that Palestinian gentleman made certain statements. I do not agree with his statements. I understand the gentleman is primarily a poet, and I am glad to concede him poetic license, but this is certainly not a permission to make statements of the kind he made yesterday. He spoke of threats allegedly issued by Israel against Arab countries. There are no such threats, there were no such threats. Israel was prepared and is prepared to enter into meaningful negotiating process, and then Israel will see if this readiness exists on the other side as well.

Today Mr. Ovinnikov introduced himself as a historian and as a diplomat. Yet he immediately managed to misquote in a most tendentious manner one of the basic provisions of Resolution 242, and he went on to say that peace could be achieved, provided at least two major points were accepted by Israel. The points he quoted were Arab claims that he said Israel should completely agree to. He did not make the slightest mention of any rights of Israel. I do not have the time to enter into a disputation with him at present here, but I would only say that this is rather significant and I would leave it at that.

Ambassador Nolte made some interesting statements. There are two points I can touch upon now. The one was when he said that the Arabs ask for justice, and one of the main injustices that has to be set aside at this stage is that we should go back, we should revert to the position obtained before the 5th of June 1967. But I believe that we all still remember that on the 4th of June 1967 there was no peace, there was no readiness for peace on the part of the Arabs vis-à-vis Israel. The more modest of the Arabs, the more moderate, would then sometimes say that their idea of removing injustice was to revert to the 29th of November 1947 situation. But the less moderate, between 1947 and 1967, and certainly before 1947, had as their slogan the cry of the Mufti Haj Amin el-Husseini, "Slaughter the Jews." These things were not, even today unfortunately, really mutually exclusive, but are cumulative. This, of course, makes things not so easy for us.

If I may, in conclusion, mention what was said by our chairman yesterday—and in this manner I really close the circle because it started off yesterday with this as well—that many difficult situations found their conclusion by means of negotiations in the course of the last year or two. One of those difficult situations posed not only political problems, but also geometric problems. There was the question of designing a suitable negotiating table in the appropriate shape. Now, the Egyptians at one point in history were pretty good at designing geometric bodies, and the pyramids still bear witness to that: so my hope is, and it is sincere, that one day we might sit down with the Egyptians and as a first step design an appropriate table, a few chairs for good measure, and then perhaps we could, if that goodwill exists, achieve a real peace, a durable and stable peace, and then it does not matter whether we call it *salaam* or *shalom*. Thank you.

MR. FINGER. Thank you, Mr. Ambassador. We now stand adjourned until dinner at seven. We will then have two statements, one by myself and one by Lord Caradon; we shall conclude with a summation by Sam Merlin and then have further opportunity for general discussion.

(End of third session.)

The Nixon Doctrine and the Middle East
by Seymour M. Finger

MR. FINGER. Ladies and gentlemen, I shall now begin my remarks on the topic, "The Nixon Doctrine and the Middle East."

You may ask the question: why did I choose this topic? The answer is, I didn't. The topic chose me. Mr. Merlin and I had prepared an outline of relevant subjects, and we were most fortunate, far beyond our expectations, in getting excellent speakers for every one of the topics except this one. Moreover, the general subject of American policy in the Middle East is one I have followed with deep interest over the years.

First, what is the Nixon Doctrine?

It was expressed succinctly in President Nixon's report of 18 February 1970 on *American Foreign Policy for the 70s* as follows:

> Its central thesis is that the United States will participate in the defense and development of allies and friends, but that America can not—and will not—conceive all the plans, design all the programs, execute all the decisions and undertake all the defense of the free nations of the world. We will help where it makes a real difference and is considered in our interest.

What is new about this doctrine in regard to American policy

209

toward the Middle East? My own conclusion has been that there is nothing essentially new about it as far as the Middle East is concerned; that, in fact, there has been a continuity of American policy going back at least till 1967. I was, therefore, much comforted when Roy Atherton confirmed that view. Essentially, the principles laid down by Lyndon Johnson on 19 June 1967 continue to be applicable to American policy, and they are consistent with the Nixon Doctrine. All except one of those principles was embodied in Resolution 242. The one that has not yet been embodied—that is, the matter of limitation of arms shipments into the Middle East—remains an objective of American policy. So I think it would be fair to say that there has been a consistency about American policy since the spring of 1967.

I don't think that that consistency is accidental, nor is it traceable to the personality or the prejudices of either President Johnson or President Nixon. One has to go back to the spring of 1967 or perhaps a little further to the fall of 1956, when all of the major members of the Security Council participated in a guarantee that, in exchange for the withdrawal of British, French, and Israeli forces, the Gulf of Aqaba would be kept open and that a U.N. force would stay on the border between Egypt and Israel in order to keep peace in an area that had not known peace for some eleven years.

I was in the Security Council during those very dramatic days of May 1967, when one by one the guarantees disappeared. The U.N. force was withdrawn; Aqaba was blockaded. And when the United States' delegation urged in May 1967 that there was an extremely serious and dangerous problem in the Middle East that required the urgent attention of the Security Council, I can recall Soviet Ambassador Fedorenko accusing American Ambassador Goldberg of being hysterical, declaring that there really wasn't much to worry about.

My purpose tonight is not to place the blame on one country or another, but simply to indicate that the American government found itself unable in that period to come through on any of the guarantees made in 1956. The United Nations Security Council did nothing to lift the blockade. The force, U.N.E.F., was removed at once. The NATO alliance did nothing, the maritime powers did nothing, and the United States did nothing. It is therefore not surprising that in June of 1967, when President Johnson made his speech, he placed particular emphasis on settlement by the parties directly concerned. He was not prepared to put the credit and faith of the United States on the line again.

It may also be that, since the country was already enmired in Vietnam, President Johnson was leery of another involvement. That is a matter of speculation. What is a matter of record is that the American government has consistently refrained from getting itself directly involved in the dispute over this six-year period and has placed its major emphasis on the parties themselves working to achieve a settlement. This position was reemphasized by President Nixon on May 3 in his fourth annual Report to the Congress on *U.S. Foreign Policy for the 1970s*:

> But a solution can not be imposed by the outside powers on unwilling governments. If we tried, the parties would feel no stake in observing its terms, and the outside powers would be engaged indefinitely in enforcing them. A solution can last only if the parties commit themselves to it directly. Serious negotiation will be possible, however, only if a decision is made on each side that the issues must be finally resolved by a negotiated settlement rather than by the weight or threat of force. This is more than a decision on the mechanics of negotiation; it is a decision that peace is worth compromise.

As Roy Atherton pointed out earlier, there have been variations in the degree of activity. There was a period of some months following June 1967 when the United States refrained from activity in the hope that in some way the parties themselves would come to a settlement. I can recall at that time that there was bitter criticism from governments in the area, and particularly the Arab governments, that this showed a lack of interest or a lack of concern. This was followed by the cooperative effort that resulted in Resolution 242 of the Security Council, which as of this moment remains the only anchor or guideline, whatever its ambiguities, on which any efforts toward peace can be built. Then, as Mr. Atherton also pointed out, there was the effort at Four-Power talks that, at least from the way I read the telegrams—and now that I am out of government I can be perfectly frank about it—never got anywhere and never stood much chance of getting anywhere. But I suppose they were a gratifying exercise for some of those who participated.

The next major step taken—and here we get into the period of President Nixon and what might, therefore, be called part of the *Nixon Doctrine*—was the statement made on 9 December 1969 by Secretary Rogers, of which we have again heard from Mr. Atherton. I think this represents a very substantial effort, because in the context of many of the speeches we have been hearing—some of which have veered to one extreme, some to the other—one would not have expected the Secretary of State of the United States, speaking with the full authority of his government, to say that the boundaries to be negotiated should represent only insubstantial changes from the armistice lines. For a country that was supposed to be blindly obedient to whatever Israel wanted, this was indeed a surprising statement, and the very bitter and sharp reaction from Israel reflects that fact. It was, as I understand it, the view of Secretary Rogers that only by giving that kind of assurance could there be some sort of negotiation among the parties; that is, that the Arab governments would be reluctant to get into negotiations, even indirect negotiations, unless they felt that the stakes had somehow been limited to insubstantial border changes.

For a similar move to come from the other side, we could imagine the Soviet government and Foreign Minister Gromyko making a statement that there must be direct negotiations between the parties. Because, in effect, the deviation between what Secretary Rogers said on 9 December 1969 and the Israeli position is virtually as great as the deviation between the Arab position and the statement that there should be direct negotiations. So I think that the step should not be underestimated.

I might add also that, despite the protests of the Israeli government, the position stated by Secretary Rogers has never to this date been countermanded, amended, revised, or changed. I would then have to add that all of the great powers in this age have learned, as we witnessed again last summer, for example, that a small, friendly power has its own views. It is one thing for the United States to state a view on what Israel should do. It is quite another thing for Israel, as a sovereign country, to take a decision to accept that viewpoint. It is understandable in the light of what had happened earlier and what happened in the spring of 1967, when all outside assurances were swept aside, that Israel would have certain misgivings about accepting advice from outside. Be that as it may, it does seem to me that the statement by Secretary Rogers was a push in the direction of negotiation.

The key factor, of course, is whether there should be any territorial adjustment at all. You can refer to either Resolution 242 or to the Charter to prove opposite conclusions. I shall deal with the territorial adjustment question later.

However, one provision of the Charter that seems to be generally overlooked is Article 33, and I would like to read that :

> The parties to any dispute the continuance of which is likely to endanger the maintenance of international peace and security shall first of all seek a solution by negotiation, inquiry, mediation, con-

ciliation, arbitration, judicial settlement, resort to regional agencies, or other arrangements, or other peaceful means of their choice.

It seems to me that the policy of the United States under both the Johnson administration and the Nixon Doctrine has been aimed precisely at achieving the implementation of that article. One speaker earlier mentioned that the Israeli position had shifted from wanting *secure* boundaries to wanting *defensible* boundaries. I must confess that it is difficult for me to see the difference. If we lived in a world where there was true collective security, in the sense that every nation of the world felt bound to go to the defense of every other nation, where alliances would be overlooked, where the U.N. had a force superior to that of any member nation, where the U.N. could truly guarantee to any country in the world that its security was fully protected, then borders might become unimportant; heights and plateaus and plains would become of little significance. But as long as we live in a world where states have not matured to that point —and I happen to hold that point as an ideal that may take us some time to reach—it is not surprising that states seek to have such frontiers as will enable them to protect their security.

Therefore, while I certainly would refrain from endorsing any particular claims of the government of Israel, I think one has to understand that a country that found all international guarantees swept away in 1967 would give some concern to having a peace settlement that is virtually self-enforcing. In the present context *self-enforcing* would mean that all parties have accepted the settlement. It does not mean a peace imposed by Israel. It does not mean a peace imposed by Egypt. Certainly it does not mean a peace imposed by the Soviet Union, the United States, the Security Council, or any other combination of powers. It is all very well to say that nothing less than total withdrawal to the June 4 lines will do. The question is, how do you get there? The question arises, what means could one envisage to force a withdrawal to the June 4 boundaries, given the feelings of the governments concerned, and what assurance is there that such boundaries are desirable, given what happened during that particular period?

As a number of representatives noted during the June 1967 meetings of the Security Council, the situation prior to June 5 was not one of stability or peace, and it is hard to believe that the whole solution consists in a policy of total withdrawal. Nor is that what Resolution 242 says. The terms of that resolution were negotiated very carefully. The absence of the word *the* and *all* from *withdrawal from territories* was negotiated carefully over some time. Consequently, it would not be a correct statement to say that implementation of the resolution necessarily involves total withdrawal. Indeed, wherever the borders might be, it is hard to escape the conclusion that the only formula for genuine peace is for the parties somehow to settle their differences.

All right, people will say, this is utopian; their differences are irreconcilable. This I heard many times during our discussion yesterday and also today. It is not a matter of communication. The parties understand each other; they each know what the other wants, but they want different things. Consequently, you cannot reconcile the differences.

I would accept that if I had not lived through the last twenty-five years. The Austrian state treaty took ten years to negotiate. Who would have expected five or six years ago that the two German governments would agree jointly to enter the U.N.? Who would have expected the government of Willy Brandt to recognize the Oder-Neisser frontier, thus ratifying the loss of large areas of formerly German territory as part of a deal to give the Soviet Union what it regarded as defensible frontiers? Who would have expected that a chancelor of the Federal Republic of Germany would sign a treaty recognizing that? I think it proves that the qualities of Lord Caradon, especially his patience and optimism, are the indispensable tools of anyone engaged in the business of international relations. One can not give up, one can not simply conclude that there is no agreement possible between the parties.

Now the question is: what sort of negotiating process might lead to an agreement?

Proximity talks are one thing that have been suggested, most often by the United States, perhaps because the original armistice agreement was worked out at Rhodes through proximity talks. Under whose auspices? Could it be Dr. Jarring? Or if the parties do not agree on Dr. Jarring, how about Roberto Guyer, who now has a position similar to that which Dr. Bunche occupied some years ago. How about Lord Caradon, who after all has shown his considerable skills as a conciliator? I find it hard to believe that no way can be found to get some sort of proximity discussions going. I was interested that Ambassador Doron, when he spoke earlier, did not speak exclusively of bilateral discussions. I forget the exact words he used, but it seemed to me that a meaningful negotiating process was what he mentioned, and if this represents the position of the government of Israel, I can conceive of a meaningful negotiating process that would not necessarily be bilateral talks or would not necessarily begin as bilateral talks.

A second suggestion is that of a coordinated effort by the Soviet Union and the United States. I think that type of cooperation is always helpful when it works. When there was Soviet-United States cooperation in 1965, the Security Council was able to stop the war between India and Pakistan. When the Soviets and the United States disagreed in 1972, the U.N. could not stop the fighting in that same area of the world. Soviet-American cooperation is often useful, and it could certainly be useful in reducing the arms supply to the area.

Insofar as interpretation of Resolution 242 is concerned, there is really relatively little difference between the Soviet proposal of total withdrawal and the Rogers position of insignificant and insubstantial changes in the lines as they existed. There is a difference, I admit, but not enough to prevent cooperation.

In one other way such cooperation could be useful. The less the parties directly concerned are inclined to feel that somehow they can be spared from facing hard facts, that somehow they can be spared difficult negotiations and hard decisions, the more likely they are to work toward a solution themselves.

Another approach that has been suggested is an international conference on Palestine. Personally I have not much faith in the value of an international conference in producing solutions to deeply complicated disputes of this type, unless in the corridors of the conference some real talks could be managed. All of us who have been around the United Nations know that it is very, very rare—perhaps one time in a thousand—that anything really gets settled on the floor of the United Nations. The real agreements take place in the private discussion.

What is absolutely necessary, however, is to consider the situation of the Palestinians, to consider self-determination for Palestinians, as well as for Israelis. Self-determination could take the form of a separate West Bank state or a United Kingdom of Palestine and Jordan or federation, thus providing a national state of Palestine.* That problem certainly must be taken care of.

There is also the question of ambiguity on both sides. I was struck by the fact that, on the one side, criticism was made of Israel because of its ambiguity on just exactly where it feels defensible borders would be, and on the other side criticism of the Arab states because in certain broadcasts aimed outside their own countries, their emphasis was on willingness to live in peace, whereas within the country the

* For specific proposals, see Appendixes 6 and 7.

emphasis was quite different. I can see where a state such as Israel would feel that the very unwillingness of parties to sit down face-to-face and talk with each other implies that there is not a willingness to grant full recognition and to live as good neighbors in peace in terms of the Charter. So I can see how Israel would wish that ambiguity to be cleared up either through final face-to-face talks or through some other means. Likewise, I can see where the Arab states, confronted with various possible maps drawn according to statements by various Israeli spokesmen, some official, some unofficial, might feel that to engage in negotiations before some of those ambiguities are cleared up might be dangerous from their standpoint. Yet, how will these ambiguities be cleared up unless the parties communicate with each other?

And so I return to the question that I asked yesterday when we began our proceedings. If the Cubans and the Americans can negotiate, if East and West Germany can negotiate, and if Poles and Germans can negotiate, why must the Middle East be the only area where peace can not be sought through negotiations.

And another question: Is there any other way to find a stable solution except through negotiations?

I do not feel at all optimistic about the status quo and its endurance. From an Israeli standpoint, I don't feel at all sure that, given ten, twenty, thirty years, the military position of Israel will be secure if hostility remains in the area. During the discussion yesterday, reference was made to how wrong people had been about Israeli military capabilities in 1948. I can remember how wrong American experts were about Chinese capabilities in 1950. The notion that people who have not yet modernized can not learn to fight is a delusion if one looks at history; therefore, I would see no long-term security for Israel in a continuation of the status quo, no matter how pretty the borders may look on the map.

With those remarks I leave the real solutions to Lord Caradon.

I believe Lord Caradon is much too well known to all of you to require any extensive introduction. He is a man who is impatient to get things done and yet has enormous patience in overcoming difficulties. Also, he is a man who certainly is one of the outstanding orators ever to appear at the U.N.

Is Peace Possible? What Are the Options?

by Lord Caradon

LORD CARADON. I am grateful to all of you for allowing me to come
and join you this evening. My qualification for speaking is that I did
spend fifteen years when I was very young in the Middle East. I was
for seven years, for instance, in Nablus, two or three years in Amman,
and then in Irbid and Aqaba. All of us are faithful to our first loves,
and my first love was Jerusalem. And therefore I do feel strongly
about the questions we discuss, and when I go back, as I did a week
or two ago, it was a matter of intense feelings to see the lovely
plain outside Nablus covered with the huts of the refugees, many
of them refugees for twenty years. And I also went to Natanya where
so many years ago I was cooperating with those who were establishing
the settlement in their difficult early days. I was proud to see that
there is still a Foot Square in Natanya. My name originally was Foot,
and the other day I accused the Mayor of Natanya of having taken
that sign down. He said, "No, we keep it there as a historic relic."

Then I have been associated with the Middle East while I have
been in the United Nations, and I have been involved in efforts to
find some advance toward a general settlement. Moreover, I did have
the great excitement of going back to both sides of the Jordan a

week or two ago, and I have many recent impressions very clear in my mind. It is therefore difficult for me to select a particular topic, except that I would like to speak to you on one main theme. I speak to you as an advocate of the need for an independent initiative.

I do not believe that it is likely that we shall wake up one morning and find that the Israeli government has put forward proposals that are acceptable to the Arabs. I certainly don't think it is likely that the Arabs are going to put forward proposals acceptable to the Israelis. I do not believe it is likely or possible that the Soviet Union is going to offer proposals that will be acceptable to everyone. And I myself think, speaking with respect, that there is no possibility that I can see that the United States, with all its commitments and with its constituency, will put forward its own proposals that will be acceptable to all. But I do not exclude the possibility of an independent initiative, and I think it may be worthwhile to go back for a few minutes to speak of the initiative that we took in 1967.

The Resolution that we speak of, Resolution 242, could never have been proposed by the United States, and it certainly could not have been proposed by the Soviet Union, but it could be proposed by a third party and accepted by both; therefore, I believe that the solution may be that something will be offered that can be accepted by both, but that could be presented by neither side. Therefore, I wish to speak out on the principle of the independent initiative. And since you all speak Arabic, I would say that I speak to the principle of *Sulh,* and that is what I have been speaking of in Hebron and Nablus and Bethlehem and Amman and Jerusalem and Natanya in the last few weeks, the idea of an independent initiative.

So to go back for a moment to what happened when we did propose an independent initiative in 1967, when people really thought there was no prospect of making any progress at all. We had been all that summer in the General Assembly. Nothing had come out of it except bad feeling and bad language. I remember walking one day from my delegation on Third Avenue to call on Foreign Minister Abba Eban in the Plaza Hotel. I know him well, and we went over all the ground together thinking of any way forward. At the end, before I left, I said to him, "Do please sum up the Israeli case; what is it? How can I get it clear in my mind what you mainly need?" And he said, "Remember what I say. . . . What Israel needs is permanent peace." Not unreasonable it seemed to me, and I remember it from time to time: what Israel mainly needs is permanent peace.

I walked from the Plaza Hotel to the Waldorf Towers and called on Mahmoud Riad of the then United Arab Republic and had a full discussion with him. I know him equally well, and at the end I put the same question to him, "What is it the Arabs must have? What is it that it is difficult for you to go back to Cairo without getting?" And he said, "Easy to tell you, of course; we must see a withdrawal of Israeli troops from occupied Arab territory."

Not surprising it seemed to me that he should say that. All the Arabs would wish to see the restoration of Arab territory, and one does not justify the permanent acquisition of territory by war.

A lot of things had to be thought about: the Straits of Tiran and Suez and demilitarized zone, certainly the great problems of the Palestine refugees. But the essence of what we suggested was a withdrawal to permanent peace.

When an independent initiative has been taken, you are usually beset by both sides and we were at once assailed by the parties concerned. Both sides did their utmost to drive us off the initiative we intended to take. But in the end, we thought we had the nine votes needed for passage.

It was a Sunday evening and we were going in to the Security Council to vote on Monday. They called me up from my delegation late that Sunday night and said that it was no good. What had happened? At the last moment there was a new resolution put down by the Soviet Union. I immediately began to calculate how the votes would fall and who would vote for the Soviet resolution, who would stay with the British resolution, who would take refuge in abstention. One doesn't go to bed of course. All night long the telegrams were going to all the main capitals of the world. At the Council and on a Monday evening to vote, people were lying in wait for me, particularly the Indian delegation I remember, urging that we should make some amendment at the last moment. No, it was too late. We must go through to a finish. But then Deputy Foreign Minister Kuznetsov of the Soviet Union wanted to see me. Would I see him alone? Certainly. We went into a little room by the Security Council and he said, "I want you to give me two days."

"Oh, no, ask me anything else but don't ask me that. We haven't been to bed for several nights, and we think we have the nine votes." We spoke to each other very frankly. He said, "I am not sure that you understand what I am saying to you. I am personally asking you for two days."

We have certain working understandings together, and reluctantly, of course—I wondered what my delegation would say, what my government might say—I went back into the Council and said a last-minute request had been made for a postponement of this all-important vote, and therefore I asked for an adjournment to the following Wednesday.

So on Wednesday we are back in the Council. There can be no more delay now; this is it. We had been debating the Middle East for three weeks. But everybody is holding back; the only one down to speak is Syria. So we settle down to listen to a speech from Syria. We don't expect the solution to the Middle East problem to come from a Syrian speech, so every now and then I send round to the President's table to discover who else is down to speak. The Syrian speech is drawing to an end and no one else is down. Sometimes it happens in the United Nations that something that has been awaited for a long time and, suddenly, unexpectedly, the crisis comes. And so Syria finishes, the President calls for a vote on the British resolution and the vote comes. Then there is a sort of ragged cheer from the back of the press gallery and I suddenly realize it was a unanimous vote.

Thus, on the 22nd of November 1967, the Russians, the Americans, the Latin Americans, the Africans, the Asians, and the Europeans, all of us, voted together for the principles of settlement in the Middle East. The Soviet Union withdrew its own resolution. In my country there was some tendency to self-congratulation. Not easy to get a unanimous vote on a British resolution on the Middle East. I wrote immediately to the London *Times* to say that yes, credit for the unanimity should go to Deputy Foreign Minister Kuznetsov. He was prepared to go back to his government and to work for full agreement instead of backing the resolution his country had offered.

I think it worthwhile telling that story, because I think it has some bearing on the way that I believe things might again progress toward a settlement. I believe in the independent initiative. I believe that it is possible that something can be proposed that neither side could think of inaugurating on its own nor could the advocates of either side. But if it would be put forward by an independent authority, an independent delegation, an independent individual, conceivably, it could be accepted by both.

When I was back in the Middle East the other day I was asked wherever I went to explain exactly what this Resolution 242 means. I defended the resolution; it was carefully drawn, correctly drawn, and I think it is sometimes misunderstood. There are three main provisions about boundaries in the resolution. First, the principle is stated in the preamble that there can be no acquisition of territory by force, no justification of the acquisition of territory by war. That is a basic principle. Therefore, it follows, and it is said in the operative section of the resolution, that there must be a withdrawal of Israeli troops from occupied territories, territories occupied in the recent conflict. But then the third point is also of vital consequence: where to? And people say we did not say. Oh, yes, we did. We said in the Resolution that the withdrawal must be to secure and recognized boundaries. And when we chose those words we chose them carefully. The boundaries can not be secure unless they are recognized: a country does not get security except by agreement; that is the only security it can get. And therefore it was well to repeat this. When I said it in Hebron and in Nablus, it was well understood what I was saying, and it was even well received in the Israeli press. I know the 1967 boundaries; I know them very well; I know them as well as anyone as the boundaries that existed before the war, before the 1967 war. They are not suitable boundaries. They are where the troops happened to be on a certain night way back in 1948. The Arab Legion was across the road from Tel Aviv to Jerusalem, and therefore there has been a detour ever since. They are not suitable boundaries. What about Mount Scopus? It was an absolutely undefensible boundary.

Of course, the boundaries must be redrawn. I know them too well to believe that they are satisfactory permanent international boundaries. And therefore we said there must be new boundaries, they must be secure and they must be recognized. And security does not come except by negotiation for agreement.

When in Jerusalem the other day, I met an Israeli general and I said to him that I had served through the Arab rebellion of 1936–38, and I knew something about security in these parts. "Surely you must realize that this idea of security being obtained by putting down a camp, a fort in Sharm el-Sheik or a row of forts down the Jordan Valley in hostile territory, or a couple of forts on the Golan Heights against the wishes of the local inhabitants, is not security? A boy scout knows that is not security; that is insecurity; it is a guarantee of insecurity. Surely you must know, you are a general. We have respect for the Israeli army, surely you know that that is not the way to achieve security. I used to sit in the Nablus fort in 1936, and they used to come and fire at us from the hills. Every night they fired at us from the hills and would go home for breakfast in the morning. A fort in hostile territory is an inducement to insecurity, and that is known by every military authority in the world. "Surely," I said, "you can not believe this nonsense."

He said, "I don't believe it is. The only security that Israel has is its air force." Security by forts in hostile territory is of no use; it goes back to the northwest frontier, something that is entirely out of date, something that is ridiculous in modern times.

I was much struck by the spirit in Jordan. I expected to find a miserable state of affairs there: a kingdom cut in half with revenues largely lost. I thought Jordan would be in a wretched condition. Not at all. Jordan is now set on a go-ahead economic development, something exciting to see. They took me in a helicopter to show me the high-level canal down the Jordan Valley to irrigate the valley on the Jordan side and to see the great Zerka Dam. Then, even more exciting, I saw in the desert east of Zerka the use of subterranean water, as far as the eye can see are the wells that are bringing the water from a water table that is usable for irrigation over an enormous area. They tell me that in Jordan they are satisfied they are able now to get ahead in economic development quickly, in agricultural development, in a way they had never been able to contemplate before —something like a miracle.

And then I found something else that was also encouraging and unexpected, a result of the occupation on the West Bank and to that extent a credit to all concerned: the people on the spot, the people who matter do not believe any longer that the borders must be barriers. I think that the essential change that has taken place, partly as a result of the occupation, is that the Arabs certainly—and I spoke to them in the refugee camps and the villages and the towns—don't speak now as if it were a necessity to establish barriers between one side and the other, not at all. They know that there is going to be a living relationship between Israel on the one side and the Arab areas on the other, and this is an entirely new attitude, and a most encouraging one.

The third thing that struck me was that I went around and spoke to the Palestinians in the camps on both sides of the Jordan and spent two weeks talking and also listening and hearing the unanimity of the Palestinians. No one actually hears them, of course; they have no voice. But I went there particularly to hear what they had to say; it seemed to me it was important. The Israelis are not inarticulate, and the Fedayeen can be heard, but the Palestinians, the people living in the camps and in the villages, are not heard. I found that on the main issues there was a practical unanimity, which again I find encouraging. And what is the unanimity about? I was surprised that there was agreement from both sides of the Jordan, the refugee camps and the towns and villages tell me the same things.

The first thing they say is that they dread the prospect of a partial peace. The proposal to open the canal and leave the Palestinians to rot in the mud and misery of their camps is something that is intolerable to them. When King Hussein said he would regard that as a stab in the back, I know what he meant. If the Egyptians come back into the canal towns and the canal is open, people may be apt to say, well, it's all over. Not all over. The main issue is the future of a million and a half Palestine refugees and what is going to happen to them. If the canal is settled, a great temptation would then arise to say that nothing more need be done. And this is a persistent view among every one of the Palestinians I could speak to; they want a *comprehensive* peace.

The second thing they are quite determined about is that they are not going to take a *dictated* peace by direct negotiations. What does direct negotiations mean? Where the Israelis occupy all the Arab territories and where they have stated and continue to state day by day that they intend to hold them? That they intend to hold Jerusalem; that they intend to put down their settlements wherever they wish in Arab territory? When they say that they not only hold the cards, but they are also going to keep them—is that fair direct negotiation? When you go cap in hand and beg them to give you something that they are prepared in their generosity to allow you? That is not negotiation; that is dictation. The Arabs demand that there shall be some holding of the ring, some impartial acceptance of the necessity of a settlement that is just and not merely something grudgingly granted by the victors. They will not tolerate merely to be told. They would rather stay as they are than be told that they can be given a few stretches of the land that they know are their own anyway.

And third they have their intense views on the subject of Jerusalem.

Now before I come to that and finish, I would ask how we can break out of the deadlock? This is a matter of method, of means. It is very urgent because there is to be a meeting in the Security Council, a special meeting called with all the foreign ministers to be there. If that meeting takes place and there is no progress and nothing except a standard exchange of abuse, then I think the prospect is indeed extremely gloomy, and it would be better not to call the meeting at all. But there is an opportunity within two or three weeks, not more than three weeks from now, to deal with this question on substance. We are not now going to deal with the substantial methods of the future, but it will be possible, if there is a means and a method of escape from the deadlock, to find it now. It seems to me tremendously important; we should not wait for the meeting and hope that something may happen, because nothing will happen if we don't think about it beforehand, if we don't examine every possibility of a new method of escape. And surely there are other methods.

Ambassador Jarring advanced his proposals three years ago, and since then nothing has happened. But does that exhaust all the processes of conciliation and arbitration? Aren't there other methods of finding some way to proceed to compose a comprehensive peace? Is one method the panacea? Are we to sit down and give up as we have done for three years to our shame?

We have an opportunity and we have a necessity now to think of the actual means. I think there are a score of ways in which progress could be made if we are prepared to think again on the basis of a method of approach. Someone spoke a little scornfully just now of the possibility of a peace conference. There has got to be a peace conference. We have to deal with all the great issues that arise from Jerusalem downwards. They all have to be dealt with and we are not going to deal with them only in hotel bedrooms. We have got to have a peace conference. We can not possibly have a peace without a peace conference. Moreover it must be an international conference. But what steps should be taken? I agree we are not going to get a peace conference next week. If there is going to be a conference in the end and agreement is reached and security comes from the agreement, how do you proceed in that direction, how do you make the preparations? Is it beyond the wit of man that we should find some means or method toward the time when the parties concerned and others can sit down together? All sorts of methods can be used. They have not been properly explored. The original approach was, I think, the right one. We recommended that there should be an intermediary in the form of Dr. Jarring, that he should seek to establish understanding and agreement. He made an effort, I admire the effort he made, but when that effort could not be continued, should everything be abandoned? Should we just leave it? It might well be that an initiative from the nonpermanent members of the Jewish Council might not be a bad idea. There are many different means of going forward. Is the international community barren of solutions?

If we are going to have a peace conference, how would it be to appoint the chairman of the peace conference in order for him to prepare the way with the parties concerned and to lay the common ground on which they could eventually come together?

Finally there is a question of primary importance. And here it may be that there will be very strong feelings of difference, but so much the better.

I think the core of the whole question is in Jerusalem and that we not only want ingenuity in dealing with the methods, but we also want magnanimity in dealing with the substance. I would say that if the Arabs thought they could reconquer Israeli Jerusalem, it would be a ridiculous delusion. But if the Israelis think they are to hold Arab Jerusalem indefinitely against the wishes of all Muslims, all Arabs, and, indeed, the overwhelming majority of the international community, then I think we can forget about talk of peace. There won't be any; it is not possible. I tell you from my knowledge of speaking to the people concerned. It is not possible that they are prepared to consider that Arab Jerusalem should be conquered and held by force forever against the wishes of the Muslim community, the world, and all Arabs. All Arabs will be united on this issue.

I think that it may be that Jerusalem is not the *barrier* to peace but is the *gateway* to peace. There is an Arab Jerusalem, it is well defined, and why should it not be that the Arabs administer their own affairs in their own town? Why should it not be that they should not have an Arab administration, an Arab Jerusalem, with Arab sovereignty. There will also be an Israeli Jerusalem, of course, which will be the capital of Israel, with Israeli sovereignty and Israeli administration—an undivided city with freedom of movement between the two. There is freedom of movement now. Could not that be a pattern for the relationship, a different relationship of equality and even friendship that is not now impossible between the two communities on the basis of equality. Equality is very important, for I don't think we will ever get peace if it is to be merely dictated to a subject people conquered in war. The idea of Jerusalem becoming the center of justice, peace, equality, freedom of movement, with a United Nations' presence in order to insure that that freedom of movement is contained. I am not in favor, nor is anyone else, of a fully internationalized city. It was proposed by the U.N. originally, but it will be opposed by the Arabs, and certainly opposed by the Israelis. Is it not worthwhile thinking about the possibility that the breakthrough will come when the Israelis say yes? When they say there is no reason why we should ensure permanent animosity of all our neighbors in order that they should administer an Arab city?

Therefore, the very intransigence of the present position may provide the starting point for the eventual settlement. But I have no doubt in my mind, there will be no peace if there is no hope, if there is no disposition to move on the question of Jerusalem. I had talks with Teddy Kollek, the Mayor of Jerusalem, whom I greatly respect; he does not take my view, but he himself has spoken about Arabs in a free city, which is not so very different. You then come down to the question of sovereignty. What is sovereignty? It is a sort of abstraction. Is it worthwhile enduring enmity and ensuring bloodshed and mounting arms forever in order to maintain an abstraction? I do not think so. And so I would suggest to you that there is a way that we can go forward in making the holy city the gateway to peace instead of its barrier.

I have said it everywhere I have gone; I said in Arab towns as well as Israeli centers that I don't blame the Israelis. I would not give an inch myself until I knew what I was going to get, not an inch. And I don't blame the Arabs for saying that they will not go cap in hand and just take what they are given by a victorious army. I don't blame either side. I blame ourselves, and I think it is we who should be considering and thinking all the time about the independent initiative and where it can come from and where it should be: first of all on the question of method and then on the question of substance. I believe that that is how it must come out, and that is what our task is in the next week or two and thereafter.

MR. FINGER. Thank you very much, Lord Caradon. Your vivid account of the birth of Resolution 242 and thoughtful proposals for new approaches to peace are a notable contribution to our proceedings. As for a conference, I would hope that a peace conference would come at the *end* of the negotiations. What I had doubts about was the notion of an international conference now on Palestine as a separate thing. But even that, if it would help, why not? ?

One other thing I must say in defense of Secretary Rogers: while I can understand the feelings of those on the West Bank, Secretary Rogers as recently as 15 February reiterated that he conceives of the Suez agreement as an interim step toward a final solution, which is the full implementation of Resolution 242. He sees it, therefore, as an attempt at arriving at the same thing you envisage. So while this may not be the best method, it is an attempt made, I believe, in good spirit.

It is now my privilege to call on another distinguished and recognized authority on the Middle East, the Executive Director of the Institute for Mediterranean Affairs, Samuel Merlin. I should also like to take this occasion to express well-deserved appreciation to Dr. Merlin, who so ably bore the brunt of preparing and organizing this colloquium.

Summation and Projections

by Samuel Merlin

MR. MERLIN. The general theme of this colloquium was: how can one fit the Middle East into the new world balance? One may perhaps ask whether the Nixon administration really was instrumental in bringing about a new world balance. One may perhaps answer that in life and in history there is always a new balance and that it is always precarious. Nor has the present one yet crystallized. We do not really know what conformation it will take or even if it will take on a definite form. One is, however, justified to assert that there is a new policy of the United States, and in this respect I don't think I agree with some speakers who emphasized that the global strategy of the present administration is nothing but a nuanced continuation of the policies of its predecessors. I believe on the contrary that the policy of the Nixon administration is based upon new concepts and proceeds from new origins. It seems to me that the policy aims at restoring to the United States—hence, at least to some extent, to other powers—a better sense of reality, a better sense of proportion, as well as of the limitations upon American power and American financial, political, and military capabilities—thus, a sense of the

227

inherent limitations upon American aspirations and American aims on a global scale.

In view of all this, American foreign policy is bound to become, at least psychologically, less aggressive and less provocative and less dogmatic. It is not any longer a crusade against would-be and worldwide conspirators, real or imaginary. Nor is it anymore a crusade for certain dogmas. It is no longer a drive to bring freedom and democracy to far-flung places, regardless of whether their inhabitants are already mature for freedom and democracy. It is no longer a policy that strives to bring salvation to the whole world. It is rather a policy that aims at creating a global structure with built-in safeguards for peace and stability—from a long-range point of view.

In the Middle East especially, there is quite an innovation of this new strategy, namely, that America does not deny any more the right of other powers, and especially of Russia, to exert influence and to be present in that region. President Nixon on more than one occasion very clearly and very emphatically declared that America recognizes the right of Russia and of any other power to be present in the Middle East, to exert its own influence, and to try to create friendships with the peoples, with the governments in that area. What America would not be willing to tolerate is the predominance of one power against the right of any other.

Then there is the Nixon Doctrine. Of course, it is still not crystallized, it is still tentative, it is still in an experimental stage, but generally speaking it has been interpreted, and I believe rightly so, in the sense that the United States will no longer intervene directly in various conflicts, but will help its friends, if they are capable, to help themselves. But, so far, this is understood only militarily. For example: If President Thieu of South Vietnam will demonstrate the reasonable assurance that he is in a position to withstand the pressures of the North and the Vietcong, then the United States will provide large-scale military assistance, that is, it will send him lots of hardware. If not, then it is too bad.

In the Middle East the United States will help Israel to defend itself as long as it will not require direct participation of American manpower in its wars with its neighbor.

Here, however, I have to remark, because I believe that I have to take exception to a widespread idea that almost became a truism: that the United States is an unconditional ally of Israel. I think that this is a misconception. Israel fought three wars. In 1948 it won, thanks to Czechoslovak arms. It won that war mainly because of the political and military help of the eastern communist bloc, while the supposedly greatest friend of Israel, President Truman, in the moment of Israel's greatest need, when an attempt was undertaken by several Arab states to nip the new nation-state in the bud, at that crucial juncture, President Truman declared and imposed a very effective arms embargo. The second war in 1956 was won, not only thanks to French arms, but also because of a collusion with Great Britain and France, who in combined operations attacked Egypt. The third war in 1967 was won thanks to French Mirages. Whether there will be a fourth round, we don't know. But if another war breaks out, it will be for the first time that American Phantoms will appear as a decisive factor in the Middle East military balance. Perhaps in the unforeseeable future, some kind of an alliance between Israel and the United States will take shape.

But to come back to the Nixon Doctrine, I believe that it has to be given a deeper meaning than just extending military assistance to friendly nations who are capable of taking care of their security. I think this Doctrine is much more than that. It has a global meaning in the sense that nations should behave responsibly in international affairs, that they should not be obsessed by military preoccupations, and that their national policies should pursue constructive aims of political stability, economic development, and social progress. This is the profound meaning of the concept "capable of helping oneself." And it is such nations who will deserve to get assistance from the U.S. and other powers in order to maintain their security, to preserve their independence, and to achieve economic and social progress. In terms of the Middle East, it may mean that both Israel and the Arabs should consider their military requirements not as the only national preoccupation exclusive of anything else, but they should also consider the more inclusive and long-range requirements of peace and stability—and this not only in their own interests, but also in the interests of the world community. It is with such a perspective and on such a basis that both can expect far-reaching assistance from the United States and from other powers.

There is also the widespread idea that if it were not for the great powers, everything would be just fine and dandy. The Arabs say the actual enemy is the United States. What would Israel be without the United States? Israel says the enemy is Russia, because what would the Arabs be without Russia? The fact is there was a conflict between Arab and Israeli nationalism long before the United States and Russia were on the scene. The conflict has to be viewed and analyzed not as something artificially provoked by the maneuvers of the big powers. On the contrary, the conflict is deeply rooted in the geopolitical realities of the region itself. It is a clash between two opposing forces in the region. Though local in origin and nature, its scope transcends the region because both sides try to enlist the support of the superpowers, who are not averse to exploit the situation to their own advantage. It would therefore be in the interests of the antagonists directly involved to seek ways and means toward a mutual accommodation and conciliation.

Then there is the widespread idea stipulating that the present impasse is a result of the mutually irreconcilable attitudes of Israel and the Arabs. In my mind, it does not exactly fit the true nature of the conflict in its present phase. Attitudes can be irreconcilable only if the antagonists themselves know what their attitudes are and are willing to define them. This is not the case now in the Israeli-Arab conflict. Neither side has a clear idea yet what it wants, what its aim is, what objectives it wishes to achieve. If there are irreconcilable attitudes that can not be bridged, it is *within* the attitudes of *each* of the parties respectively. Generally speaking, it is probably fair to say that the policymakers of Israel, supported by the majority of public opinion, would like to keep all or most of the territories conquered in 1967. Yet the Israeli government is reluctant to make this its official policy, because this is not the only thing Israel wants. It wants also to remain a predominantly Jewish state—that is, demographically Jewish. But keeping the territories with its inhabitants threatens the demographic character of the state. Therefore, the Israelis would like to keep the territories, but not the Arabs. This is like squaring the circle. Since the Israelis did not find a solution to their irreconcilable attitudes, they stick to the status quo, which in their view absolves them from arriving at a decision one way or another.

A similar predicament plagues the other side. Egypt, for instance, would like to arrive at a peaceful settlement with Israel. But at the same time it finds itself committed to the "just cause of the Palestinian people." However, the Palestinians who speak both in words and terror not only do not want peace with Israel, but also consider their just cause as nothing less than the dismantling of the State of Israel and substituting in its place a Palestine-Arab state. Of course this is not a basis for peace, by the farthest stretch of the imagination. Yet the Egyptians consistently refuse to divulge what *they* understand by the phrase *the just cause of the Palestinians*. More than that, they never repudiate the definition of the Palestinian Fedayeen organizations, asserting time and again that it is up to the Palestinians to define their own terms. But until then, there will be no peace agreement between Egypt and Israel either. This, too, is like squaring the circle. The tragic complication in the Middle Eastern conflict is that neither the Arabs nor the Israelis are yet clear in their own minds as to what their aims are, what their objectives are, and how they intend to go about achieving a settlement.

A few words need to be said about the emotional climate in which the Israel-Arab conflict is being discussed in both camps, as well as among their respective friends and apologists outside the region. We know of the torrents of hatred and abuse coming from the Arab side. No invective against the Israelis is too strong. No restraint upon atrocity propaganda is imposed and no murderous deed committed by the Fedayeen is ever genuinely condemned. But there is also contempt and denigration on the part of many Israelis and their friends abroad, vis-à-vis the Arabs. Some voice the opinion that the Arabs, at least from a military-technological point of view, are congenitally or innately inferior. I, for one, got the impression that echoes or hints of these attitudes of contempt could be discerned yesterday in some of the discussion on the military balance in the Middle East. Such statements, regardless of how well documented or academic they may sound, are disturbing, especially when voiced by Israelis or their Jewish defenders abroad. We should remember that anti-Semites preached for centuries the congenital or generic inferiority of the Jews. Learned authors like Arthur Gobinaue published his essay on the subject and titled it, "The Inequality of the Human Races." This was also the thesis of Stuart Chamberlain in his, "Foundations of the Nineteenth Century." But there is no need to go back a century to find examples of this philosophy of contempt. It is in the work of our own contemporary Arnold Toynbee, who referred to the Jews as the fossils of historic civilizations, postulating that they are not creative and referred to Israel as some kind of a reincarnation of Nazism. In my view, Jewish scholars, even if motivated by a sincere search for truth and having a wealth of documentation at their disposal, must pause before indulging in sweeping and generic statements that are certain to be regarded by the Arabs as offensive, racist, or contemptuous.

There is yet another aspect to this psychological climate. In Israel there is a learned man—a general and a professor, the author of several well-documented and exhaustive studies—whose publications all deal with one subject: the hatred of the Arabs toward Israel and the Jews. It has become an obsession with him. For a decade he has dedicated his life to this task of selecting and collecting Arab atrocity utterances—whether speeches or articles or excerpts and summaries from books—in any and all countries—all dripping with poisonous hatred. His historiophilosophical conclusion is that there is just no way and thus no chance to arrive at a conciliation with the Arabs.

I personally have very little sympathy for this single-minded dedication. I do not think it is a constructive effort. I guess that in the Arab countries parallel studies are being undertaken to select and collect everything derogatory and contemptuous that was said by Israelis or Jews against the Arabs. That is not a constructive effort either. I don't believe it is even illuminating. I don't accept the premise that hatred is eternal. As a student of history, I long ago came to the opposite conclusion—that hatred is not eternal, not even among Semites.

This brings us to yet another aspect of the problem we were discussing in this forum : should one pay attention to what the other side, the antagonist, the enemy says? Should one believe him? Of course one should, if the utterances are taken in the right perspective and within their context. Generally, I think it is wiser and more prudent to take seriously what people say. The Jews especially should adhere to this rule. Had the Jews taken *Mein Kampf* seriously, subsequent events might not have been the same as they were. When the Arabs say that they want to destroy the State of Israel, all the Arab apologists and all the Arab friends say that the Arabs do not mean it, that they say 'it for internal consumption. I reject that. I say that if Nasser in May 1967 said that the next war will bring the situation back to status quo ante 1956, and that after that he would start a campaign to bring the situation back to status quo ante 1948, it meant that he spoke of the destruction of the State of Israel. Conversely, if President Sadat says he is ready to make peace with Israel and will sign a peace agreement and recognize Israel's sovereignty, its boundaries, and so forth, I believe that what one has at least to do is to look into it very seriously, because this is great news, this is sensational news.

It seems to me that there is only one way to get out of the impasse, if at all : negotiations. I don't believe that the status quo can endure and last forever or even for a long time. I am old enough to know that no status quo lasts in private life, and I do not think that it lasts in history. And then I am not so sure that the status quo would work only in favor of Israel.

Many Israelis and their friends abroad are convinced that the status quo will last many years and that time works in their favor because of the Arab's inability to fight a modern war. Whenever I hear this I am quite surprised, because for centuries the Jews were often depicted as a nonmartial people, totally lacking military prowess. Their enemies accused them of cowardice. Yet, not only were they to become a nation capable of defending itself, but in the process they also developed the best army in the world. And it is my hunch that they have the best army in the world precisely because of their self-consciousness in this particular field of human endeavor. The Jews have for so long been accused by their enemies of lacking martial virtues and have for so long poked fun at themselves, (and this was always the saving grace of the Jews—to joke about themselves), on the same subject, it was their determination to overcome this weakness and surpass everybody else in the art and spirit of warfare.

Conversely, the Jews who were so creative in the fields of art and science in the Diaspora; who, in the first decades of the twentieth century brought about an effervescence and explosion of culture, literature—both in Eastern Europe among the traditionalist communities, as well as in Central and Western Europe among the assimilationists—that gave birth to the Yiddish and Hebrew masterpieces in modern literature and from whose spiritual milieu a Freud and an Einstein arose; yet the Jews, when established in their own country, living the life of an independent nation, have not thus far produced any world-shaking masterpiece, nor any individual spiritual giant of world renown. Of course, Israel is only a quarter-of-a-century old and one may expect that in the future she may still astonish the world not only in the field of military triumphs, but also by victories in the battlefield of the spirit. My hunch is that this lack of a spectacular spiritual or artistic breakthrough is due to the fact that the Israelis took it for granted that in these fields they have nothing much to worry about—after all, they are the eternal people of the Book. By the way, the Jews are known and pride themselves as astute economists. I do not think that the strongest part of Israel is its economy. All this is just to warn against thinking of the Arabs as destined or doomed to remain forever inferior in the art of modern warfare.

Military feats from one side or another will not bring a solution to the impasse. Other avenues have to be tried. First, and above all, we have to confront the issues squarely and realistically.

The best way to get out of the impasse is to start negotiating. And negotiations should not be obsessive about territories, but about the nature, the scope, and the instruments of peace. Territories are only one aspect of these negotiations.

Professor Kerr spoke about the ambiguities in the attitudes of the protagonists. I believe he touched upon the heart of the problem. Somehow all the parties to the conflict get away with murder in the sense that they say things in such an ambiguous manner that can be interpreted in contradictory ways and deprive the proclaimed attitudes of both Arabs and Israelis of any serious meaning. Only in the process of negotiation can each side test the sincerity of its antagonist. Only in the process of negotiation can one try to discern the meaning of the professions of peace on either side. Israel can not claim that the Arabs do not want any kind of peace with Israel, for the simple reason that Israel did not really try to clarify the issue: what actually do the Arabs mean and propose from the point of view of Israel's security and destiny when they speak of a *just and durable peace*?

One of the great difficulties in this whole situation is that in so many respects the Jews and the Arabs are so similar. The Jews suffer from what is called the *Massada complex*. Massada is indeed a disturbing symbol. Of course it is primarily a symbol of heroism, of national self-sacrifice. But what is its meaning, even when you add the words "Massada shall not fall again"? Ultimately, it is a symbol of suicide and defeat.

The Arabs, on their part, suffer from what may be referred to as the *Phoenix complex*—that is, of being burned and then rising from the ashes. This, too, is some kind of irrational desperation. For in this warped psychological attitude, the punishment is certain—to be defeated and humiliated—while the redemption is uncertain.

For rational analysts, these emotional or mystical attitudes are puzzling. When all is said and done—or not done—what remains for certain is the need of the parties to the conflict to embark upon a process of negotiations. According to the Nixon Doctrine, only those who help themselves are worthy of assistance on the part of the United States and the international community at large.

MR. FINGER. Thank you, Mr. Merlin, for your highly illuminating comments. I have on my list ten people who have asked to speak. In United Nations' language, "I am in the hands of the committee." But may I suggest that if you would like to go on for fifteen minutes and hear a few speakers, we may do that with the understanding that anyone who wants to leave . . . .

PROFESSOR SINAI. Mr. Chairman, I would just like to protest against Mr. Merlin's complete distortion of what I had said.

MR. MERLIN. Did I mention your name?

professor sinai. It was obvious.

mr. finger. The floor is not yet open. I am sorry, but if we are going to have a discussion, it must be fair and orderly.

professor sinai. But in fact, I was attacked by implication, and I think you should give me the opportunity of a rebuttal to a comment that is really beyond contempt. In any case, I would just like to say that I never used the words *congenital, innate,* or *inherent,* or any other terms of that kind. I merely spoke about the fact that the Arab world at the present moment is in decay. I have now completed a book about the decadence of the modern world and the decadence of the United States, and that does not mean to say that I am talking about something congenital or inherent. And if you, Mr. Merlin, do not understand concepts like the rise and fall, or the rise and maturity, and decadence or fall of empires and civilizations, then you should hesitate before entering into these complicated matters.

mr. finger. Now we come to the question of whether we have a discussion and how long it should last. May I suggest that fifteen minutes would be a suitable period. All right. I have ten speakers down, so I would say that perhaps two minutes would be the time allotted to each. I realize it is difficult.

professor gruen. May I make a suggestion, Mr. Chairman? I would suggest that the stated positions of the excellencies, representatives of the various states, who have had an opportunity to air their views on many occasions not be reiterated here, but rather in the limited time remaining that you will decide to call upon those people here whose views are unknown to most of us and who have not yet been heard.

mr. finger. Thank you, I shall try to follow that suggestion and hopefully people will feel that I have selected accordingly. The first person, and I will apply strictly a two-minute limitation, is Mr. Selden.

mr. selden. This afternoon I was heartened to hear Mr. Osman invoke international law, and I intend to address myself briefly to that. This evening I must confess that I was appalled to hear Lord Caradon express a disdain for international law. If I drew a wrong inference from what he said, then I earnestly apologize, but when I heard him say that sovereignty was an abstraction that may be ignored and that there is an Arab presence in Jerusalem that must be recognized, then I must confess that I feel justified in my inference. Sovereignty is what determines territorial title and integrity, not mere possession. Possession as a sanctity for title is jungle law, and under that jungle law Israel is in possession and entitled to remain there until she is dispossessed. But Israel is not there by virtue of possession. Israel is there by virtue of sovereignty that followed an orderly course in pursuance of international law.

Arabs had never, never, never in history any sovereignty in Palestine until the end of the First World War. The sovereignty over the Middle East was in the Ottoman Empire. The Ottoman sultan at the end of the First World War, pursuant to international law, orderly international law, surrendered title to those lands to the principal Allied powers. They in turn delivered that title in various ways to a variety of emirs and sheiks and sharifs, including the honorary Arab land of Egypt. Three major territories were not considered quite ready for sovereignty, and former Mesopotamia (now Iraq) was mandated to Britain; Lebanon, and Syria, were entrusted to the fiduciary control of France. Palestine, the whole of Palestine, with no distinction as regards to Trans-Jordan, was entrusted to the British for the stated purpose of developing a national home for the Jews, with a secondary reservation that the rights of the non-Jewish community then existing in that territory should not be disparaged in any way. The United Nation, which succeeded to the League of Nations, subsequently gave title to Palestine, by then truncated to some 10,000 square miles, to Israel. In defiance of that international, very carefully stated legal precept of legal sovereignty, the Arab members of the United Nations invaded Israel. The situation now is that there is no sovereignty; there are no borders. Israel has not done anything in violation of the law because none exists. The borders have not been settled. The borders that prevail under international law are the ones that were laid down in 1947 by the United Nations.

MR. FINGER. I have both Mr. Osman and Ambassador Doron on my list, but I should like to give the floor to other speakers who are previously inscribed. I will call on Mr. de la Gorce.

MR. FRANCOIS DE LA GORCE. I do want to underline the interest of my country in the problem of the Middle East. We are bound to the future by many links, intellectual, cultural, and political. This is an important region for our security and also for our economy. But there is a name that has hardly been mentioned in this debate : the name of Europe. I think, and this is the sincere wish of our delegation, that the cooperation of European countries and their consultation may one day bring some substantial contribution to the settlement of the problem. We recognize that the power is not in our hands, it is in the hands of the United States and the Soviet Union, but I really think that the part that Europe will play has to be kept in mind, and it will certainly make great efforts to play its part successfully.

My second point is with respect to the necessary involvement of the international community for a settlement. Of course, our dearest wish is that the parties concerned may get together and find a solution, but past experience from this point of view is certainly not encouraging, and we are inclined to believe that some external stimulation, perhaps a little more than simply influence, can play an important part in this endeavor. From this point I must say that I do not agree completely with what Ambassador Finger said about the Four-Power consultation. I think this could be very useful. In any case, we welcome the efforts of the United States and of the major powers in order to bring about a settlement, and we have our interests in regard to all the possibilities of bringing the support of the international community to bear for a settlement. We really think that the problem is of such magnitude that it can not be left entirely in the hands of the parties, but others must enter the situation to see that the present deadlock is broken. This does not mean that peace should be imposed, of course.

My third point is just to repeat what some speakers have already said about a certain sense of urgency. It is an unfortunate circumstance that, in the case of a problem like this, when we are in the phase of confrontation and acute crisis, it is argued that nothing can be done, that no attempt can be made to try to reach settlement. When we are in the phase of relaxation, it is argued that it is not necessary to act. I think it is time to break this vicious circle. We hope that the present phase of relaxation of tension, of growing cooperation between East and West, and especially between the United States and the Soviet Union, but also between Western Europe and Eastern Europe, will foster a general feeling of confidence that is growing and that could offer the opportunity for new efforts that are more determined. That the opportunity will not be lost this time. Thank you, Mr. Chairman.

MR. FINGER. Thank you, Minister de La Gorce. I am so impressed with the ability of the French representative to say so much so clearly and so concisely: It has been demonstrated again. I regret that because Senator Javits had to speak yesterday instead of today, Mr. de La Gorce did not hear his statement on Western Europe and tension in the Middle East.

I now call on Mr. J. C. Moberly, Counselor of the British Embassy in Washington.

MR. MOBERLY. The point I wish to make is not made in my official capacity in any way, but is purely a personal one, and part of it has already been made this evening. But there is one thing

I think that did not really come out sufficiently, it seemed to me, in the discussion here yesterday and earlier today: that is, the answer to why the Middle East situation should be different from the Korean, the Vietnam, the two parts of Germany, and so on. What is different, why is there an obstacle to negotiation? I submit that the real basis, the real difficulty about negotiation is a psychological one; that one party in this case was so overwhelmingly defeated that there is a psychological barrier that has to be broken down. Any attempt or agreement to enter negotiation is seen as an intolerable humiliation that can not be borne. This is why I think the argument that, when President Sadat sees that he has no military road to follow and that there is no way to make progress from his present unenviable position except through entering an unconditional negotiation, he will not draw what seems to us to be the logical conclusion and say, "I shall go and discuss it with the Israelis and see what we can get by going that road." He has to be given a lifeline to get him there, and that lifeline has to be something that will remove that sense of defeat and humiliation.

In looking at the situation between Egypt and Israel, how is there to be such a lifeline? I think it would be illusory to suppose that the Egyptians will be able to enter negotiation in circumstances where they don't feel that they are at least going to recover at some stage at the end of the road what they regard to be and what has always been Egyptian territory. I don't think that need be incompatible with Israeli security. It is a question more of giving Sadat some sort of formula that need not exclude special arrangements in Sinai and elsewhere, strips of lands as you heard in a formula, but will at least give some kind of reassurance at the end of the road. One way of approaching this would be if the Israeli government, instead of stating their security requirements in a negative way, (for example, we will not return to the June boundaries), could say, rather, in dealing with Sinai, that we are prepared at the end of the road to restore Egyptian sovereignty in this area after a negotiation where we are satisfied that our security requirements are met. In such circumstances, perhaps that terrible psychological blockage might be overcome. But I don't think we shall find any negotiations until some way, there may be other ways people can think of, that can break down this psychological barrier.

MR. FINGER. I thank you, Mr. Moberly.

I now call on Dr. Riebenfeld.

DR. RIEBENFELD. A two-minute limit makes it possible to forego those circumlocutions that out of politeness make statements often less than clear. May I then start by saying that it is typical that in an assembly like ours, an English representative would rise to proclaim the age-old Egyptian character of the Sinai, an absolute matter of Arab honor. Surely, the British of all people know best that before 1906 the Sinai was not Egyptian and that it was British imperial policy that added the peninsula to British-Egyptian administration. This does not necessarily mean that Israel has to keep the Sinai; it only means that there are certain great power habits that are not abandoned easily.

Lord Caradon, who once was a District Commissioner in Palestine, threatens fire and bloodshed, all over Islam unto India and Pakistan—one is reminded of those British speeches during the thirties—unless Jerusalem comes partly under Arab sovereignty. I doubt whether the reaction of Islam or even of the Arab world must tend in this direction unless, of course, British and other professional Arabists in this meddlesome tradition make it their business and travel the world to preach such ideas.

God preserve us from "independent initiatives." The peoples of the Middle East are quite capable of starting the process of negotiation by themselves. However, I agree with my Arab friends that the Palestinian question is the core of the problem of Middle East peace. But the Palestinian question embraces all of the territory of historic Palestine. If it is a question of justice that preoccupies the Arab mind, it would seem that it is only in all of the former Palestine Mandate area that a just agreement can be accomplished.

There does exist a Palestinian Jewish state that is called *Israel* and there does exist a Palestinian Arab state called *Jordan*. There are not one million and a half refugees who are "homeless." One may doubt whether King Hussein thinks of reducing Amman again to the townlet of 30,000, which it was in 1948, and of sending the bulk of his people—economically as productive as described by Lord Caradon—back to Israel. The Palestinian question has been solved, in fact. It has been solved in the Jordan that is Eastern Palestine. What remains is a question of psychology, of explanation, or reconciliation. There the greatest and most fruitful contribution could be made exactly by British statesmen and scholars by explaining truthfully : "We have made certain promises to the Arabs. We could not keep them all. We made certain promises to the Jews. We could not keep them all. The Partition principle announced in 1937, in the Peel Report, aimed at an honorable solution. Although we abandoned it before the war, the international community later arrived at the same principle. What ensued was conflict and war. However, the

British government had already in 1922 taken measures to secure the Arab character of the Trans-Jordan part of Palestine, which now has developed into a flourishing community. It is time for the two communities to sit down together and settle the problems outstanding between them."

What I suggest is that nations which have influence and special knowledge—especially nations that have once been in charge of strife-ridden territories—have a responsibility to foster peace instead of prolonging issues of divisiveness. I have read Lord Caradon's articles in the London *Times*. He is very enthusiastic about King Hussein's scheme for a "United Arab Kingdom" that would establish a small "Province of Palestine" on the West Bank, as a part of the kingdom. This sort of proposal looks very much like a humiliation of the Arab people of Palestine. Why, out of the 45,000 square miles that constituted the area of the Palestine Mandate until 1946, the Palestinian Arabs should only call 2,000 square miles their own? While the Jews of Palestine have over 8,000 square miles and the kingdom of Jordan occupies 35,000 square miles? If I were a Palestinian Arab leader, my first thought would be : how to break out of these 2,000 square miles? Into Israel? Into Jordan? In any event, this is a prescription for continuous warfare. Those who think differently should think again.

I suggest that once it is realized that Palestine, in history and under the Mandate, covered the territory east and west of the Jordan —not just until 1922, but during the whole lifetime of the League of Nations—the solution of the outstanding Palestine issues becomes much easier. There exists already a Palestinian Arab state. Here diplomats, British and others, could apply their skills—so could scholars.

MR. FINGER. Thank you. Now there are a couple of criticisms that have been made of certain points made by Lord Caradon. I do not know whether he wishes to reply or not. One request has been made to put a ten-second question to him. I call on Dr. John Stoessinger.

DR. STOESSINGER. Thank you. I have no statement, only a question of Lord Caradon. Do you, Lord Caradon, see any virtue in the possibility of a small U.N. presence in Jerusalem before the holy places in a quasi-extraterritorial role, which would not disturb the secular jurisdiction by Israel over Jerusalem, but would give Jordan a role again in some form of internationalization?

LORD CARADON. I will refrain from answering other questions that have been raised that must be well pursued, but we can not pursue them tonight. But I would like to answer that particular question. I am especially interested in the proposal that there should be a Statute of Jerusalem, not as originally proposed for the internationalization of the city, but to ensure that there is freedom of access for everyone to the holy sites and freedom of worship throughout the holy city. This is possible within whatever political structure is eventually accepted. Therefore I think that this is a proposal that should be pursued, limiting the question to freedom of access for all to all holy sites and freedom of worship within the holy city. Whatever happens, and even with almost any conceivable answer to the political situation, such a statute might well be accepted by all concerned. I believe there is a method of advancement that will not solve the political issue, but may, indeed, provide what the world would wish, whatever political answer is obtained. that the holy city is, in fact, accessible to all.

MR. FINGER. Thank you, Lord Caradon. I have now just two speakers left, Mr. Osman and Ambassador Doron.

MR. OSMAN. Thank you once again, Mr. Finger. Very reluctantly I am taking the floor simply to rectify some of the historical statements that have been made just now. I should have got this intervention mainly to reply to the reckoning of the issue of direct negotiations, as stated by the representative from Israel. However, I am constrained to refer to the simple distortions of what has been said now about the Sinai and its belonging to Egypt. I believe that no individual of good faith, and I stress this, *of good faith,* of minimum level of learning, would dispute that the Sinai has been, is, and will continue to be a part of Egypt.

Now you are talking again about this question of negotiations, and I am glad that the Honorable Lord Caradon has saved me the trouble of answering that. We can not negotiate as long as a part of our country is occupied. This will not be a negotiation then, it will amount to simply—and I am using the words of Lord Caradon—*capitulation and dictation.* Let Israel spell out its real intentions. Is she really and genuinely willing to make peace or is it just a camouflage and is the real intention rather to gain more lands?

And as for Resolution 242, we are privileged that Lord Caradon is among us tonight. He stated in the preamble paragraph to the resolution the inadmissibility of acquisition of land by war. Of course, it took Israel a long time to acknowledge that resolution or even to accept it as a whole. And then, if we come to a matter of interpretation, nobody can dispute that the Sinai Peninsula is a part of Egypt.

Mr. Doron, as long as the bulldozers change the demographic

structure of the occupied lands, as long as the assimilation policies and coercive policies are observed in the occupied lands, Sinai mainly, do not expect peace, do not anticipate peace. Peace can not be gained by occupation. Peace can be gained by justice, and that is why we have accepted Resolution 242 and that is why we have answered favorably to Ambassador Jarring.

Now about designing tables : yes, we are good at that and we are proud of the fact that we are good designers, but the impasse is not attributed to a lack of tables. The table is there and I am referring to Ambassador Jarring's table that Israel abandoned long ago because she made every effort to render Jarring's mission abortive, with the result that this distinguished diplomat was sitting idle doing nothing for the last three years. We have accepted his memorandum. What has Israel done to Ambassador Jarring's mission? She told him she would not return to the 4th-of-June lines. And unless a favorable answer comes from her, and she admits the sovereignty of Egypt over Sinai, the impasse will still continue.

I must say that I am thankful to Ambassador Finger because he referred to and invoked Article 33 of the Charter that stipulates, among other things, the role of meditation. Ambassador Jarring is in fact the mediator assigned to bring peace in the Middle East through his mission that is based and emanates from Resolution 242. Thank you, Mr. Chairman.

MR. FINGER. I now call Ambassador Doron.

AMBASSADOR DORON. Mr. Chairman, ladies and gentlemen, I think the hour is too far advanced tonight to start going into repetitious argument or even to embark on new arguments. I still have one minute to my credit from my previous intervention this afternoon. All I would need now is perhaps a minute and a half to read out something that covers one-and-a-quarter typewritten pages, and I think it is only fair if I tell you now what it is. I would like to read to you, with your kind permission, Mr. Chairman, an excerpt from a message by Prime Minister Golda Meir on the anniversary of Israel's twenty-fifth year of independence and statehood. It is dated 27 April 1973, and this year we are celebrating our twenty-fifth anniversary on the seventh of May. The excerpt reads as follows:

> We crave for peace with all our hearts. We have left no stone unturned in our constant pursuit of it. Tragically, throughout these past twenty-five years we have not been granted its blessings. Three times in 1948, 1956, and 1967 the whole nation was compelled to take up arms in defense of its very existence. National defense and national building have had to proceed simultaneously. Though we

have had to accept the reality of no peace, we persist in the faith that peace will one day come, because it is also a fundamental need of all the peoples in our area. Conflicts elsewhere are moving toward their solution through negotiation by the nations involved. We, too, shall continue to work and strive for the day when negotiations with our neighbors will begin and a reconciliation will finally be reached. Certainly these are long overdue. They will arrive once the option of war is eliminated and the realization that Israel is home for good is accepted. Until that prayed-for day approaches, we are forced to maintain our military strength not for its own sake, but to protect what we have built by deterring our neighbors from resorting to war again. On the twenty-fifth anniversary of our reborn statehood, Israel again stretches out the hand of peace to its neighbors. We call upon them to join us as equals at the negotiating table, the only place where true reconciliation is ever possible. We make no prior commitments to them, just as we expect them to make none to us. Our mutual goal is a secure peace, a lasting peace, a peace that will remove forever the temptation of renewed war. This surely is an Arab interest as much as it is an Israeli one. I am convinced that peace will come to the Middle East just as it will come to other areas of the world.

Thank you very much.

MR. FINGER. I think this promise that peace will come to the Middle East is a good note on which to end. I want to thank you one and all. To me it has been a very stimulating and most enlightening colloquium. Thank you.

Appendix 1

The Arab-Israeli Problem and the United Nations*

SEYMOUR M. FINGER

The United Nations has lived with crises between Arabs and Jews in the Middle East almost since its birth. As with chronic illness, commentaries vary along a wide range—from appreciation that the patient has been kept alive at all to condemnation because the problem is still there—from urging the doctor to do more to telling him to go away so that nature may take its course. Yet it is generally acknowledged today that the U.N. must be involved, directly or indirectly, in any further efforts to work toward genuine peace or at least to forestall a resumption of fighting.

The history of U.N. involvement is on record and need not be recounted in detail. Briefly, it is as follows. On 29 November 1947, the General Assembly adopted a resolution on the future government of Palestine that provided for the partition of the country between separate Jewish and Arab states, bound together by a system of

* Reprinted from the *Middle East Information Series* 17 (February 1972): 2–14.

economic union, with an international area for Jerusalem. This resolution was rejected by the Arabs and fighting in Palestine ensued. Through repeated resolutions of the Security Council and determined efforts by the Acting Mediator, the late Ralph Bunche, armistices were finally agreed to between Israel and neighboring Arab countries, resulting in de facto partition of Palestine along lines substantially maintained until 4 June 1967.

The next major fighting erupted in 1956. Following Nasser's nationalization of the Suez Canal, (closed to Israel on grounds of belligerency), British, French, and Israeli forces invaded Egypt. The U.N. again intervened, with strong and active U.S. support, to bring about their withdrawal and to attempt to stabilize the situation. A U.N. Emergency Force (U.N.E.F.) stood guard on the border between Israel and Egypt in the Gaza Strip and at Sharm-el-Sheik (overlooking the entrance to the Gulf of Aqaba). This was the most peaceful border between Israel and its Arab neighbors during an entire decade marked by repeated incidents of violence and reprisal.

Then suddenly, in May 1967, President Nasser called for the withdrawal of U.N.E.F. and announced a blockade of the Gulf of Aqaba, Israel's lifeline to Asia and Africa—again, as with the Suez Canal, on the grounds of a state of belligerency. The events of 1967 and the U.N.'s actions in response thereto have a direct and highly important bearing on the situation today; consequently, it might be well to look at the significant developments of that period.

Israel, under threat of strangulation, saw one outside guarantee after another vanish. She had withdrawn her forces from Sinai on two understandings: (1) that a U.N. force would keep her border with Egypt tranquil and the Gulf of Aqaba open; (2) that the major maritime powers would guarantee access to Aqaba.

On the first guarantee, Secretary-General U Thant acceded promptly to Nasser's request for withdrawal of the force—an action subsequently attacked sharply by critics and defended staunchly by U Thant.

There is no roubt whatsoever that U Thant had to withdraw the force if Nasser was sufficiently determined to oust it. A lightly armed force of 5,000 men had been sent to keep peace, not to fight, and were dependent for logistics on the Egyptians—such a force could not have resisted a determined Egyptian army. If the two sides were determined to fight, leaving U.N.E.F. would only have exposed its troops to fruitless casualties and might have done permanent damage to the willingness of states to provide contingents for any future U.N. peacekeeping.

Moreover the contingents of India and Yugoslavia—countries tightly aligned with Egypt as leaders of the nonaligned—had already pulled out of the line without waiting for the Secretary-General to act, leaving only about half the force.

The only real question, therefore, is whether U Thant had to respond so promptly. I felt at the time—and still do—that he should have stalled for more time. President Nasser, following the Six-Day War, told Eric Rouleau, a correspondent of *Le Monde,* (19 February 1970), that he did not want the whole force withdrawn, only part of it. Whether or not this statement is taken at face value, U Thant might have volunteered to go to Cairo to discuss the matter, perhaps giving Nasser a face-saving way to back down. This is speculation, of course, but it is hard to see why even this slight possibility was left unexplored.[1]

So the force was withdrawn, and the first outside guarantee, dating back to 1956–57, vanished.

On the second guarantee, the U.S. consulted the other Western maritime powers about action to fulfill the pledge that Aqaba would be kept open to all shipping. I saw the replies. One government after another found reasons not to act. It was said around the U.S. Mission to the U.N., not entirely in jest, that the fleet of maritime powers that could be assembled would consist of a Dutch admiral commanding an American destroyer (our Navy was heavily committed to Vietnam and elsewhere). London and Washington did issue statements on behalf of the maritime powers, protesting the announced blockade of Aqaba, but these were peremptorily rejected by the U.A.R.[2]

U Thant learned of the blockade while en route to Cairo on 22 May, following the decision to terminate U.N.E.F. Upon his return to New York, he alerted the Council to the fact that Israel considered the blockade a casus belli. He then stated:

> In my view, a peaceful outcome to the present crisis will depend upon a breathing spell which will allow tension to subside from its present explosive level. I therefore urge all the parties concerned to exercise special restraint, to forego belligerence, and to avoid all other actions which could increase tension, to allow the Council to deal with the underlying causes of the present crisis and to seek solutions.[3]

The U.S., along with Argentina, Brazil, Canada, Denmark, and the United Kingdom consulted other Council Members on a draft

[1] For U Thant's rationale, *see* Security Council document S/7906, 26 May 1967, paras 1–8.
[2] Security Council Document S/7925, 2 June 1967.
[3] Security Council Document S/7906, 26 May 1967, para 14.

resolution calling on all parties "to forgo belligerence," (for example, not to blockade Aqaba), in order to provide a "breathing spell" that would "allow the Council to deal with the underlying causes of the present crisis and to seek solutions." This proposal had the support of at least nine of the fifteen members—the required majority, unless a Permanent Member cast a veto. In the Council, when Ambassador Arthur Goldberg pleaded for such action without delay, the Soviet Representative, Nikolai Fedorenko—echoed by Bulgaria—accused him of creating "hysteria" and argued that there was no cause for excitement. India, apparently reflecting Nasser's views, also denied any urgency. Thus the Council was stymied right up to the very eve of the outbreak of fighting—another fact that Israel remembered.

The General Assembly's Emergency Session

When fighting broke out on June 5, the U.S. delegation moved promptly that morning to get Council agreement on a resolution calling, as a first step, for an immediate cease-fire. Once again there was opposition from the U.S.S.R., Bulgaria, and India, who all insisted that the resolution also call for withdrawal to the June 4 positions. The entire day and evening were spent in wrangling and negotiations, while both the Israelis and the Egyptians told Council members around the fringes of the Chamber that their armies were having great success. The most intensive negotiations took place between the U.S. and the U.S.S.R., the latter apparently carrying the proxy of the U.A.R. These were adjourned overnight at Fedorenko's request.

By June 6, the rout of Egyptian forces was evident. The Soviets, acting apparently at the behest of the U.A.R. accepted the draft resolution initially suggested by the U.S. and the Council promptly adopted it. It is interesting to conjecture what might have happened if this resolution had been adopted on the morning of June 5, when it was originally proposed, and Israel had not yet advanced very far into Sinai. Later that week similar cease-fire resolutions called for a halt to the fighting between Israel and Jordan and Syria respectively.[4] These were accepted by all the parties, although there were numerous sporadic violations in the ensuing weeks and systematic violations along the Suez Canal for more than a year prior to the negotiation, with U.S. assistance, of a new truce along the Suez in August 1970.

[4] For an account of the Soviet and U.S. roles during negotiations, see *The Big Powers and the Present Crisis in the Middle East*, ed. Samuel Merlin (South Brunswick, N.J.: Associated University Presses, 1968), pp. 92–140.

The Soviets then requested an Emergency Session of the General Assembly—ironically, under a rule of procedure introduced by the "Uniting for Peace" resolution of 1950, a resolution they had so often denounced because it was related to the U.N. action in Korea and because Moscow maintains, as a matter of principle, that only the Security Council may take action to deal with the maintenance of peace or threats to international peace and security.

One hour before the Assembly began its first substantive session, on 19 June, 1967, President Johnson made a speech over all media, laying down the fundamental policy of the United States. He declared that peace in the Middle East must be made by the parties themselves and that it must be based on five principles:

First, the recognized right of national life;
—second, justice for the refugees;
—third, innocent maritime passage;
—fourth, limits on the wasteful and destructive arms race,
—fifth, political independence and territorial integrity for all.

American policy since that date has been based on those principles as well as on the concept that peace must be made by the parties themselves. Variations have occurred, mainly on the question of how much outside assistance, mediation, or prodding might be helpful.

Discussion at the 1967 Emergency Session centered largely on two draft resolutions—one, sponsored by Yugoslavia, India, and a group of "nonaligned" countries, was close to the U.A.R.'s desiderata, for example, immediate-unconditional withdrawal of all Israeli forces to June 4 positions; the second, sponsored by a group of Latin American countries, linked withdrawal by Israel of "all its forces from the territories occupied by it as a result of the recent conflict" to ending "the state of belligerency."[5] The vote on the first was 53 in favor, 46 against, with 20 abstentions; on the second, 57 in favor, 43 against, and 20 abstentions. Since this was an important question requiring a two-thirds majority, neither was adopted. The superficial observer might conclude that the session was thus a failure. In my view, it was a highly significant exercise, more so than at other sessions, when resolutions were adopted that obviously could have no effect. The result was a general recognition that if Israel were to act as if there were a state of peace, by withdrawing from good, defensive positions, the Arab states concerned could not persist in a state of belligerency vis-à-vis Israel. Thus the groundwork was laid for Security Council

[5] G. A. Documents A/L572/Rev. 3 and A/L523/Rev. 1 of the Fifth Emergency Special Session.

Resolution 242 of 22 November 1967—the only basis for solution accepted unanimously by the Council and by the parties concerned.

Another significant result of the Emergency Session was the decisive rejection of Soviet and Albanian resolutions that sought to brand Israel as an aggressor.

In the latter stages of the Emergency Session, the Soviets initiated bilateral negotiations with the U.S. in an endeavor to find a generally acceptable formula. The Soviets chose their Ambassador to Washington, Anatoly Dobrynin, to lead their side, apparently because they had more confidence in him than in Nikolai Fedorenko, their Ambassador to the U.N. But when Dobrynin suggested negotiations with U.S. Secretary of State, Dean Rusk, he was advised that Ambassador Goldberg had the responsibility for the U.S. The Dobrynin-Goldberg negotiations proceeded very well in New York; a draft resolution was worked out that was acceptable to the U.A.R., Jordan, the Soviets, and the U.S.—but not to Israel. The U.S. was nevertheless ready to go forward with it; however, when violent opposition from Algeria and Iraq caused the U.A.R. to draw back, the Soviets—with evident reluctance and discomfort—abandoned the endeavor, much to the relief of Israel.

Yet these negotiations were not in vain. Along with the Latin American resolution referred to above, they helped to pave the way for Security Council action in November.

During the general debate of the twenty-second general session of the General Assembly that began in September 1967, progress was made toward understanding among the prime ministers and foreign ministers of the interested countries. Consequently, when the Security Council met in November to consider the Middle East question, it was able to build upon the Latin American resolution of the Emergency Session, the Soviet, American, U.A.R., and Jordan discussions of July, and the discreet private sessions that had taken place during the general debate.

The Security Council Resolution

The resolution finally agreed upon unanimously in the Securtiy Council was worked out by Lord Caradon, the British representative. As he pointed out, it was far from being a one-man job. Virtually all fifteen members of the Council engaged in the consultations that resulted in the agreed text.

Since the various parties have given different interpretations to the text, it might be well at this point to refer to the Security Council records of the discussion that took place there. Most of the controversy about Resolution 242 has revolved around Paragraph One concerning "withdrawal of Israeli armed forces from territories occupied in the recent conflict." The Arabs and Soviets have claimed that this means *all territories*. I know, from my own experience with the negotiations, that the resolution would not have been accepted by a substantial number of members of the Security Council and certainly not by Israel if the word *all* had appeared. This is what Lord Caradon alluded to when he introduced the draft resolution to the Security Council on November 20. He said :

> Since then I have been strongly pressed by both sides—I emphasize, by both sides—to make changes, particularly in the provisions regarding withdrawal. But I came to the conclusion that to make variations under pressure from one side or the other at this stage would destroy the equal balance which we had endeavored to achieve and would also destroy the confidence which we hope to build on our effort to be just and impartial.

Another important fact frequently overlooked is that the truly operative paragraph of the entire Resolution is Paragraph Three, requesting the Secretary-General :

> to designate a special representative to proceed to the Middle East to establish and maintain contacts with the states concerned in order to promote agreement and assist efforts to achieve a peaceful and accepted settlement in accordance with the provisions and principles in this resolution.

The man chosen by the Secretary-General as his special representative was the Swedish Ambassador to Moscow, Gunnar Jarring. Jarring held many quiet discussions with the key governments on both sides—Israel, Jordan, and the United Arab Republic, but with no success.

In an effort to assist Jarring, France proposed that the Big Four —the United Kingdom, France, the Soviet Union, and the United States—should meet in New York. These Big-Four discussions had been going on for more than two years (1969–1971) without any apparent progress. The differences within the Big Four appeared to mirror those among the parties themselves.

Simultaneously, the United States held bilateral discussions with the Soviet Union. At one point during the fall of 1969, it appeared that the two were making progress toward an agreed interpretation of Resolution 242. Unfortunately, Moscow did not confirm the *ad referendum* (for example *tentative*) position of its representatives and the talks were therefore not successful.

The U. S. Initiative

The next major step taken by the American side came in a speech by Secretary Rogers to the Galaxy Conference on 9 December 1969. Rogers reaffirmed the basic U.S. stand taken by President Johnson in June 1967 that peace must be made by the parties to the conflict:

> The efforts of the major powers can help; they can provide a catalyst; they can stimulate the parties to talk; they can encourage; they can help define a realistic framework for agreement; but an agreement among other powers can not be a substitute for agreement among the parties themselves.

But Rogers added something very new and significant. He stated that, in the U.S. view, the secure and recognized boundaries to be negotiated under Resolution 242 of the Security Council should represent only insubstantial changes in the armistice line.

The Rogers's view was sharply attacked by the Israelis. Apparently they felt that it gave away most of their cards before negotiations even began.

Despite Israel's expressed displeasure, the United States has never modified this position on boundaries. Evidently, Washington has felt that the Arabs would not engage in negotiations for peace, direct or indirect, unless they had some assurance of Israeli withdrawal from virtually all the occupied territory. During the next six months there was no movement toward negotiations. On the contrary, the cease-fire was increasingly violated, particularly along the Suez Canal. In June the United States, realizing that the situation along the canal was growing increasingly dangerous, took the initiative in proposing to Israel, Jordan, and the United Arab Republic that they resume their negotiations, under Ambassador Jarring's auspices, on the basis of agreement to mutual acknowledgment of each other's sovereignty, territorial integrity, and political independence. That they also agree to Israel's withdrawal from territories occupied in the 1967 conflict and that, to facilitate agreement, they observe a cease-fire for three months in the case of Israel and the U.A.R., a strict military standstill in specified zones adjacent to the cease-fire lines.

The three governments accepted this initiative. The cease-fire and standstill went into effect on 8 August 1970. Unfortunately, Israel reported shortly thereafter that the United Arab Republic had violated the agreement by moving additional missiles and constructing additional missile sites in the Suez area. Independent U.S. reconnaissance confirmed the Israeli accusations. This violation delayed the resumption of the talks. Nevertheless, the cease-fire did become effective and has remained effective on the Suez Canal to date.

Israel, Egypt, and the Jarring Mission

In February 1971, Ambassador Jarring resumed his efforts to promote agreement between the parties. On February 8, he addressed to the governments of the United Arab Republic and Israel a request for certain prior commitments, to be given simultaneously and on condition that the other party make its commitment, subject to the eventual satisfactory determination of all other aspects of a peace settlement. The most important provisions of his request were that Israel would give a commitment to withdraw its forces to the international boundary between Egypt and the British Mandate of Palestine, on the understanding that satisfactory arrangements were made for: a) establishing demilitarized zones; b) practical security arrangements in the Sharm-el-Sheik area to guarantee freedom of navigation through the Straits of Tiran; c) freedom of navigation through the Suez Canal. On its side, the United Arab Republic was to make commitments for: a) termination of all claims or states of belligerence; b) respect for and acknowledgment of each other's independence; c) respect for and acknowledgment of each other's right to live in peace within secure and recognized boundaries; d) responsibility to do all in their power to insure that acts of belligerency or hostility do not originate from or are not committed from within the respective territory against the population, citizens, or property of the other party; e) noninterference in each other's domestic affairs.

The Egyptian reply to Jarring was positive on most points. With respect to freedom of navigation in the Suez Canal, however, it made the qualification: "in accordance with the 1888 Constantinople Convention." Likewise, concerning the Straits of Tiran, it made the qualification, "freedom of navigation *in accordance with the principles of international law*." Egypt also accepted the stationing of a U.N. peacekeeping force at Sharm-el-Sheikh, and the establishment of demilitarized zones.

The Egyptian position was taken on the understanding that Israel would make certain commitments, including the establishment of demilitarized zones *astride the borders in equal distances* and withdrawal of the Israeli armed forces from *all* the territories occupied since 5 June 1967.

Israel did not respond to the Jarring letter and has, in fact, taken strong exception to its terms. It appears unlikely that Israel would accept the U.A.R. response as satisfactory. Given the enormous difference in the size of the two countries, demilitarized zones astride the borders in equal distances would be manifestly unsatisfactory to Israel. Moreover, Israel would certainly not accept the withdrawal of its forces from all territories occupied since June 5 in advance of any negotiated peace. The Israeli position remained as stated by Foreign Minister Abba Eban when he addressed the Security Council on 20 November 1967 :

> The policy of the Israel government and nation remains as it was when I formulated it in the Security Council on 13 and 16 November [1,375th and 1,379th meetings], namely, that we shall respect and fully maintain the situation embodied in the cease-fire agreements until it is succeeded by peace treaties between Israel and the Arab states ending the state of war, establishing agreed, recognized, and secure territorial boundaries, guaranteeing free navigation for all shipping, including that of Israel, in all the waterways leading to and from the Red Sea, committing all signatories to the permanent and mutual recognition and respect of the sovereignty, security, and national identity of all Middle Eastern states, and ensuring a stable and mutually guaranteed security. Such a peace settlement, directly negotiated and contractually confirmed, would create conditions in which refugee problems could be justly and effectively solved through international and regional cooperation.

After it became clear that Israel would not respond to Jarring's letter, the United States undertook a new initiative to get agreement of the parties to the reopening of the Suez Canal as a first step toward a full solution on the basis of Resolution 242. While both parties showed some interest in this proposal, serious difficulties soon arose. Israel would not accept the presence of Egyptian troops on the east side of the Suez Canal when Israeli troops withdrew therefrom and insisted that a reopened canal must be open to ships of all countries, including Israel. Egypt insisted on moving its military forces to the east side of Suez, offered no guarantee of Israeli passage, and insisted that, as part of the agreement on Suez, Israel give a commitment for prompt withdrawal of its forces to the lines of 4 June 1967. There was also disagreement as to how far Israel would withdraw in the interim. As months passed, there was no evidence that either side had moved from these mutually contradictory positions.

Prospects for the Future

As 1972 opens, there are three existent approaches to the problem:
1. *Negotiations through Ambassador Jarring*

Israel has rejected Jarring's initiative of February 1971 and GA Resolution 2,799 (XXVI) of 20 December 1971, calling upon her to respond favorably to it. Yet there are certain circumstances under which Israel might find it possible to consider that initiative. If the demilitarized zones include all of Sinai, if practical security arrangements are made in the Sharm-el-Sheikh area for guaranteeing freedom of navigation through the Straits of Tiran, and if freedom of navigation through the Suez Canal is guaranteed, Israel might not find it disadvantageous to withdraw its forces to the former international boundary between Egypt and the British Mandate of Palestine—on the clear understanding that the secure and recognized boundary between Egypt and Israel would be a matter for separate negotiation.[6] Obviously Israel can not accept Egypt's interpretation, given in the latter's reply of 15 February 1971, but perhaps an Israeli reply along the lines suggested above would, at long last, start the process of negotiations between the parties, direct or indirect, that Israel considers essential to the attainment of peace and security.

A very persuasive argument for another Israeli look at the Jarring proposal was made in a *Life* article by Charles Yost,[7] now retired after an outstanding career as a diplomat, including two years as U.S. Permanent Representative to the U.N., 1969–71. Ambassador Yost's ideas comprehend a U.N. presence, including Big-Four contingents at Sharm-el-Sheikh and other strategic points. While I agree wholeheartedly with Yost's main point—that a viable peace with its Arab neighbors offers better long-term security for Israel than holding large chunks of territory incurring bitter Arab hostility—I do not see the slightest chance that Israel would relinquish the Golan Heights or East Jerusalem, as he appears to suggest. The strategic part of the Golan Heights contains no substantial Arab population; hence, the parallel Yost makes with Alsace-Lorraine is not correct. Also, Germany had not been threatened with extinction, as Israel was in 1948 and 1967.

Arrangements can be worked out for a united Jerusalem, with

---

[6] The idea of separating withdrawal from final boundaries is suggested in an article by Gidon Gottlieb, "Of Suez, Withdrawal, and Jarring: The Search for a Compromise." *New York University Center for International Studies Policy Papers* 5, no. 1

[7] "Last Chance for Peace in the Mideast," *Life* 70, no. 4 (9 April 1971).

Arab control over Moslem holy places. And in Sinai it should be left to Egypt and Israel to negotiate secure and recognized boundaries, as provided in Resolution 242, perhaps limiting changes to the "insubstantial alterations" mentioned by Secretary Rogers in his speech of 9 December 1969.

2. *Agreement on opening the Suez Canal*

This would be a step toward complete and full implementation of Resolution 242, within a reasonable period of time, as proposed by Secretary Rogers.

Neither party has so far responded to Rogers's statement to the U.N. General Assembly of 4 October 1971. In fact, Cairo has, on a number of occasions, pronounced the idea dead. Yet, as Rogers pointed out, such an interim agreement:

> would make the next step toward peace less difficult for all the parties to take;
> —would restore the use of the Suez Canal as a waterway for international shipping;
> —would reestablish Egypt's authority over a major national asset;
> —would separate the combatants;
> —would produce the first Israeli withdrawal;
> —would extend the cease-fire;
> —would diminish the risk of major power involvement;
> —would be an important step toward the complete implementation of Resolution 242.

Perhaps Jerusalem and Cairo should take a second look at this proposal.

3. *Committee of African Heads of State*[8]

Both parties have responded favorably to the aproaches of this Committee. Perhaps it could explore, with the parties, some elements of the Jarring and Rogers's proposals, without attaching a name to them.

All of these proposals present enormous difficulties for both parties. But the dangers of letting things fester and drift toward war will not go away. It might be temporarily easier to avoid facing difficult choices, but this is a formula for disaster in the long run. It is crucial that Paragraph Three of Resolution 242 be carried out—that there be *agreement* among the parties based on the principles set forth in Paragraph Two thereof. If the Egyptians will not negotiate directly at this time, then indirect negotiations must start the ball rolling, as suggested by Jarring, Rodgers, and the African Heads of State.

[8] For documents relating to the African initiative, *see* the *Special Supplement to the Bulletin of the American Professors For Peace In the Middle East* 11, no. 2 (January 1972).

The U.N. can not impose an agreement, but it can encourage efforts, in the words of Paragraph Three of Resolution 242, "to promote agreement." Meanwhile, it can provide the parties with a rationale for not resuming hostilities. And its Observer Mission, by observing and reporting violations, helps to maintain the truce. If agreement in substance is reached among the parties, a U.N. role in endorsing such an agreement and in reinforcing its peace and security guarantees might provide a limited but crucial margin.

Israel has shown understandable reluctance to depend on U.N. guarantees, bearing in mind the abrupt withdrawal of U.N.E.F. in May 1967. Yet, as Secretary Rogers observed in a television interview on 5 January 1972, there are ways to insure that a U.N. peacekeeping force could not be withdrawn at the wish of one of the parties; for example, the Security Council resolution establishing the force could stipulate that it could be withdrawn only by a decision of the Council—as Yost suggests.[9] In effect, such a resolution would

[9] Yost, *Life.*

give any Permanent Member a veto on withdrawal. The other requirement, of course, would be that the troops comprising the force would have to be reliable, at least in substantial part, and prepared to hold firm until a Council decision was taken to remove them. (Incidentally, both parties have now lived for more than four years with a U.N. Observer Mission along the Suez Canal.) Naturally, the type of U.N. peacekeeping force required, if any, would depend on the nature of the agreement reached between the parties.

There are, admittedly, risks for the parties in pursuing any of these avenues toward the negotiation of peace. But inaction also has its risks and, in the long run, I believe they are graver and more dangerous risks than is the risk of grappling now with the difficult issues that divide the parties. It is the parties directly concerned who must overcome those difficulties and reach agreement, but—as indicated above—there are many significant ways they can be helped by the U.N. and other countries, both in reaching agreement and in guaranteeing it, if they are willing to try.

* * * * *

The Basis for and Function of the U.N.E.F.

Aide-Memoire on the Basis for the Presence and Functioning of the U.N.E.F. in Egypt, 1956 (excerpted):

The Government of Egypt and the Secretary General of the U.N. have stated their understanding on the basic points for the presence and functioning of U.N.E.F. as follows:

(1) The Government of Egypt declares that, when exercising its sovereign rights on any matter concerning the presence and functioning of U.N.E.F., it will be guided, *in good faith,** by its acceptance of General Assembly Resolution 1000 (ES-D) of 5 November 1956.

(2) The U.N. takes note of this declaration of the Government of Egypt and declares that the activities of U.N.E.F. will be guided, *in good faith.** by the task established for the force in the afore-mentioned resolutions; in particular, the U.N., understanding this to correspond to the wishes of the government of Egypt, reaffirms its willingness to maintain U.N.E.F. until its task is completed.

(Report of the Secretary-General on Basic Points for the Presence and Functioning in Egypt of the U.N.E.F.; Original Text English. 20 November 1956.)

A Memorandum of Important Points in the Discussion Between the Representative of Israel and the Secretary General, 25 February 1957 (excerpted):

A. The Representative of Israel, stating that his government's primary concern in the area was in measure designed to reduce the risk of reoccurance of acts of belligerency after the with-drawal of Israel, raised the following . . . questions:

1. Following the withdrawal of Israel's forces, would the function of the Emergency Force be . . . the prevention of possible acts of belligerency?

2. In connection with the duration of U.N.E.F.'s deployment in the Sharm-el-Sheik area, would the Secretary-General give notice to the General Assembly of the U.N. before U.N.E.F. would be withdrawn from the area, with or without Egyptian insistence or before the Secretary-General would agree to its withdrawal?

1. With regard to the function of U.N.E.F. in the prevention of belligerency, the answer is affirmative, subject to the qualification that U.N.E.F. is never to be used in such a way as to force a solution of any controversial political or legal problem.

2. On the question of notification to the General Assembly the Secretary-General wanted to state his view *at a later meeting.** An indicated procedure would be for the Secretary-General to inform the Advisory Committee on the U.N.E.F., which would determine whether the matter should be brought to the attention of the Assembly.

(U.N. Document A/3563; Note by the Secretary-General Annexes.)

* Author's italics.

Appendix 2

Resolution 242 and Interpretations of Its Withdrawal Provisions

On 22 November 1967, the Security Council adopted Resolution 242, which reads as follows:

The Security Council:
  Expressing its continuing concern with the grave situation in the Middle East,
  Emphasizing the inadmissibility of the acquisition of territory by war and the need to work for a just and lasting peace in which every state in the area can live in security,
  Emphasizing further that all member states in their acceptance of the Charter of the United Nations have undertaken a commitment to act in accordance with Article 2 of the Charter,
  1) *Affirms* that the fulfilment of Charter principles requires the establishment of a just and lasting peace in the Middle East which should include the application of both the following principles:
    (i) Withdrawal of Israeli armed forces from territories occupied in the recent conflict;
    (ii) Termination of all claims or states of belligerency and respect for and acknowledgment of the sovereignty, territorial integrity, and political independence of every state in the area and their right to live in peace within secure and recognized

boundaries free from threats or acts of force;

2) *Affirms further* the necessity

(*a*) For guaranteeing freedom of navigation through international waterways in the area;

(*b*) For achieving a just settlement of the refugee problem;

(*c*) For guaranteeing the territorial inviolability and political independence of every state in the area, through measures including the establishment of demilitarized zones;

3) *Requests* the Secretary-General to designate a Special Representative to proceed to the Middle East to establish and maintain contacts with the states concerned in order to promote agreement and assist efforts to achieve a peaceful and accepted settlement in accordance with the provisions and principles in this resolution;

4) *Requests* the Secretary-General to report to the Security Council on the progress of the efforts of the Special Representative as soon as possible.

Interpretations of the "Withdrawal" Phrase

The Phrasing of Draft Resolutions Rejected by the Security Council in 1967

1) "The Security Council . . . demands that Israel should immediately and unconditionally remove all its troops *from the territory** of these states(for example, the U.A.R., Jordan, and Syria) and withdraw them *behind the armistice lines** and should respect the status of the *demilitarized zones,** as prescribed in the General Armistice Agreement."

(U.S.S.R. draft resolution [S/PV 1,358] 13 June 1967.)

2) "Israel's armed forces should withdraw *from all the** territories occupied as a result of the recent conflict."

(Draft resolution submitted by India, Mali, Nigeria [S/8,227], 7 November 1967.)

3) "Withdrawal of armed forces *from occupied territories** . . . respect for the right of every state in the area to . . . secure and recognized boundaries."

(U.S. draft resolution [S/8,229], proposed 7 November 1967.)

4) "The parties to the conflict should immediately withdraw their forces *to the positions they held before 5 June 1967**."

(U.S.S.R. draft resolution [S/8,253] submitted after the passing of the British draft that became Resolution 242.)

* Author's italics.

The Resolution as Interpreted by U.N. Representatives in the Security Council (1967)

1) "[The resolution] is a balanced whole. To add to it or to detract from it would destroy the balance and also destroy the wide measure of agreement we have achieved together. . . . I suggest that we have reached the stage when most, if not all, of us want the draft resolution, the whole draft resolution, and nothing but the draft resolution."

   (Lord Caradon, United Kingdom Representative, [S/PV 1,382].)

2) "For us, the resolution says what it says. It does not say that which it has specifically and consciously avoided saying."

   (Abba Eban, addressing the Security Council after the adoption of the British draft resolution [S/PV 1,382].)

3) "To seek withdrawal without secure and recognized boundaries . . . would be just as fruitless as to seek secure and recognized boundaries without withdrawal. Historically there have never been secure or recognized boundaries in the area. . . . An agreement on that point is an absolute essential to a just and lasting peace just as withdrawal is. . . . History shows that imposed boundaries are not secure and that secure boundaries must be mutually worked out and recognized by the parties themselves as part of the peacemaking process."

   ((Arthur Goldberg, U.S. Representative, [S/PV 1,377].)

4) "If our aim is to bring about a settlement or a political solution, there must be withdrawal to secure and recognized borders."

   (George Ignatieff, Canadian Representative, [S/PV 1,373].)

5) "We keep constantly in mind that a just and lasting peace in the Middle East has necessarily to be based on secure permanent boundaries freely agreed upon and negotiated by the neighboring states."

   (Geraldo de Carvalho Silos, Brazilian Representative, [S/PV 1,382].)

6) "Phrases such as 'secure and recognized boundaries.' What does that mean? What boundaries are these? Secure, recognized—by whom, for what? Who is going to judge how secure they are? Who must recognize them? . . . There is certainly much leeway for different interpretations that retain for Israel the right to establish new boundaries and to withdraw its troops only as far as the lines that it judges convenient."

(U.S.S.R. Representative, Vasliy Kuznetsov, in the discussions preceeding the adoplion of Resolution 242 [S/PV 1,373].)

7) "While there is a mention of the withdrawal of Israeli forces, this reference is almost nullified by the absence of any time limit or any modus operandi. . . . Even in the very mandate entrusted to the special representative-to-be, the call for withdrawal of the Israeli occupying forces is not provided for."

(Syrian Representative, Dr. George J. Tomeh, in the discussion preceeding the adoption of Resolution 242 [S/PV 1,382].)

As Interpreted by Egypt

"Our actions will be bound by nothing but our principles. What has been taken by force will be restored by force only. Any resolution adopted by the Security Council means nothing by itself."

(Presidest Nasser, addressing the Egyptian National Council, 23 November 1967.)

"Jarring's mission is to implement the U.N. Resolution concerning Israel's unconditional withdrawal."

Al-Ahram, 1 January, 1968.)

As Interpreted by Israel

"If there is any desire at all to move forward . . . there is only one method to do it—it is the method of direct meeting, of direct negotiations leading to an unequivocal, unambiguous peace treaty.

We will cooperate to the full in this direction. We will cooperate with the representative of the Secretary-General to the United Nations, whose functions has been defined as promoting agreement between the parties."

(Prime Minister Levi Eshkol, in a speech in New York, 11 January 1968.)

"Does the U.A.R. accept the need for agreement between itself and Israel? In particular, does it accept the authoritative interpretation of the British Foreign Minister, whose delegation sponsored the Security Council Resolution of 22 November 1967, and who stated the following: It is recognized that all aspects of the Resolution must be accepted by the parties and that there should be agreement on all of them and on the program under which all of them will be put into effect. . . ."

(Abba Eban, in a memorandum dated 27 November 1968 to the Israel Knesset with regard to the Jarring Mission, citing his memorandum of 4 November 1968 to Mahmud Riad.)

Appendix 3

The Rogers Plan

"The basic and related issues might be described as peace, security, withdrawal, and territory. Peace between the parties: . . . we believe that the conditions and obligations of peace must be defined in specific terms. . . . Respect for sovereignty and obligations of the parties to each other must be made specific.

Security: . . . a lasting peace must be sustained by a sense of security on both sides. To this end, as envisaged in the Security Council Resolution, there would be demilitarized zones and related security arrangements, more reliable than those that existed in the area in the past. The parties themselves, with Ambassador Jarring's help, are in the best position to work out the nature and details of such security arrangements.

Withdrawal and territory: the Security Council Resolution endorses the principle of the nonacquisition of territory by war and calls for withdrawal of Israeli armed forces from territories occupied in the 1967 war. We support this part of the Resolution, including withdrawal, just as we do its other elements.

We believe that while recognized political boundaries must be established and agreed upon by the parties, any change in the preexisting lines should not reflect the weight of conquest and should be confined to insubstantial alterations required for mutual security. . . ."

(Secretary of State William P. Rogers, addressing an Adult Education Conference, 9 December 1969.)

The Response of the United Arab Republic

"Last November we were informed of the Rogers Plan, and we found lots of points there, but we did not reply. But now we feel ourselves . . . in a position of strength :

a) The increased capabilities of our armed forces.

b) The increased military and political support of the Soviets. . . . Our aim is a definite and limited one. It is concentrated on two points :

1) withdrawal from all the conquered Arab territories;

2) restoration of the legitimate rights of the Palestine people.

The enemy treated the U.N. Resolution as a program for direct talks between us and them. We refused, and we continue to refuse. . . ."

(President Nasser then declared that the Foreign Minister of Egypt had replied to the Secretary of State as follows:

We agree to implementation of the Security Council Resolution, which means withdrawal from all Arab territories, and also restoration of the rights of the Palestine people in accordance with U.N. Resolutions. . . .)

"If political action succeeds, so much the better. But if it does not, we sons of the Egyptian nation will have no choice but to fight for our freedom, for the liberation of our soil and the conquered Arab lands."

(President Nasser, addressing the opening session of the Fourth Arab Socialist Union, 23 July 1970.)

The Response of Israel

"1. Israel is prepared . . . to designate a representative to discussions to be held under Ambassador Jarring's auspices with the U.A.R. (Jordan). . . .

2. Israel's position in favor of a cease-fire on a basis of reciprocity on all fronts, including the Egyptian front, in accordance with the Security Council's cease-fire Resolution, remains unchanged. . . .

3. The discussions under Ambassador Jarring's auspices shall be held within the framework of Security Council Resolution 242, on

the basis of the expression of readiness by the parties to carry out
the Security Council Resolution 242 in all its parts, with the object
of achieving an agreed and binding contractual peace agreement . . .
that will ensure:

(a) termination by Egypt (Jordan) and Israel of all claims or
states of belligerency and respect and acknowledgment of
the sovereignty, territorial integrity, and political independence
of each other and their right to live in peace within secure
and recognized boundaries free from threats or acts of force;

(b) withdrawal of Israeli armed forces from territories occupied
in the 1967 conflict to secure, recognized, and agreed boundaries to be determined in the peace agreements.

4. Israel will participate in these discussions without any prior
conditions. . . ."

**(From the text of the Israeli government's reply to the government of the
U.S., 4 August 1970 to President Nixon's message of 24 July 1970.)**

Appendix 4

The Jarring Proposal

*Document S/10,403**

Report of the Secretary-General on the activities of his Special
Representative to the Middle East

[Original: English]
[30 November 1971]

Introduction

1. By its Resolution 242 (1967) of 22 November 1967, the
Security Council affirmed the principles and provisions which should
be applied in establishing a just and lasting peace in the Middle East
and requested me to designate a special representative to establish
and maintain contacts with the states concerned in order to promote
agreement and assist efforts to achieve a peaceful and accepted settlement in accordance with these provisions and principles. I designated
Ambasador Gunnar V. Jarring of Sweden as my Special Representa-

* Also circulated as a General Assembly document under the symbol A/8,541.

tive and submitted progress reports from time to time to the Security Council on his efforts.

2.   By its Resolution 2,628 (XXV) of 4 November 1970, the General Assembly, after expressing its views on the principles that should govern the establishment of a just and lasting peace in the Middle East, called upon the parties directly concerned to resume contact with the Special Representative of the Secretary-General with a view to giving effect to Security Council Resolution 242 (1967) and requested me to report to the Security Council within a period of two months, and to the General Assembly as appropriate, on the efforts of the Special Representative and on the implementation of Security Council Resolution 242 (1967).

3.   In accordance with my responsibilities under Security Council Resolution 242 (1967) and with the request contained in General Assembly Resolution 2,628 (XXV), I submitted to the Security Council on 4 January 1971 a comprehensive report [*S/10,070*] on the activities of the Special Representative up to that date. Subsequently, on 1 February and 5 March, I submitted further progress reports [*S/10,070/Add. 1 and 2*] on his activities.

4.   In view of the fact that the General Assembly is about to debate again the situation in the Middle East and of the request contained in General Assembly Resolution 2,628 (XXV) that I should report to it as appropriate on the efforts of the Special Representative and on the implementation of Security Council Resolution 242 (1967), I am arranging to have my report of 4 January 1971 available to the Members of the General Assembly; I am also submitting the present report on the implementation of Security Council Resolution 242 (1967) to both the Security Council and the General Assembly in order to give a more comprehensive account of the activities of the Special Representative at the beginning of 1971 than that given in documents S/10,070/Add. 1 and 2 and to bring that account up to date.

The Holding of Discussions under the Special Representative's Auspices (January–March 1971)

5.   It will be recalled that at the close of 1970 it was possible to arrange for the resumption of the discussions under the auspices of Ambassador Jarring with Israel, Jordan, and the United Arab Republic for the purpose of reaching agreement on a just and lasting peace between them.

6.   Ambassador Jarring resumed his discussions with the parties at Headquarters on 5 January 1971 and pursued them actively. He

held a series of meetings with the representatives of Israel (including meetings with the Prime Minister and Foreign Minister during a brief visit to Israel made from 8 to 10 January 1971 at the request of that government), of Jordan, and of the United Arab Republic. In addition, he held meetings with the Permanent Representative of Lebanon, which is also one of the states directly concerned with the Middle East settlement.

7. At an early stage in these meetings, Israel presented to Ambassador Jarring, for transmission to the governments concerned, papers containing its views on the "Essentials of peace." Subsequently, the United Arab Republic and Jordan having received the respective Israeli views, presented papers containing their own views concerning the implementation of the provisions of Security Council Resolution 242 (1967).

8. During the remainder of January, Ambassador Jarring held further meetings with the representatives of Israel, Jordan, and the United Arab Republic, in the course of which he received further memoranda elaborating the positions of the parties. Unfortunately, these indicated that the parties held differing views on the order in which items should be discussed. More importantly, each side was insisting that the other should be ready to make certain commitments before being ready to proceed to the stage of formulating the provisions of a peace settlement.

9. On the Israeli side there was insistence that the United Arab Republic should give specific, direct, and reciprocal commitments toward Israel that it would be ready to enter into a peace agreement with Israel and to make toward Israel the various undertakings referred to in Paragraph One of Security Council Resolution 242 (1967). When agreement was reached on those points, it would be possible to discuss others, including the refugee problem; such items as secure and recognized boundaries, withdrawal and additional arrangements for ensuring security should be discussed in due course.

10. The United Arab Republic continued to regard the Security Council Resolution as containing provisions to be implemented by the parties and to express its readiness to carry out its obligations under the Resolution in full, provided that Israel did likewise. However, it held that Israel persisted in its refusal to implement the Security Council Resolution, since it would not commit itself to withdraw from all Arab territories occupied in June 1967. Furthermore in the view of the United Arab Republic, Israel had not committed itself to the implementation of the United Nations' Resolutions relevant to a just settlement to the refugee problem.

11. The papers received by Ambassador Jarring from Israel and Jordan relating to peace between these two countries showed a similar divergence of views. Israel stressed the importance of Jordan's giving an undertaking to enter into a peace agreement with it which would specify the direct and reciprocal obligations undertaken by each of them. Jordan emphasized the inadmissibility of the acquisition of territory by war and expressed the view that the essential first step toward peace lay in an Israeli commitment to evacuate all Arab territories.

12. Ambassador Jarring felt that at this stage of the talks he should make clear his views on what he believed to be the necessary steps to be taken in order to achieve a peaceful and accepted settlement in accordance with the provisions and principles of Security Council Resolution 242 (1967), which the parties had agreed to carry out in all its parts. He reached the conclusion, which I shared, that the only possibility of breaking the imminent deadlock arising from the differing views of Israel and the United Arab Republic as to the priority to be given to commitments and undertakings—which seemed to him to be the real cause for the existing immobility in the talks—was for him to seek from each side the parallel and simultaneous commitments that seemed to be inevitable prerequisites of an eventual peace settlement between them. It should thereafter be possible to proceed at once to formulate the provisions and terms of a peace agreement not only for those topics covered by the commitments, but with equal priority for other topics, and in particular the refugee question.

13. In identical aide-mémoires handed to the representatives of the United Arab Republic and Israel on 8 February 1971 Ambassador Jarring requested those governments to make to him certain prior commitments. Ambassador Jarring's initiative was on the basis that the commitments should be made simultaneously and reciprocally and subject to the eventual satisfactory determination of all other aspects of a peace settlement, including in particular a just settlement of the refugee problem. Israel would give a commitment to withdraw its forces from occupied United Arab Republic territory to the former international boundary between Egypt and the British Mandate of Palestine. The United Arab Republic would give a commitment to enter into a peace agreement with Israel and to make explicitly therein to Israel, on a reciprocal basis, various undertakings and acknowledgments arising directly or indirectly from Paragraph One (ii) of Security Council Resolution 242 (1967). [For the full text of the aide-mémoires, *see* annex I.]

14. On 15 February, Ambassador Jarring received from the representative of the United Arab Republic an aide-mémoire in which it was indicated that the United Arab Republic would accept the specific commitments requested of it, as well as other commitments arising directly or indirectly from Security Council Resolution 242 (1967). If Israel would give, likewise, commitments covering its own obligations under the Security Council resolution, including commitments for the withdrawal of its armed forces from Sinai and the Gaza Strip and for the achievement of a just settlement for the refugee problem in accordance with United Nations' Resolutions, the United Arab Republic would be ready to enter into a peace agreement with Israel. Finally, the United Arab Republic expressed the view that a just and lasting peace could not be realized without the full and scrupulous implementation of Security Council Resolution 242 (1967) and the withdrawal of the Israeli armed forces from all the territories occupied since 5 June 1967. [For the full text of the United Arab Republic reply, *see* annex II.]

15. On 17 February, Ambassador Jarring informed the Israeli representative of the contents of the United Arab Republic reply to his aide-mémoire.

16. On 26 February, Ambassador Jarring received a communication from the representative of Israel, in which, without specific reference to the commitment he had sought from that government, Israel stated that it viewed favourably "the expression by the United Arab Republic of its readiness to enter into a peace agreement with Israel" and reiterated that it was prepared for meaningful negotiations on all subjects relevant to a peace agreement between the two countries. Israel gave details of the undertakings that in its opinion should be given by the two countries in such a peace agreement, which should be expressed in a binding treaty in accordance with normal international law and precedent. Israel considered that both parties, having presented their basic positions, should now pursue the negotiations in a detailed and concrete manner without prior conditions.

17. On the crucial question of withdrawal on which Ambassador Jarring had sought a commitment from Israel, the Israeli position was that it would give an undertaking covering withdrawal of Israeli armed forces from "the Israeli-United Arab Republic cease-fire line" to the secure, recognized, and agreed boundaries to be established in the peace agreement; Israel would not withdraw to the pre-5 June 1967 lines. [For the full text of the Israeli paper, *see* annex III.]

18. On 28 February, Ambassador Jarring informed the United Arab Republic representative of the contents of the Israeli com-

munication. The latter held that it was improper for the Israeli authorities to have responded to his government's reply, which had been addressed to Ambassador Jarring and would have full effect only if the Israeli authorities gave the commitment requested of them by Ambassador Jarring.

19. In accepting the United States' proposal for renewed discussions under Ambassador Jarring's auspices [see S/10,070, paras. 33 and 34], the parties had agreed that they would observe strictly, for a period of ninety days from 7 August 1970, the cease-fire resolutions of the Security Council. In response to the recommendation of the General Assembly in Resolution 2,628 (XXV), the cease-fire had been extended for a further period of three months. In my report of 1 February submitted as that period was expiring, I appealed to the parties at that stage of the discussions, to withhold fire, to exercise military restraint, and to maintain the quiet which had prevailed in the area since August 1970.

20. In response to that appeal, the Foreign Ministry of Israel, in a communiqué released in Jerusalem on 2 February, announced that Israel would observe the cease-fire on a mutual basis; in a speech to the National Assembly on 4 February, the President of the United Arab Republic declared the decision of the United Arab Republic to refrain from opening fire for a period of thirty days ending on 7 March.

21. In submitting my report of 5 March 1971, I commented as follows:

> Ambassador Jarring has been very active over the past month and some further progress has been made toward a peaceful solution of the Middle East question. The problems to be settled have been more clearly identified and on some there is general agreement. I wish moreover to note with satisfaction the positive reply given by the United Arab Republic to Ambassador Jarring's initiative. However, the government of Israel has so far not responded to the request of Ambassador Jarring that it should give a commitment on withdrawal to the international boundary of the United Arab Republic.
>
> While I still consider that the situation has considerable elements of promise, it is a matter for increasing concern that Ambassador Jarrings's attempt to break the deadlock has not so far been successful. I appeal, therefore, to the government of Israel to give further consideration to this question and to respond favorably to Ambassador Jarring's initiative.
>
> To give time for further consideration and in the hope that the way forward may be reopened, I once more appeal to the parties to withhold fire, to exercise military restraint, and to maintain the quiet which has prevailed in the area since August 1970. [S/10,070/ Add. 2, paras. 14–16.]

Further Developments (March–November 1971)

22. In response to my appeal, the Israeli government once again made clear its willingness to continue to observe the cease-fire on a basis of reciprocity. The President of the United Arab Republic, in a statement to the nation on 7 March 1971, declared that his country no longer considered itself further committed to a cease-fire or to withholding fire. This did not, however, mean that political action would cease.

23. On 11 March, the Israeli representative informed Ambassador Jarring that his government was awaiting the reaction of the United Arab Republic government to the Israeli invitation in its reply of 26 February to enter into detailed and concrete discussions. When that statement of the Israeli representative was brought to the attention of the United Arab Republic representative, he maintained that his government was still awaiting an Israeli reply to Ambassador Jarring's aide-mémoire.

24. Subsequently, the talks under Ambassador Jarring's auspices lapsed. He therefore left Headquarters to resume his post as Ambassador of Sweden in Moscow on 25 March.

25. Although he returned to Headquarters from 5 to 12 May and from 21 September to 27 October and has held certain consultations elsewhere, he has found himself faced with the same deadlock and with no possibility of actively pursuing his mission.

26. Indeed, during much of this time the promotion of agreement between the parties was the object of two separate initiatives: first, an effort by the United States of America to promote an interim agreement providing for the reopening of the Suez Canal, which has not, so far, achieved any positive results; second, a mission of inquiry conducted by certain African Heads of States on behalf of the Organization of African Unity, which is still in progress as this report is being prepared. Both initiatives were described to Ambassador Jarring and myself by the sponsors as designed to facilitate the resumption of Ambassador Jarring's mission. Nevertheless, while they were being pursued, they obviously constituted an additional reason for him not to take personal initiatives.

27. In the introduction to my report on the work of the Organization, I expressed certain views on the situation in the Middle East. After recalling the responses of the United Arab Republic and Israel to Ambassador Jarring's initiative of February, I said that I continued to hope—as I still do—that Israel would find it possible before too long to make a response that would enable the search for a peaceful settlement under Ambassador Jarring's auspices to continue.

28.   After noting the relative quiet which has continued to exist in the area, I went on to say:

> It is not possible to predict how long this quiet will last, but there can be little doubt that, if the present impasse in the search for a peaceful settlement persists, new fighting will break out sooner or later. Since the parties have taken advantage of the present lull to strengthen considerably their military capabilities, it is only too likely that the new round of fighting will be more violent and dangerous than the previous ones, and there is always the danger that it may not be possible to limit it to the present antagonists and to the confines of the Middle East.
>
> I see no other way to forestall such a disastrous eventuality than by intensifying the search for a peaceful and agreed settlement. I believe there is still a chance of achieving such a settlement. I do not overlook the formidable difficulty of the problems to be tackled, but there exist several important assets on the side of peace efforts as well. The Security Council's cease-fire resolution of June 1967 and its Resolution 242 (1967) of 22 November 1967, if implemented simultaneously and fully, should provide the framework for achieving a peaceful and agreed settlement of the present conflict. To promote agreement for such a settlement, we are fortunate to have the services of Ambassador Jarring, who is uniquely qualified for this almost impossible task.
>
> Ambassador Jarring has clearly defined the minimum conditions that are required to move the peace talks ahead and, until those conditions are met, it is hard to see what else he can do to further his efforts. Steps to ensure that those conditions are met must be taken by the parties concerned and, failing this, by the Security Council itself or by states members of the United Nations and, particularly, the permanent members of the Security Council, both because of their special responsibility within the United Nations and of their influence on the parties concerned.[1]

29.   Recent developments have added to the urgency of my remarks. It therefore seems to me that the appropriate organs of the United Nations must review the situation once again and find ways and means to enable the Jarring mission to move forward.

Annexes

Annex I

Aide-mémoire presented to Israel and the United Arab Republic by Ambassador Jarring on 8 February 1971[2]

I have been following with a mixture of restrained optimism and

---

[1] Official Records of the General Assembly, Twenty-sixth Session, Supplement no. 1A, paras. 221–3.

[2] In presenting the aide-mémoire, Ambassador Jarring added the following interpretation:

growing concern the resumed discussions under my auspices for the purpose of arriving at a peaceful settlement of the Middle East question. My restrained optimism arises from the fact that in my view the parties are seriously defining their positions and wish to move forward to a permanent peace. My growing concern is that each side unyieldingly insists that the other make certain commitments before being ready to proceed to the stage of formulating the provisions to be included in a final peace agreement. There is, as I see it, a serious risk that we shall find ourselves in the same deadlock that existed during the first three years of my mission.

I therefore feel that I should at this stage make clear my views on what I believe to be the necessary steps to be taken in order to achieve a peaceful and accepted settlement in accordance with the provisions and principles of Security Council Resolution 242 (1967), which the parties have agreed to carry out in all its parts.

I have come to the conclusion that the only possibility to break the imminent deadlock arising from the differing views of Israel and the United Arab Republic as to the priority to be given to commitments and undertakings—which seems to me to be the real cause for the present immobility—is for me to seek from each side the parallel and simultaneous commitments which seem to be inevitable prerequisites of an eventual peace settlement between them. It should thereafter be possible to proceed at once to formulate the provisions and terms of a peace agreement not only for those topics covered by the commitments, but with equal priority for other topics, and in particular the refugee question.

Specifically, I wish to request the governments of Israel and the United Arab Republic to make to me at this stage the following prior commitments simultaneously and on condition that the other party makes its commitment and subject to the eventual satisfactory determination of all other aspects of a peace settlement, including in particular a just settlement of the refugee problem.

1. *Israel*

Israel would give a commitment to withdraw its forces from occupied United Arab Republic territory to the former international boundary between Egypt and the British Mandate of Palestine on the understanding that satisfactory arrangements are made for:

(*a*) establishing demilitarized zones;

"I interpret *practical security measures* in the Sharm-el-Sheikh area for guaranteeing freedom of navigation through the Straits of Tiran to mean arrangements for stationing a United Nations force in the area for this purpose."

(*b*) practical security arrangements in the Sharm-el-Sheikh area for guaranteeing freedom of navigation through the Straits of Tiran;

(*c*) freedom of navigation through the Suez Canal.

2. *United Arab Republic*

The United Arab Republic would give a commitment to enter into a peace agreement with Israel and to make explicitly therein to Israel, on a reciprocal basis, undertakings and acknowledgments covering the following subjects:

(*a*) termination of all claims or states of belligerency;

(*b*) respect for and acknowledgment of each other's sovereignty, territorial integrity, and political independence;

(*c*) respect for and acknowledgment of each other's right to live in peace within secure and recognized boundaries;

(*d*) responsibility to do all in their power to ensure that acts of belligerency or hostility do not originate from or are not committed from within their respective territories against the population, citizens, or property of the other party;

(*e*) Noninterference in each other's domestic affairs.

In making the abovementioned suggestion, I am conscious that I am requesting both sides to make serious commitments, but I am convinced that the present situation requires me to take this step.

Annex II
Aide-mémoire presented to Ambassador Jarring by the United Arab Republic on 15 February 1971

The United Arab Republic has informed you that it accepts to carry out—on a reciprocal basis—all its obligations as provided for in the Security Council Resolution 242 (1967) with a view to achieving a peaceful settlement in the Middle East. On the same basis, Israel should carry out all its obligations contained in this resolution.

Referring to your aide-mémoire of 8 February 1971, the United Arab Republic would give a commitment covering the following:

1. termination of all claims of states of belligerency;

2. respect for and acknowledgment of each other's sovereignty, territorial integrity, and political independence;

3. respect for and acknowledgment of each other's right to live in peace within secure and recognized boundaries;

4. responsibility to do all in their power to ensure that acts of belligerency or hostility do not originate from or are committed from within the respective territories against the population, citizens, or property of the other party;

5. noninterference in each other's domestic affairs.

The United Arab Republic would also give a commitment that:

6. it ensures the freedom of navigation in the Suez Canal in accordance with the 1888 Constantinople Convention;

7. it ensures the freedom of navigation in the Straits of Tiran in accordance with the principles of international law;

8. it accepts the stationing of the United Nations peacekeeping force in the Sharm-el-Sheik;

9. to guarantee the peaceful settlement and the territorial inviolability of every state in the area, the United Arab Republic would accept:

(a) the establishment of demilitarized zones astride the borders in equal distances;

(b) the establishment of a United Nations' peacekeeping force in which the four permanent members of the Security Council would participate.

Israel should, likewise, give a commitment to implement all the provisions of Security Council Resolution 242 (1967). Hence, Israel should give a commitment covering the following::

1. withdrawal of its armed forces from Sinai and the Gaza Strip;

2. achievement of a just settlement for the refugee problem in accordance with United Nations' resolutions;

3. termination of all claims of states of belligerency;

4. respect for and acknowledgment of each other's sovereignty, territorial integrity, and political independence;

5. respect for and acknowledgment of each other's right to live in peace within secure and recognized boundaries;

6. responsibility to do all in their power to ensure that acts of belligerency or hostility do not originate from or are committed from within the respective territories against the population, citizens, or property of the other party;

7. noninterference in each other's domestic affairs;

8. to guarantee the peaceful settlement and the territorial inviolability of every state in the area, Israel would accept:

(a) the establishment of demilitarized zones astride the borders in equal distances;

(b) the establishment of a United Nations' peacekeeping force in which the four permanent members of the Security Council would participate.

When Israel gives these commitments, the United Arab Republic will be ready to enter into a peace agreement with Israel containing all the aforementioned obligations as provided for in Security Council Resolution 242 (1967).

The United Arab Republic considers that the just and lasting peace can not be realized without the full and scrupulous implementation of Security Council Resolution 242 (1967) and the withdrawal of the Israel armed forces from all the territories occupied since 5 June 1967.

Annex III
Communication presented to Ambassador Jarring by Israel on 26 February 1971

Pursuant to our meetings on 8 and 17 February, I am instructed to convey the following to you, and through you to the United Arab Republic.

Israel views favorably the expression by the United Arab Republic of its readiness to enter into a peace agreement with Israel and reiterates that it is prepared for meaningful negotiations on all subjects relevant to a peace agreement between the two countries.

The government of Israel wishes to state that the peace agreement to be concluded between Israel and the United Arab Republic should, *inter alia,* include the provisions set out below.

A. *Israel*

Israel would give undertakings covering the following:

1. declared and explicit decision to regard the conflict between Israel and the United Arab Republic as finally ended, and termination of all claims and states of war and acts of hostility or belligerency between Israel and the United Arab Republic;

2. respect for and acknowledgment of the sovereignty, territorial integrity, and political independence of the United Arab Republic;

3. respect for and acknowledgment of the right of the United Arab Republic to live in peace within secure and recognized boundaries;

4. withdrawal of Israel armed forces from the Israel-United Arab Republic cease-fire line to the secure, recognized, and agreed boundaries to be established in the peace agreement—Israel will not withdraw to the pre-5 June 1967 lines;

5. in the matter of the refugees and the claims of both parties in this connexion, Israel is prepared to negotiate with the governments directly involved on: :

(*a*) the payment of compensation for abandoned lands and property;

(*b*) participation in the planning of the rehabilitation of the refugees in the region—once the obligation of the parties toward the settlement of the refugee issue has been agreed, neither party shall be under claims from the other inconsistent with its sovereignty;

6. the responsibility for ensuring that no warlike act or act of violence by any organization, group, or individual originates from or is committed in the territory of Israel against the population, armed forces, or property of the United Arab Republic;

7. noninterference in the domestic affairs of the United Arab Republic;

8. nonparticipation by Israel in hostile alliances against the United Arab Republic and the prohibition of stationing of troops of other parties which maintain a state of belligerency against the United Arab Republic.

B. *United Arab Republic*

The United Arab Republic undertakings in the peace agreement with Israel would include :

1. declared and explicit decision to regard the conflict between the United Arab Republic and Israel as finally ended and termination of all claims and states of war and acts of hostility or belligerency between the United Arab Republic and Israel;

2. respect for and acknowledgment of the sovereignty, territorial integrity, and political independence of Israel;

3. respect for and acknowledgment of the right of Israel to live in peace within secure and recognized boundaries to be determined in the peace agreement;

4. the responsibility for ensuring that no warlike act or act of violence by any organization, group, or individual originates from or is committed in the territory of the United Arab Republic against the population, armed forces, or property of Israel.

5. noninterference in the domestic affairs of Israel;

6. an explicit undertaking to guarantee free passage for Israel ships and cargoes through the Suez Canal;

7. termination of economic warfare in all its manifestations, including boycott, and of interference in the normal international relations of Israel;

8. nonparticipation by the United Arab Republic in hostile alliances against Israel and the prohibition of stationing of troops of other parties which maintain a state of belligerency against Israel.

The United Arab Republic and Israel should enter into a peace agreement with each other to be expressed in a binding treaty in accordance with normal international law and precedent, and containing the above undertakings.

The government of Israel believes that now that the United Arab Republic has through Ambassador Jarring expressed its willingness to enter into a peace agreement with Israel, and both parties have presented their basic positions, they should now pursue their negotiations in a detailed and concrete manner without prior conditions so as to cover all the points listed in their respective documents with a view to concluding a peace agreement.

Appendix 5

U.N. Security Council Resolutions on Cease-fire,
Peacekeeping, and Disengagement of Forces
Following the October War

Resolution 338 (1973)

Adopted by the Security Council at its 1,747th meeting, on
21/22 October 1973

The Security Council:

1. calls upon all parties to the present fighting to cease all firing
and terminate all military activity immediately, no later than twelve
hours after the moment of the adoption of this decision, in the
positions they now occupy;

2. calls upon the parties concerned to start immediately after the
cease-fire the implementation of Security Council Resolution 242
(1967) in all of its parts;

3. decides that, immediately and concurrently with the cease-fire,
negotiations start between the parties concerned under appropriate

auspices aimed at establishing a just and durable peace in the Middle East.

Resolution 339 (1973)

Adopted by the Security Council at its 1,748th meeting, on 23 October 1973

The Security Council:
Referring to its Resolution 338 (1973) of 22 October 1973,
1. Confirms its decision on an immediate cessation of all kinds of firing and of all military action, and urges that the forces of the two sides be returned to the positions they occupied at the moment the cease-fire became effective;
2. Requests the Secretary-General to take measures for immediate dispatch of United Nations observers to supervise the observance of the cease-fire between the forces of Israel and the Arab Republic of Egypt, using for this purpose the personnel of the United Nations now in the Middle East and first of all the personnel now in Cairo.

Resolution 340 (1973)

Adopted by the Security Council at its 1,750th meeting on 25 October 1973

The Security Council:
Recalling its Resolution 338 (1973) of 22 October and 339 (1973) of 23 October 1973,
Noting with regret the reported repeated violations of the cease-fire in noncompliance with Resolutions 338 (1973) and 339 (1973),
Noting with concern from the Secretary-General's report that the United Nations military observers have not yet been enabled to place themselves on both sides of the cease-fire line:
1. Demands that immediate and complete cease-fire be observed and that the parties return to the positions occupied by them at 16:50 hours *GMT* on 22 October 1973;
2. Requests the Secretary--General, as an immediate step, to increase the number of United Nations military observers on both sides;
3. Decides to set up immediately under its authority a United Nations Emergency Force to be composed of personnel drawn from

states members of the United Nations, except the permanent members of the Security Council, and requests the Secretary-General to report within twenty-four hours on the steps taken to this effect;

4. Requests the Secretary-General to report to the Council on an urgent and continuing basis on the state of implementation of the present resolution, as well as Resolution 338 (1973) and 339 (1973);

5. Requests all member states to extend their full cooperation to the United Nations in the implementation of the present resolution, as well as Resolution 338 (1973) and 339 (1973).

Resolution 341 (1973)

Adopted by the Security Council at its 1,752nd meeting, on
27 October 1973

The Security Council : :

1. Approves the report of the Secretary-General on the implementation of Security Council Resolution 340 (1973) contained in document S/11,052/Rev. 1 dated 27 October 1973;

2. Decides that the force shall be established in accordance with the abovementioned report for an initial period of six months, and that it shall continue in operation thereafter, if required, provided the Security Council so decides.

Resolution 344 (1973)

Adopted by the Security Council at its 1,760th meeting, on
15 December 1973

The Security Council :

Considering that it decided by its Resolution 338 (1973) of 21/22 October 1973 that talks among the parties to the Middle East conflict for the implementation of Resolution 242 (1967) of 22 November 1967 should be held under "appropriate auspices,"

Noting that a Peace Conference on the Middle East situation is to begin shortly at Geneva under the auspices of the United Nations :

1. Expresses the hope that the conference will make speedy progress toward the establishment of a just and durable peace in the Middle East;

2. Expresses its confidence that the Secretary-General will play a full and effective role at the Peace Conference, in accordance with

the relevant resolutions of the Security Council, and that he will preside over its proceedings, if the parties so desire;

3. Requests the Secretary-General to keep it suitably informed of the developments in negotiations at the Peace Conference in order to enable the Council to review the problem on a continuing basis;

4. Requests the Secretary-General to provide all necessary assistance and facilities for the work of the conference.

Resolution 346 (1974)

Adopted by the Security Council at its 1,765th meeting, on
8 April 1974

The Security Council:

Recalling its Resolution 340 (1973) of 25 October 1973 and 341 (1973) of 27 October 1973 and the agreement reached by members of the Security Council on 2 November 1973 (S/11,072),

Having reviewed the functioning of the United Nations Emergency Force set up under these resolutions as reported by the Secretary-General,

Noting from the report of the Secretary-General of 1 April 1974 (S/11,248) that in the present circumstances the operation of the United Nations Emergency Force is still required:

1. Expresses its appreciation to the states which have contributed troops to the United Nations Emergency Force and to those which have made voluntary financial and material contributions for the support of the Force;

2. Expresses its appreciation to the Secretary-General for his efforts in implementing the decisions of the Security Council regarding the establishment and functioning of the United Nations Emergency Force;

3. Commends the United Nations Emergency Force for its contribution to efforts to achieve a just and durable peace in the Middle East;

4. Notes the Secretary-General's view that the disengagement of Egyptian and Israeli forces is only a first step toward the settlement of the Middle East problem and that the continued operation of the United Nations Emergency Force is essential not only for the maintenance of the present quiet in the Egypt-Israel sector, but also to assist, if required, in further efforts for the establishment of a just and durable peace in the Middle East and accordingly decides that, in accordance with the recommendation in paragraph 68 of the

Secretary-General's report of 1 April 1974 (S/11,248), the mandate of the United Nations Emergency Force, approved by the Security Council in its Resolution 341 (1973) of 27 October 1973, shall be extended for a further period of six months, that is, until 24 October 1974;

5. Notes with satisfaction that the Secretary-General is exerting every effort to solve in a satisfactory way the problems of the United Nations Emergency Force, including the urgent ones referred to in paragraph 71 of his report of 1 April 1974 (S/11,248);

6. Further notes with satisfaction the Secretary-General's intention to keep under constant review the required strength of the Force with a view to making reductions and economies when the situation allows;

7. Calls upon all member states, particularly the parties concerned, to extend their full support to the United Nations in the implementation of the present resolution;

8. Requests the Secretary-General to report to the Security Council on a continuing basis as requested in Resolution 340 (1973).

Report of the Secretary-General

1. I wish to transmit to the Council the text of the Agreement on Disengagement between Israeli and Syrian forces, which is attached as Annex A to this report, and the Protocol to the Agreement between Israeli and Syrian forces concerning the United Nations Disengagement Observer Force, which is attached as Annex B.

2. The Security Council will note that this Agreement and the Protocol, which are to be signed in Geneva not later than 31 May 1974, calls for the creation of a United Nations Disengagement Observer Force. I shall take the necessary steps in accordance with the provisions of the Protocol, if the Security Council so decides.

3. It is my intention that the United Nations Disengagement Observer Force will be drawn, in the first instance at any rate, from United Nations military personnel already in the area.

4. I shall keep the Council fully informed of future developments in this regard.

Annex A
Agreement on Disengagement Between Israeli and Syrian Forces

A. Israel and Syria will scrupulously observe the cease-fire on land, sea, and air and will refrain from all military actions against each other, from the time of the signing of this document, in implementation of United Nations Security Council Resolution 338 dated 22 October 1973.

B. The military forces of Israel and Syria will be separated in accordance with the following principles :

1. All Israeli military forces will be west of the line designated as Line A on the map attached hereto, except in the Quneitra area, where they will be west of Line A–1.

2. All territory east of Line A will be under Syrian administration and Syrian civilians will return to this territory.

3. The area between Line A and the line designated as Line B on the attached map will be an area of separation. In this area will be stationed the United Nations Disengagement Observer Force established in accordance with the accompanying protocol.

4. All Syrian military forces will be east of the line designated as Line B on the attached map.

5. There will be two equal areas of limitation in armament and forces, one west of Line A and one east of Line B as agreed upon.

6. Air forces of the two sides will be permitted to operate up to their respective lines without interference from the other side.

C. In the area between Line A and Line A–1 on the attached map there shall be no military forces.

D. This Agreement and the attached map will be signed by the military representatives of Israel and Syria in Geneva not later than 31 May 1974, in the Egyptian-Israeli Military Working Group of the Geneva Peace Conference under the aegis of the United Nations, after that group has been joined by a Syrian military representative, and with the participation of representatives of the United States and the Soviet Union. The precise delineation of a detailed map and a plan for the implementation of the disengagement of forces will be worked out by military representatives of Israel and Syria in the Egyptian-Israeli Military Working Group who will agree on the stages of this process. The Military Working Group described above will start their work for this purpose in Geneva under the aegis of the United Nations within twenty-four hours after the signing of this Agreement. They will complete this task within five days. Disengagement will begin within twenty-four hours after the completion of the task of the Military Working Group. The process of disengagement will be completed not later than twenty days after it begins.

E. These provisions shall be inspected by personnel of the United Nations comprising the United Nations Disengagement Observer Force under this Agreement.

F. Within twenty-four hours after the signing of this Agreement in Geneva all wounded prisoners of war which each side holds of the other as certified by the I.C.R.C. will be repatriated. The morning after the completion of the task of the Military Working Group, all remaining prisoners of war will be repatriated.

G. The bodies of all dead soldiers held by either side will be returned for burial in their respective countries within ten days after the signing of this Agreement.

H. This Agreement is not a Peace Agreement. It is a step toward a just and durable peace on the basis of Security Council Resolution 338 dated 22 October 1973.

Annex B

Protocol to Agreement on Disengagement Between Israeli and Syrian Forces Concerning the United Nations Disengagement Observer Force

Israel and Syria agree that:

The function of the United Nations Disengagement Observer Force (U.N.D.O.F.) under the agreement will be to use its best efforts to maintain the cease-fire and to see that it is scrupulously observed. It will supervise the agreement and protocol thereto with regard to the areas of separation and limitation. In carrying out its mission, it will comply with generally applicable Syrian laws and regulations and will not hamper the functioning of local civil administration. It will enjoy freedom of movement and communication and other facilities that are necessary for its mission. It will be mobile and provided with personal weapons of a defensive character and shall use such weapons only in self-defence. The number of the U.N.D.O.F. shall be about 1,250, who will be selected by the Secretary-General of the United Nations in consultation with the parties from members of the United Nations who are not permanent members of the Security Council.

The U.N.D.O.F. will be under the command of the United Nations, vested in the Secretary-General, under the authority of the Security Council.

The U.N.D.O.F. shall carry out inspections under the agreement, and report thereon to the parties, on a regular basis, not less often than once every fifteen days, and, in addition, when requested by either party. It shall mark on the ground the respective lines shown on the map attached to the agreement.

Israel and Syria will support a resolution of the United Nations Security Council which will provide for the U.N.D.O.F. contemplated by the agreement. The initial authorization will be for six months subject to renewal by further resolution of the Security Council.

Resolution 350 (1974)

Adopted by the Security Council at its 1,774th meeting on
31 May 1974

The Security Council:

Having considered the report of the Secretary-General contained
in document S/11,302 and Add. 1, and having heard his statement
made at the 1,773rd meeting of the Security Council:

1. Welcomes the Agreement on Disengagement between Israeli
and Syrian Forces, negotiated in implementation of Security Council
Resolution 338 (1973) of 22 October 1973;

2. Takes note of the Secretary-General's report and its annexes
and his statement;

3. Decides to set up immediately under its authority a United
Nations Disengagement Observer Force, and requests the Secretary-
General to take the necessary steps to this effect, in accordance with
his abovementioned report and the annexes thereto. The Force shall
be established for an initial period of six months, subject to renewal
by further resolution of the Security Council;

4. Requests the Secretary-General to keep the Security Council
fully informed of further developments.

Appendix 6

A Trusteeship for Palestine?

By Seymour M. Finger

In the search for peace in the Middle East, it is widely recognized that one essential element is self-determination for the Arabs on the West Bank and in Gaza. This is the minimum demand of Arab nations seeking peace, and of the Palestinians, and it has been endorsed overwhelmingly by the General Assembly of the United Nations. It has also been endorsed by Nahum Goldmann, President of the World Jewish Congress. (Interview in *Le Monde,* Paris, 9 January, 1975.)

In Israel, it is true, there is a substantial group in the L.I.K.U.D. coalition that holds, on biblical and strategic grounds, that Israel should keep the West Bank. But this has never been the official position of the government of Israel. The late David Ben-Gurion, Israel's first premier, stated firmly that the West Bank and Gaza should revert to Arab control in exchange for real peace. The present government of Israel has taken forcible steps to prevent any large-scale Jewish settlement in the West Bank. And a recent article by

287

Naomi Shepherd (*New York Times*, 23 March, 1975) indicates that a group of prominent kibbutz members, intellectuals, and public figures are advocating that Israel publicly recognize Palestinian aspirations and declare its willingness to give up territory to that end.

The major external roadblock for such an Israeli policy is the P.L.O. The Arab States and the United Nations General Assembly have recognized the P.L.O. as "the representative of the Palestinian people." Israel has refused to negotiate with the P.L.O. on the grounds that it is a terrorist organization and that its covenant calls for the liquidation of Israel.

How can this impasse be resolved.

One way could be the use of the United Nations Trusteeship system. Under this system ten formerly dependent territories have achieved self-determination, either through independence or freely chosen association with an existing state (for example, Cameroon). The eleventh, the Trust Territory of the Pacific Islands, is now in process of attaining self-determination.

Article 81 of the United Nations Charter provides that a trusteeship agreement "shall in each case include the terms under which the trust territory will be administered and designate the authority which will exercise the administration of the trust territory," and that the administering authority may be one or more states or the Organization itself. Thus, the administering authority could be Jordan and Egypt, which held the West Bank and Gaza prior to 5 June, 1967, or Jordan alone, or the United Nations itself. Israel could be party to the negotiation of the trusteeship agreement and, accordingly, have a say in who the administering authority shall be, as well as other terms and conditions.

The Palestinians of the West Bank and Gaza could immediately begin to set up their own instruments of government. The P.L.O. and other groups would have the opportunity to compete for the support of the electorate, under the supervision of the United Nations. (and their fellow Palestinians there) or federation with Jordan (and their fellow Palestinians there) or federation with Israel. The The electorate could choose independence, federation with Jordan timing of self-determination could be flexible, depending on developments both inside the territory and in neighbor states.

Given the strategic position of the West Bank and Gaza, the trusteeship agreement could designate them as strategic areas. This would mean, under Article 83 of the United Nations Charter, that the UN's functions would be exercised by the Security Council. Under the same article, the Trusteeship Council (consisting of China, France, the Soviet Union, the United Kingdom and the United States plus Jordan and/or Egypt if they become the administering authority) would assist the Security Council by performing the UN's functions relating to political, economic, social, and educational matters in the area. The agreement could provide that the area be demilitarized and that the administering authority take all necessary action to prevent acts of terrorism against neighboring states.

Such a trust territory might include the Moslem quarter of Jerusalem, with appropriate access. Final arrangements for Jerusalem would be worked out as part of the agreement under which the trusteeship is terminated.

The trusteeship idea would not meet the demands of either side fully, but it might offer a reasonable and honorable way out of the present deadlock. It would assure self-determination for the Palestinians in the West Bank and Gaza, while providing security guarantees for Israel. It would allow for negotiations on secure and recognized boundaries on Israel's eastern frontier. The arrangements for terminating trusteeship would have to be approved by the Security Council, where the veto power of the Soviet Union and the United States would assure both sides that their vital interests will not be sacrificed. (For example, the guarantees of demilitarization and against terrorism could be insisted upon as part of the termination agreement, itself carrying Security Council endorsement.)

Moving out of the present deadlock is essential to peace in the area, which is in turn closely linked to world peace and stability. There will, of course, still be the difficult problems of settlement with Egypt and Syria, involving—as provided in Resolution 242—troop withdrawals, the negotiation of secure and recognized boundaries, an end to belligerency, and the recognition of the right of all states in the area, including Israel, to an independent existence solidly guaranteed. But a start must be made somewhere and, given the breakdown of Kissinger's mission on the Egypt-Israel disengagement issue, it might be worth trying for a solution of the Palestinian question as the next step.

Appendix 7

Guidelines for an Alternative

A FOUR-YEAR PLAN: A CONSTITUTION FOR ISRAEL AND PEACE WITH HER NEIGHBORS

By H. Kook and S. Merlin

The repeated victories of Israel's Armed Forces have prevented our enemies from annihilating us. But our military successes alone did not and could not bring about peace and normalization in the relations with our neighbors. More important, our victory in the Six-Day war of June 1967, not only failed to guarantee our security, but also, paradoxically, exposed us to a major enemy attack on two fronts for which we were not prepared psychologically, politically, even militarily. Indeed, our extraordinary victory of 1967 left us with a time bomb that we refused to recognize and did not defuse. All this happened because we regarded the military triumph as something of an end in itself instead of an instrument to shape a political stategy for achieving peace and stability in the region.

---

* Translation from the Hebrew (with minor omissions) of a memorandum sent on 10 March 1975 to Prime Minister Rabin and circulated among a select group of personalities in Israel.

Mysticism and Military Force—A Dead End

Historically our policy has been based on two principal elements: mystical Zionism and military power. This combination, however, has not brought us nearer to our desired goals—neither from the point of view of security, nor in our social life and certainly not in the realm of the spirit. In fact, we have reached a dead end. It will be impossible to extricate ourselves from this cul-de-sac by repeating the same mistakes, by continuing the same line of thought, and by perpetuating a regime that has failed us and brought political defeat and total isolation in the international arena.

There is no other way to overcome our troubles and to weather the crisis than to undertake a thorough analysis of what went wrong and to draw the necessary conclusions. This requires probing not merely the initial military setbacks of the October 1973 war but also the political, psychological, and philosophical attitudes that prevailed since the establishment of the State.

In a detailed survey, of which this memorandum is only a summary of conclusions, we will offer a critical analysis of the principles that have so far guided our State and determined our very lives. Building on this analysis we will develop guidelines for the future on two levels: First, a formulation of an authentic Israeli peace plan and a political offensive with the aim of moving toward the solution of the conflict between us and our neighbors. Second, we offer a program for the transformation of the State of Israel from its present character, essentially as part of the Jewish dispersion, into a sovereign nationstate.

Simultaneous Elections both in Israel and among the Palestinians

This program is visualized from both a short-range and long-range perspective:

1. *The short-range* : to prepare in the course of one year general elections both in Israel and among the Palestinian Arabs.

2. *The long-range,* during the term of the next Knesset (Israeli Parliament): to implement a four-year plan leading to the transformation of Israel into a sovereign nation-state that functions in accordance with principles defined in a written constitution. Finally to bring about a settlement of the conflict between Israel and her neighbors, sanctioned in an all-inclusive peace treaty.

FOREIGN AND DEFENSE POLICY

We and the Palestinians

An Authentic Israeli Peace Plan as an Alternative to Dr. Kissinger's Initiatives

Regardless of the future of Secretary of State Kissinger's initiative, and despite his good intentions and friendly attitude toward Israel, it is already clear that the step-by-step method will not bring the hoped-for peace. Nor is the alternative to a step-by-step approach *necessarily* the Geneva Conference. Every initiative based upon external factors must, by its very nature, result in pressures and, ultimately, in imposed conditions upon Israel. Therefore, sooner or later, Israel will feel compelled to abandon the policy of partial settlements. Instead, it will be incumbent upon us to offer a comprehensive peace plan of our own and pass over to a diplomatic offensive with a view to convincing the Arabs, our friends in the world and public opinion everywhere, of our sincere determination to bring to an end the intolerable status quo that leads us from one war to the next.

Israel should simultaneously offer a plan for an immediate settlement of the Palestine conflict, as well as a vision of the development of good-neighborly relations between the two peoples, through cooperation and friendship in the framework of a Palestinian-Israeli confederation in the whole of Palestine on both banks of the Jordan.

To Reverse the Order: A Solution to the Problem of the Palestinians Prior to Negotiations with Egypt

Israel should express its readiness to enter peace negotiations, directly or indirectly, with each of her neighbors, if any of them feel that they can isolate such a settlement from the Palestinian question.

Since, however, all of them believe that a bilateral peace settlement is contingent upon a solution of the problem of the Palestinians, it makes no sense to enter into such negotiations with our neighbors *before* that question is settled. In such a case the procedure should be reversed : first we have to seek a solution to the problem of the Palestinians and only then to enter negotiations with Egypt, Syria, and Lebanon.

*To Call Upon the Security Council to Supervise the Election
of a Legitimate Representation of the Palestinian People*

Since the P.L.O. has never established itself as a legitimate representative of the Palestinian people and since King Hussein at present refuses to act as their representative, Israel should address itself to the Security Council of the United Nations and offer a plan to initiate, in cooperation with Jordan, elections to a Constituent Assembly of the Palestinians, to be held within one year's time. Thus, the Palestinians will, at long last, have a legitimate body to represent them, capable of entering negotiations with Israel toward a peace settlement.

*The Palestinian People—East and West of the Jordan—Are a
Single Entity: No Reason to Split Them*

It is not possible to isolate the Palestine problem from the Kingdom of Jordan. No verbal acrobatics, no sophistry will do away with the organic connection and identity between the two. The conquest of the West Bank by King Abdullah was not a historical monstrosity. On the contrary, it was a natural development under the given circumstances. From 1948 on, new realities emerged in both the Israeli and the Jordanian parts of Palestine. Lod, Ramleh, Jaffa were transformed into towns inhabited by Israelis. Jordan, on the other hand, held the largest concentration of Palestinians. In Transjordan are also concentrated the vast majority of the refugees, whose rehabilitation is most urgent from a humanitarian, moral, and practical point of view.

To sanction a Palestine State in the West Bank (and in Gaza) does not solve the Palestine problem, it exacerbates it. Such a State would not contribute to peaceful relations between us and the Palestinians. It would become a stormcenter of tensions, conflicts, confrontations, and wars between various elements of the Palestinians. As demonstrated in September 1970, civil war between the Palestinian people waged along our own frontiers can also endanger our peace and security. We can not be indifferent to these inter-Palestinian confrontations and wash our hands of them. We have a direct interest in what is going on in the whole of Palestine, on both sides of the Jordan. We have to do everything to bring about an easing of inter-Palestinian tensions and find a solution to the Palestine problem in its totality.

In this connection it is worth noting the paradox of Israel recognizing the existence of a Jordanian nation but ignoring the existence of a Palestinian nation. Realities and common sense would idicate an opposite position, since most, if not all of the "Jordanians" are in fact Palestinians.

The Problem of the Legitimate Representation of the Palestinians

The most important problem is that of evolving a plausible and legitimate representation of the Palestinians.

Historically the legitimate authority to deal with concerning the Palestine conflict has been King Hussein. This is not to ignore the criticism, at times extremely severe, leveled against the King. Nor is it to disregard the hatred, at times deep, of the King on the part of certain segments of the Palestinian population, and especially among the Fedayeen. But the relevant fact is that King Hussein ruled the Palestinians for a whole generation—more than twenty years. His grandfather, Abdullah, ruled them before that. Good, bad, or indifferent, the Hashemites were the rulers of those parts of Palestine where most of the Palestinians lived.

Hence, if despite the Rabbat summit and despite all the pressures and threats King Hussein is subject to, he is nonetheless willing and self-confident enough to make commitments of a lasting nature; if he feels strong enough to enter negotiations with Israel on behalf of the Palestinian people and will not hesitate to sign a peace agreement with us concerning the territories that we conquered in the Six-Day war—we, on our part, should take the calculated risk of negotiating a peace agreement with him. In other words, if Hussein decides to fight for the right to represent the Palestinian people in their entirety, and making all the allowances for the inherent dangers to him in such a course, there is no compelling reason why we, too, should not take the risk of recognizing him as our partner for negotiation and peace.

If Not Hussein—Who?

Since, however, King Hussein, for the time being, refuses to act as spokesman for the Palestinian people, we should express readiness to enter negotiations with an alternative body representing the Palestinians. This must be on the condition, however, that such an alternative representation possesses a plausible mandate from the Palestinian people, and is not just an artificial creation, as is the P.L.O., appointed and financed by foreign governments, whose common motivation is religious and fanaticism and political totalitarianism so characteristic of pan-Arabism.

A Constituent Assembly of the Palestinian People

Such a mandate can be obtained by a simple procedure of electing a Constituent Assembly of the Palestinian people. The elections should take place in the West Bank (Judea and Sumaria), in Gaza, and Transjordan.

The elections should take place under the aegis and supervision of the Security Council. The government of Israel will offer maximum cooperation with the Security Council in carrying out this most important and decisive undertaking.

The Israeli government will guarantee complete freedom of expression, association and assembly to all the inhabitants of the West Bank and Gaza during the one-year period to prepare and hold the elections.

Arafat Without a Gun

There will be no restrictions whatsoever against any person, group, or organization or party among the Palestinians, including the P.L.O. and the other Fedayeen organizations, to participate in the elections, to wage their respective propaganda campaigns. This complete freedom to participate in the election campaign will be contingent upon one condition only—that those groups who wish to be part of this democratic process will have to proclaim a suspension of violence for the whole period of the election campaign. In an atmosphere of violence no genuine elections are possible. It would indeed be desirable if Arafat, before trying to introduce secular democracy in the Israeli part of Palestine, tries his hand at the art and craft of the democratic process among his fellow Palestinians in the Arab parts of Palestine.

The only control and intervention on behalf of the government of Israel during the one-year period of the election campaign to the Constituent Assembly of the Palestinian people, will be in the prevention of violence and the smuggling of arms.

Upon the completion of the elections to the Palestine Constituent Assembly, the government of Israel will enter into direct or indirect negotiations with representatives of the newly elected Constituent Assembly of the Palestinians, regardless of who wins the election. The negotiations will be conducted on a basis of equality and mutual recognition and respect. No preconditions will be advanced by any of the two sides. The legal, international basis of reference for these negotiations will be Security Council Resolution 242.

From Refugees to Nationhood

The aim of the negotiations will be to find a solution of the Israel-Arab conflict in Eretz-Israel (Palestine) that has agitated the peoples of the region and threatened the peace of the world for more than a quarter of a century.

The two sides will try not only to reconcile their claims and counter claims, but also to adjust the principles embodied in Security Council Resolution 242 (that now deals exclusively with existing states) to the conditions of the emerging new Palestinian entity.

No Escape from Tri-partite Negotiations

Such an adjustment of the negotiations to the new conditions, and the transition of the Palestinians from a status of refugees to one of a national entity, will inevitably call for tripartite negotiations between Israel, the Palestinians, and King Hussein.

Israel's interest will not be served by splitting the Palestinian people. On the contrary, Israel is interested in its consolidation. There is just no possibility of ignoring King Hussein or avoiding dealing with him, not only because of the legitimacy of his rule, but also mainly because the majority of the population that lives under his jurisdiction is mostly if not totally Palestinian. There is no escape from this basic fact. And therefore a solution will have to be found to the Palestine problem in its totality within the framework of the original mandated territories on both banks of the Jordan. Either this, or a solution may not be achieved at all.

Though Israel can not and should not force its views on the Palestinians, either east or west of the Jordan, nor on King Hussein, it can not and should not remain indifferent either. Israel's vital national interests are inextricably involved in any such arrangements. Hence, as long as there is no unified authority over all the Palestinians on both sides of the Jordan, Israel will have to insist that the negotiations between her and the Palestinians will have to start on a tripartite basis, with a view, however, that in the last account a unified Palestinian representation will be the party in the negotiations with us.

It will do no good to sketch in advance detailed proposals or a scenario for the hoped for eventual settlement. Yet, even at this preliminary stage, it is necessary to advance three basic concepts, so that all concerned understand what the talks will be about.

A Palestinian State on Both Sides of the Jordan and an Israeli Republic to the West of It

From the point of view of tranquility in the region and its peaceful development, it would in all probability be in the best interests of all concerned if in the framework of historic and Mandated Palestine there will be two states rather than three. That is, an Arab-Palestinian state on both sides of the Jordan and Israel—west of it.

To have a third state would defy the demographic, historic, and economic realities of Palestine. Transjordan is no less Palestine than is the West Bank. One can not fail to arrive at the conclusion that both Transjordan and the West Bank constitute a single demographic and economic entity. Such a large and viable state could give Israel the necessary guarantees by offering to demilitarize areas contiguous to the agreed upon borders.

Is it not for Israel to dictate to the Palestinians the nature of the political regime that is to emerge from the new and large Palestinian entity. It is up to the Palestinians to determine for themselves the nature of the regime. Perhaps Arafat could persuade his fellow Palestinians on both sides of the Jordan to transform their country into a secular democratic republic. Or perhaps King Hussein will succeed in convincing the majority of the Palestinians that the regime best fitted to their traditions and temperament is a benign monarchy, headed by him and as outlined on 15 March 1972 when he offered his famous plan for a federated state. And perhaps another plan of Hussein will have greater appeal with the Palestinians: the one he suggested in July 1967, shortly after the Six-Day war, to transform the Hashemite Kingdom of Jordan into a Palestine Republic, headed by him not as King but as President.

The Palestinians Will Not "Liberate" the Terrorists, They Can Only Negotiate Their Future

It will be up to the Palestinians to determine their future and the form of their independence. But they must also understand that Israel is duty-bound to see to it that its security requirements are not jeopardized. The Palestinians, whatever their rhetoric, will not and can not "liberate" the West Bank. They can only negotiate for it in good faith, as indeed Israel should negotiate with the Palestinians in good faith.

The Final Aim: The Reunification of Historic Palestine in a Confederative Framework

Sooner or later the idea of reuniting the whole of Palestine on both banks of the Jordan into some kind of a confederated Israeli-Arab framework, regardless of how loose, will surface in the consciousness of both peoples. Though Israel should not make any pre-conditions for any peace settlement, and though it is incumbant upon her to enter negotiations in full freedom of give-and-take, this does not mean that Israel can not or should not voice her views concerning the future of Palestine. Israel should not be inhibited from voicing its ideal loud and clear, because in our opinion the vision of cooperation corresponds to the deepest interests and yet muted aspirations of those directly involved—the Israelis as well as the Palestinians.

Total Solution to the Refugee Problem—Is In The Vital Interests of Israel

Whatever the outcome of the tripartite negotiations, one problem can not be left open without a total solution—*the Palestine refugees.* No settlement can or should be acceptable to Israel that does not provide for a practical and formal solution of the refugee problem. Whatever the nature and scope of the future Palestine state, not one Palestinian should remain a refugee, within that state or outside it. After an Israeli-Palestinian settlement is reached, no Palestinian should be in a position to claim the status of a refugee. Of course, the implementation of transferring the Palestinians from one bank to the other, or from abroad to Palestine will take time. But from a formal and treaty point of view the total solution of the problem will be signified by the signing of the peace agreement with the Palestinians. The camps in Gaza, in Transjordan, in Lebanon, and in Syria will be liquidated, without any exception. Palestinians will either become full-fledged citizens of the Palestine State or they will be considered citizens of the countries where they have settled. The settlement of the Israeli-Arab conflict will mean that the refugee problem has been solved once and for all.

Relations with the United States

There Is No Alliance between Israel and the U.S.

The world considers the United States not only a friend, but also a staunch and abiding ally of Israel. There is, however, a great deal of ambiguity and imprecision in this relationship. The history of U.S.-Israeli relations has shown abundantly that from the very beginning we were often treated cavalierly by Washington, sometimes even with outspoken enmity. This was the case, for instance, in 1956 after our spectacular victory in the Sinai campaign. We were given an ultimatum and we submitted. There certainly was no friendship let alone alliance on the part of Amercia under the Eisenhower-Dulles administration.

Conversely, from the June 1967 war until the war of October 1973 it was Israel that treated the U.S. cavalierly, with complete disregard of America's interests, as if that superpower is committed, by force of circumstances, or for some obscure reason, to submit to any wish and whim of the Israeli government. This was an absurd and surrealistic situation. Such an attitude stemmed in great part from our unrealistic evaluation of the influence and power of American Jewry in shaping the policy of America. This false evaluation contains the seeds of possible disasters to come.

Though Israel's attitude, generally speaking, may not have caused any great harm to the interests of the United States (as Washington understands them), it had detrimental effects upon our own fortunes. The Yom-Kippur war was to a great extent a direct result of this short-sighted and arrogant attitude.

With the shock of the "earthquake," our arrogance nearly disappeared but instead paralysis set in. The absence of any Israeli initiative created a most dangerous vacuum that permitted the Arabs to undertake a worldwide political offensive.

The Summit Conference at Rabat violated the spirit if not the letter of all the agreements reached between us and our neighbors in the wake of the October 1973 war. Pan-Arabism emerged with a strategy whose spirit and aim is the liquidation of the State of Israel. Though Sadat occasionally makes statements that may (or may not) be interpreted as moderate or even concilatory, the fact remains that never before was the climate in the Middle East so charged with hostility and evil intentions toward Israel as it is now.

To Clarify Our Relations with the United States

In view of our past experience the time has come to try to normalize our relations with the United States. First and above all we need to define, by mutual agreement, the nature and the scope of the

American commitment to the security and territorial integrity of Israel and our own commitments to the United States, on a reciprocal basis.

Among the various elements and aspects of such a formalized commitment, four are of paramount importance:

a. *Territorial Integrity*
What is the American administration's interpretation of the concept of the territorial integrity of the State of Israel? What are the boundaries of Israel agreed upon between Israel and the United States as legitimate and defensible and as defining the territorial integrity of our country?

b. *Aggression*
When and under what circumstances would the U.S. consider military action by any of the Arab states as an act of aggression against the territorial integrity of Israel?

c. *Soviet Intervention*
When and under what circumstances, and according to what criterion would the United States consider Russian military action in the Middle East as direct and unprovoked intervention in the Israeli-Arab conflict?

d. *Oil Blackmail*
To what degree, if at all, will the United States tolerate the Arab oil-producing countries using the vital commodity with the intent of determining the outcome of the Arab-Israeli conflict—both in the field of battle as well as in the international arena?

These and other important aspects of Israel-American relations can be clarified (though never absolutely and with finality) only in a process of negotiations with a view toward defining them in a formal document. A formal treaty would probably constitute the most effective instrument to serve the security interests of Israel. But it can also be in the form of a series of documents containing understandings based upon reciprocity. Israel can not remain the eternal recipient without committing itself to consulting with the administration concerning far-reaching strategic or political moves on her part against the Arabs, or against any other international factors.

One should always keep in mind that American pressures are exerted only against a background of Israeli negativism and lack of initiative, or as a reaction to lack of Israeli willingness to consult Washington. Israeli-American relations must be based on mutual understanding, and regular consultations. Otherwise, Israel's situation—militarily and diplomatically—is bound to deteriorate at an ever-increasing pace.

ISRAEL-SOVIET RELATIONS

Parallel and complementing the above—and there is no contradiction here—Israel should urgently undertake a vigorous diplomatic offensive, with a view towards improving relations with the Soviet Union. Israel should seek the renewal of diplomatic relations and normalization in as many fields as possible.

HISTORIC TRANSFORMATION: FROM PART OF THE DISPERSION INTO A SOVEREIGN NATION STATE

Toward a Reevaluation of Values and Priorities

The proclamation on 14 May 1948 of the reemergence of the State of Israel, constituted the triumph of the Hebrew war of liberation and the realization of the Zionist aim. The Zionist revolution achieved its purpose.

With the proclamation of the state, a new leaf should have been turned over in our history, and a new age of national independence ushered in. The leaf was never turned, and the new age never began. True, there was a need for a transition period for adjustments to the harsh conditions of that period. We were confronted in the very first months of our independent existence by a war of annihilation waged by all our neighbours. At the same time we were also faced with the urgent task of transferring to Israel, speedily and on a large scale, the remnants of European Jewry and most of the Jewish communities from Arab lands. These tasks required the full concentration of the energies both of the government and the people.

But this transition period became a permanent condition. What were supposed to be emergency priorities became habitual preoccupations. In order to rationalize all this, a phoney poststate-Zionist ideology was created and is perpetuated till this very day. The basic requirements of the sovereign state were neglected, as if the national revolution never took place.

After a period of almost thirty years, the time has come to put an end to a state of affairs in which all principles of an independent and normal political existence became distorted. The time is certainly overdue for a public debate concerning the basic issues of our existence, so that we can plan a more normal life and brighter future for our nation. As long as we persist in our refusal to define our identity as a sovereign nation-state, there will be no end to our internal religious divisions and the appalling gap between our various ethnic communities. Nor will we find the time and the means to rectify the present disgraceful social conditions and the ever widening gap between the haves and have nots.

There is a lack of elementary sincerity in the relationship between Israel and world Jewry. A clear and honest attempt to define the relations between us as a sovereign nation and the communities of the Jewish people in the dispersion would greatly help to crystalize and solidify our relations with the Jewish people wherever they are.

National Debate on Basic Issues

We suggest that within one year elections be held in Israel.

The election campaign should, for the first time in the history of Israel, become an occasion to debate real and basic issues concerning the nature of Israel's political constitutional regime with a view of transforming Israel from a heavily armed Jewish community into a nation-state living in peace with its neighbors.

Thus the election campaign will have to deal not only with immediate problems concerning negotiations with our neighbors and other foreign policy and domestic matters, but also with the basic questions concerning the constitutional nature of Israel. In the course of this debate we will raise the questions enumerated below and make an effort to provide satisfactory and reasonable answers.

Separation of State and Religion

Should Israel retain the theocratic aspects of its present regime, or should an honest and effective effort be made at a separation of state and religion within a constitutional framework to be drafted and promulgated during the term of the next Knesset? In other words, should Israel be launched upon a course of secularization, or remain shackled by the chains of tradition belonging to Judaism as a religion but having no justification among the constituent elements of Israel as a modern nation-state?

The Jewish religion is an ancient and universal faith for the sake of which the best of her adherents sacrificed themselves in large numbers. Millions of Jews in almost all parts of the world are attached to their religion no less than the Jews of Israel. Should the Jewish religion remain a component of the political and party system of the state? Is that not in essence, a negation of the spiritual and moral values of Judaism as a religion?

We, on our part, will advocate the separation of state and religion and the transformation of Israel into a secular republic, which of course will remain Jewish in the sense that the vast majorityy of its citizens are of the Jewish faith. Just as the United States is a Christian and France is a Catholic country.

Should Israel remain psychologically and structurally part of the *pezurah*—of the dispersed world Jewish community—or should she begin to assume an even greater autonomy, freeing herself more and more from diaspora Jewish institutions, and thus becoming a normal and sovereign nation-state? We will advocate the latter course.

In addition to the conventional notion of *the Jewish people,* we should try to advance the idea of *the Israeli people,* and thus adjust the resurgence of historic Israel to the modern age.

Protector of the Whole House of Israel the World Over—Or the Imperative of National Priorities?

Conversely : Should Israel continue to consider itself the guarantor and protector of Jewish communities the world over? Or should Israel adjust her very raison d'être to the imperative of consolidating and strengthening the infrastructure of the state as such? In other words, it is time for Israel to define her national priorities in accordance with the principle that her own destiny, her own vital needs are also her first priorities, transcending everything else, with one exception : in case of an emergency, when a Jewish community anywhere finds itself in physical danger as a result of anti-Semitic persecution.

The radical change in the philosophical, psychological, and political outlook we advocate stems from the assumption that the State of Israel is no longer the opening phase of the realization of Zionism. On the contrary, the emergence of the State of Israel is the consummation and realization of the ideal of Zionism as a national liberation movement that achieved its aim by liberating Palestine from British rule and by winning the subsequent war of independence. Thus Israel can no longer be regarded as an instrument or outpost or a vanguard of the Zionist movement. We perceive our destiny in a radically different perspective : the consolidation, the strengthening, and the development of the newly sovereign State of Israel as the supreme historic imperative.

More than that : this reevaluation of values and reordering of priorities is not only vital and natural and logical from the point of view of Israel's interests as a sovereign state, but in the last account it is also in the best interests of world Jewry. What is healthy for Israel is also good for the Jews of the world.

In the present confused state of affairs, the lines are blurred between Israel as a sovereign state and the Jews as citizens in the various countries of their dispersion. In those circumstances, Israel can not protect the Jews of the world. Rather the reverse is the case: paradoxically, it is the Jews of the dispersion who must time and again come to the defense of Israel both as a state and as a collectivity of Jews who are in danger of their lives.

On the other hand, the need for the Jews of the world to defend Israel is responsible, at least to a considerable extent, for the steady erosion of the status and the security of the Jewish communities in the Western free countries. This trend is most disturbing.

A change in national perspective and the reordering of priorities require the following:

1. As a matter of principle, Israel should be committed to a policy of noninterference in the internal affairs and policies of any other state, except, as we indicated above, in special situations when there is a physical danger to Jews being persecuted *as Jews*.

2. Israel's policy should no longer be subordinated to absorbing new immigrants as a supreme and transcedental principle ("the ungathering of the exiles"), that can not be questioned under any circumstances. We suggest harmonizing the problem of Jewish immigration with other, no less important requirements, namely, to strive for greater social justice for all our citizens. We advocate economic policy that aims at a more decent and more just socieconomic system—even if such a new policy may affect the scope of immigration into Israel, in one period or another. (Except, again, in those emergency cases we have referred to above. In such cases, the gates of Palestine will be wide open.)

We will also encourage the end of the use of the terms *Alyia* (*ascent*) and *Yerida* (*descent*). These terms do not reflect a respectful attitude toward Jews who imigrate to or from Israel. Eretz-Israel is the Holy Land only from a religious point of view. Therefore, it is not befitting to use terms that characterized the pilgrimage of Jews from the diaspora to Jerusalem during the great holidays and religious festivals, for the present day migration. A Jew who emigrates from Israel for one reason or another is not a criminal nor a traitor. He does not descend from anywhere. He migrates to a place of his choice. He remains the same Jew that he was when he lived in Israel.

3. The relations between the State of Israel and the Jewish institutions in the diaspora will have to undergo a basic change, not only philosophically but also institutionally.

To Cancel the Covenant with the Jewish Agency

We advocate the annullment of the covenant between Israel and the Jewish agency. As a result this institution will have to reorganize itself on an entirely new foundation and will assume a public rather than a state character.

It is imperative to establish a new system of relationships, sincere and honest, between Israel and the Jewish organizations in the world. This is particularly necessary for the United Jewish Appeal. The U.J.A. should organize in Israel a body of experts, who in consultation with Israeli institutions will disperse this fund for specific and proper purposes. It is also necessary to enable the newly established body of the U.J.A. to supervise and to directly control the spending of the monies that are being transferred to Israel, in such a way that the connection between Israel and the Jews will be strengthened. It will become more genuine and honest and this in all probability will also help to advance the goal of bridging the social gap now prevailing in Israel.

The Law of Return and Naturalization in Israel

We suggest basic revisions in the Law of Return ("Khok Hashevut") :

The constitutional laws that the next Knesset will debate should include legislation that stipulates that Israel is open to immigrants of all religions and all nations. Their numbers will be determined by the needs and interests of the state, and the vast majority will, in the nature of things, be Jews. The non-Jews, as in any other democratic and normal state, will also be able to become nationals and a part of the Israeli nation (like tens of thousands of Israeli emigrants who became Americans). The new legislation will also include a provision stipulating that every person who is a Jew or is designated by others as a Jew and as such is subject to persecution in the country where he lives, and who wishes to find a haven in Israel, will find the gates of our country wide open. Thus the practical requirements of the Law of Return will be met.

In the framework of an Israeli nation all nationals of the state —Jews, Moslems, Christians, and so forth—must be equal, not only in theory but also in practice, before the law; this equality includes equal rights in employment, without any restrictions, including the civil service, diplomatic appointments, and service in the army. An Israeli Arab is not an exception, unless he declares in writing that because of reasons of conscience he objects to serving in the Israeli armed forces or in any service of the state.

The principle of political asylum should be incorporated in the new legislation and given the most liberal interpretation—in the sense that Israel will become an exemplary haven for the politically oppressed.

SUMMATION

The conflict between Israel and her neighbors is not a territorial conflict, nor are frontiers the issue. It is essentially a conflict over national identity and self-determination between two peoples. Even it temporary arrangements are achieved, they will not insure true peace. True peace is conceivable only through the definition of the Palestinian entity on the one hand, and through the revision of the prevailing definition of the State of Israel on the other.

As long as Israel refuses to define itself as a sovereign nation-state, and as long as it is not clear that the government of Israel represents the Israeli people and not the totality of the Jewish people in the world, we will remain misunderstood by friends, let alone enemies. The State of Israel is not an infinite entity. It is a defined national entity within defined frontiers. It is impossible to reconcile two unique phenomena—a Zionist Jewish state on the one hand, and such a movement movement as the P.L.O. advocating the phoney slogan of a democratic secular Palestine on the other. But it is definitely possible to arrive at a compromise and understanding between two nation-states, with defined territorial and demographic identities.

To a great degree it was Israel's policy that imposed the P.L.O. upon the Palestinians. The recognition of the Palestinians' right to self-determination will in all probability lead to the decline of the P.L.O. Such a recognition on the part of Israel can result in the recognition by the Palestinians of Israel's right to exist as a sovereign nation-state.

In summing up our proposals we should like to emphasize the imperative of freeing ourselves of the political immobilism in which we stagnated for much too long. It is imperative to launch a dynamic diplomatic offensive of political initiatives with a view toward achieving peace in the region. This can not be achieved through Dr. Kissinger's process of a step-by-step approach. Even more important, it must be an Israeli initiative for many reasons not the least of whch is the Soviet Union's compelling opposition to American initiatives.

The isolation that we face today stems not from the surrender of the world to the Arab oil blackmail (we were quite isolated in the international arena before October 1973), but mainly from the fact that the world does not understand exactly what we are and what we are after. We never offered any proposals. We only rejected proposals of others. An Israeli peace offensive as suggested in this memorandum, as well as other steps that the government surely would add the moment it decides upon an independent Israeli initiative, will certainly bring about an end to the frightening erosion of our standing in the United States and in Europe. It will also help world public opinion to understand our position. It will revive friendly attitudes toward us, as was the case, for instance, when in the weeks preceding the Six-Day war in 1967, the whole free world, without any exception, was on our side. The truth is that the oil weapon is a two-edged sword. And there is a deep reservoir of anger and resentment in all of the Western countries against the Arab oil potentates, a factor that today we are not exploiting at all.

Our government makes desperate efforts to gain time. But time works against us with an ever-increasing speed. The postponement of political initiatives with the intention of gaining time constitutes a grave danger to our security. Had we undertaken a major initiative in the wake of the Six-Day war with a view toward achieving a peace settlement, we would certainly have obtained much better results than we can expect today. And of course, we would have prevented the October 1973 war from taking place. It is clear that if we persevere in our policy of procrastination, we will not be able to obtain even the limited aims our government strives to achieve. And after the next war, even if we score a clear and resounding victory, our diplomatic situation will not improve, but will become more precarious.

All this is not to say that the outlook for the future is necessarily gloomy. Just as before the Yom-Kippur war we exaggerated our power, we are now inclined to indulge in extreme exaggerations in the opposite direction. Neither of the two contrasting moods reflect objective reality. We are not a "world power," but neither are we entirely powerless.

The truth is that our situation is far from desperate, if we are sober and alert enough to remove the hurdles we ourselves have erected. We are a nation of three million living in a strong state marshalling the most potent and sophisticated weapons in the world. And we can count on the help and backing of a superpower, on the condition that we act wisely and in harmony with the United States.

We must also remember that apart from our military capabilities, we possess forces and extraordinary talents that have not been tapped. The time has come to utilize these forces for purposes befitting an ancient people reborn in its homeland. But all this is contingent upon snapping out of our lethargy, that is the greatest of all dangers. One should not, one must not, postpone any longer the redeeming initiative.

There is no denying that some of the elements of our plan contain serious concessions. But our plan requires far-reaching concessions also from the other side. The truth is that the concessions demanded of both sides are trivial when compared to the goal : to bring the conflict between us and our neighbors to a conclusion based on reciprocity, in which there are no victors nor vanquished. Only thus is a true peace possible, a peace that will enable our historic nation to fulfill the age-old vision of the prophets of Israel and to make our contribution to the whole of mankind, as a sovereign nation and a spiritual power in the Middle East.